Inclusion through Access to Higher Education

COMPARATIVE AND INTERNATIONAL EDUCATION:
A Diversity of Voices

Volume 45

Scope

Comparative and International Education: A Diversity of Voices aims to provide a comprehensive range of titles, making available to readers work from across the comparative and international education research community. Authors will represent as broad a range of voices as possible, from geographic, cultural and ideological standpoints. The editors are making a conscious effort to disseminate the work of newer scholars as well as that of well-established writers. The series includes authored books and edited works focusing upon current issues and controversies in a field that is undergoing changes as profound as the geopolitical and economic forces that are reshaping our worlds. The series aims to provide books which present new work, in which the range of methodologies associated with comparative education and international education are both exemplified and opened up for debate. As the series develops, it is intended that new writers from settings and locations not frequently part of the English language discourse will find a place in the list.

Inclusion through Access to Higher Education

Exploring the Dynamics between Access to Higher Education,
Immigration and Languages

Edited by

Marie-Agnès Détourbe
INSA Toulouse, LACES EA 7437, France

SENSE PUBLISHERS
ROTTERDAM/BOSTON/TAIPEI

A C.I.P. record for this book is available from the Library of Congress.

ISBN: 978-94-6351-225-1 (paperback)
ISBN: 978-94-6351-226-8 (hardback)
ISBN: 978-94-6351-227-5 (e-book)

Published by: Sense Publishers,
P.O. Box 21858,
3001 AW Rotterdam,
The Netherlands
https://www.sensepublishers.com/

Printed on acid-free paper

TABLE OF CONTENTS

FOREWORD

When Migration, Higher Education and Language Intersect

I happily accepted the invitation to write this preface in my capacity as a migration studies specialist focusing on Franco-British and wider European comparisons, with particular emphasis on integration, immigration, minority communities, and on the various modes of migrant inclusion, ranging from French Republican integration to multiculturalism. Migration studies constitute an interdisciplinary field *par excellence*, drawing on a wide range of disciplines, such as history, geography, politics, economics, law, sociology, anthropology or more recently postcolonial studies.

Migration studies took shape in the early 20th century, most notably with the publication of the five volumes of *The Polish Peasant in Europe and America* (1918–1920) by W. I. Thomas and F. Znaniecki, a study of a human group in transition (Polish immigrants and their families in this particular case) for the purpose of which the authors devised specific fieldwork methods, and made an extensive use of personal documents.

In the second half of the 20th century, immigrants were mostly studied through two perspectives. First, they were considered as workers. This approach obviously lent itself to Marxist analytical grids but also reflected a long-lasting trend in certain countries, notably in Germany and France, where post-war governments considered immigrants exclusively in relation to their contribution to the economy, hence the durable use of the expressions *Gastarbeiter* and *travailleurs immigrés* as a way to label immigrants, which had the effect of emphasising their being kept at a distance from German and French societies during the thirty years of sustained growth that followed the end of WW2.

Immigrants were also seen and studied through the prism of their assimilation (whether absolute or comparative) into the host society. In English-speaking countries, the interest in assimilation was gradually supplanted by a new interest in ethnicity, a trend that came later in France, given the peculiar place occupied by immigrants between the end of the war and the first oil shock.

The religious dimension to migration studies was added more recently, over the past three decades, when for the first time, certain migrants in the west started positioning themselves as religious groups and being recognised as such, notably by governments. This was notably the case in Britain, where the Rushdie Affair (1989) led certain groups from the Indian subcontinent to present themselves as "Muslims" or indeed as "the Muslim community," thus supplanting previous distinctions based on national or ethnic origin.

Since 9/11, all major immigration nations have devised stricter immigration and integration rules, leading certain analysts to talk about "neo-assimilationism," even when the actual framework for integrating migrants remained, as in the UK, by and large influenced by multiculturalism. In the UK, this has led to ever tougher rules for overseas students from developing countries, often suspected of trying to enter the country for economic rather than for academic reasons. It has also engendered a new emphasis on the mastery of English, now clearly seen as a prerequisite for integration and naturalisation.

Immigration, higher education and language are therefore intertwined and central to contemporary debates, notably in Britain. Marie-Agnès Détourbe's enlightening volume and careful editing shows how consistent the whole picture is and gives substance to a fascinating survey, where the question of migration intersects with access to higher education, while the crucial role played by language is duly considered and investigated.

This book's eight chapters tackle a wide array of migration situations (e.g., student and teaching staff mobility; the impact of tightened immigration controls on the recruitment of international students; language-related challenges for qualified workers born and trained overseas; the burning and contentious issue of refugees' access to universities, to name a few), cover a variety of geographic areas (e.g., France, England, Canada, US, Germany, Switzerland, and Japan) and rely on diverse research methods (e.g., international comparisons, qualitative methods, social network analysis, autobiographical narratives).

There lies the originality of this truly interdisciplinary volume, whose impressive scope will be of great interest to academics from a wide range of disciplines (e.g., migration and integration studies, area studies, pedagogy, contemporary history, sociology), advanced students and decision-makers.

Vincent Latour
Université Toulouse Jean Jaurès
Toulouse

MARIE-AGNÈS DÉTOURBE

CROSSING BOUNDARIES

*Insights into the Dynamics of Access to Higher Education,
Immigration, and Languages*

INTRODUCTION

A key feature of the 21st century is undoubtedly the increased flow of goods, ideas and people across geographical, cultural and political boundaries which has led to new dynamics and ever more complex forms of interconnectedness: this intense circulation simultaneously nurtures new forms of entanglement, interdependences, and cross-fertilization which reshape and redefine more traditional spaces at the regional, national or local level. While some authors have conceptualized globalization in terms of flows and interconnectedness (e.g., Derné, 2008; Munoz, 2006 or Neubauer, 2006; cited by Schröttner, 2012, pp. 22–23), putting forward concepts such as "ethnoscapes," "mediascapes," or "ideoscapes" to account for the movements of people, institutions, ideas and practices (Appadurai, 2006; cited by Schröttner, 2012, p. 24), others have tried to go beyond the globalization discourse and looked into the impact of globalization on the local, elaborating on Roland Robertson's (1992) concept of "glocalization."

The complex and challenging encounter of the global and the local is critically embodied in the situation of people on the move – migrants – and the way they are socially included in their host countries as immigrants. Understood as "the inclusion and acceptance of immigrants into the core institutions, relationships and positions of a host society" (Bosswick & Heckmann, 2006, p. 11), social integration is fundamentally "an interactive process:"

> For the immigrants, integration means the process of learning a new culture, acquiring rights and obligations, gaining access to positions and social status, building personal relationships with members of the host society and forming a feeling of belonging to, and identification with, that society. For the host society, integration means opening up institutions and granting equal opportunities to immigrants. (ibid.)

At the heart of social integration is the concept of access: it is particularly relevant in the context of growing flows of populations in that it refers to an inclusive dual movement whereby people have both the possibility *and* the ability to benefit from certain rights, services, statuses or goods, to share ideas, knowledge, to participate in networks, democratic processes, etc. It is necessarily a dual process which involves two parties – those who provide, open, or share access, either openly or under certain conditions, and those who gain, have, benefit from access, on the condition that they have the ability to do so. This holds particularly true for populations that have not necessarily gained full citizenship (yet) or developed a sense of belonging in their host countries and for whom access to certain rights and opportunities is key to integration. Equal access to housing, health and social care or education is often at the heart of the various integration policies and initiatives devised nationally and locally (Boyd, 1989; Fawcett, 1989).

Access to education is a case in point as it represents a key inclusion factor for people on the move, whatever their country of origin, mother tongue and rationale for migrating temporarily or permanently:

> In times of displacement, education is crucial. It can foster social cohesion, provide access to life-saving information, address psychosocial needs, and offer a stable and safe environment for those who need it most. It also helps people to rebuild their communities and pursue productive, meaningful lives. (UNHCR, n.d.)

Mandatory pre-tertiary education is the norm in most developed countries, with variations as to the age limit. Host nations often integrate migrant children into their national school systems as a way of including them more broadly into society, without necessarily devising specifically targeted policies. As a consequence, many primary and secondary schools are faced with the challenge of upholding similar academic standards for all while dealing with increasingly diverse languages and cultures in the classroom (Urias, 2012, p. 1). The way this diversity is handled at school level echoes broader societal debates on inclusion.

One the one hand, the proponents of multiculturalism and multilingualism advocate the maintenance of linguistic and cultural diversity in the classrooms through various teaching and learning approaches (Cummins, 1980; Kelly, 2015; Majhanovich, 2014). For instance, dual language education (DLE) initiatives have emerged in an effort to tackle "the phenomenon of language loss and the desire of immigrant communities to preserve their cultural identity, whether immigrant children settle temporarily or permanently in a host country" (Stritikus & Varghese, 2012, p. 37). Such multilingualism is also advocated at supra-national level with specific regulation such as the European "Action Plan on Promoting Language Learning and Linguistic Diversity" which was launched in 2003 and set a landmark in the acknowledgement of the inherent variety of cultural identities in Europe.

On the other hand, within the immigration and integration debate, "there is growing awareness that formation of ethnic minority identities among migrants is leading to and reinforcing ethnic stratification and ethno-cultural conflict," and that "incorporation, in equal terms, demands that migrants acquire the cultural and social competences and attitudes to participate in the society's institutions" (Bosswick & Heckmann, 2006, p. 5). For instance, Content and Language Integrated Learning

(CLIL) initiatives which combine foreign (target) language, content subject, and intercultural learning have been developed in many countries in an attempt to target simultaneously pupils' linguistic and academic skills (e.g., Räsänen, 2011). The European project INCLUDE carried out between 2013 and 2016 embodied such an attempt to "integrate language learning in social inclusion policy" by "identifying, pooling and disseminating successful practices of CLIL aimed at migrant and other 'at risk' groups" (Cullen, Bian, & Orlando, 2014, pp. 7–8). Even though CLIL programmes often target English as a Foreign Language (EFL), and have been criticized for pushing the dominant cultural norms of the English-speaking world (Stritikus & Varghese, 2012, p. 50), they do aim at providing immigrants with the sufficient cultural and social capital they need to achieve integration in the host society in the long run.

Finding the point of equilibrium between multiculturalism and integration at linguistic, cultural and social levels is both challenging and critical, as acknowledged by Androulla Vassiliou, European Commissioner for Education, Culture, Multilingualism and Youth in a 2014 speech at Harvard (cited by Leroy, this volume):

> Language serves as a useful measure of our diversity. Today, the European Union functions with 24 official languages, more than 60 regional and minority languages and more than 120 migrant languages. [...The] challenge [...] lies in striking the right balance between the respect for cultural diversity and the construction of a shared European identity – an identity that does not replace the sense of national belonging, but adds a new layer to the multiple identities of our citizens.

Despite specific efforts and initiatives at the national and local levels to promote equity and social cohesion by catering for the specific needs of migrants, they are still often at a disadvantage:

> Migrants are often faced with legal, cultural [including linguistic] and social barriers, and obstacles to accessing the full range of resources, services and opportunities that [their host country] can offer, including formal housing, employment, heath care, education and social support systems. (International Organization for Migration, 2015, p. 81)

Evidence of these multiple barriers and obstacles is found in the way they are named, officially or through popular expressions, to differentiate them from the native population, however long their family history in the host country and however diverse their origins: ethnicity is the most common rationale for differentiating them, with phrases like "ethnic minorities" definitely indicating "a status of belonging to a society that in many ways rejects the notion of inclusion" (Scholten et al., 2015, p. 191). In the UK for instance, "young migrants and second-generation children born in Britain [...] are collapsed into the category of black and minority ethnic" citizens for statistical purposes (ibid., p. 245); the Dutch have coined the term *allochtonen* to refer to "those people whose ethnic roots lie outside the Netherlands," with the statistical category of *niet-westerse allochtonen* referring to "both first-generation migrants and persons who were born in the Netherlands, but have at least one parent born in a 'non-western' country" (ibid., p. 217); and in Japan (see Henault-Morrone, this volume), the names "*zainichi-Nihonjin*" (in-Japan Japanese) and "*dekasegi*" have been coined to designate people from non-Japanese descent, or whose ancestors left Japan at some point in time to seek work elsewhere, thereby setting in stone their ethnic past at the expense of their current national identity and status.

When taking stock of the increased circulation of people worldwide, and looking at the various ways the social distance and differences between them and other groups in society can be lessened so as to achieve greater inclusion, access to education and the handling of diverse languages and cultures stand out as central issues. Against such a backdrop and at a time when the issue of immigration is "strongly politicized" (Scholten et al., 2015, p. 2) and revolves around questions of borders, wall building and increased control over population flows, this book frames the issue of inclusion of immigrants through their access to higher education and looks at the role played by languages in the process. While most migrant children, whatever their status and origin, are given access to primary and secondary education as part of the mission of most state-funded school systems to educate the young under a certain age, accessing higher education tells a different story. First, it represents a strategic issue in the endeavors of adult immigrants to integrate a new society in the long run, with lifelong learning representing a key opportunity (e.g., van der Linden, 2017). For those who have completed their secondary education successfully in their host country or back home, it stands as an opportunity for them to obtain higher qualifications which, in turn, can provide access to higher statuses and positions in the labour market home or abroad. Moreover, the diversity of immigrants is echoed by a similar variety amongst higher education institutions: contrary to often standardized national systems of primary and secondary education, higher education consists of a wide range of institutions which follow different models of governance – ranging from state-controlled models to more market-oriented ones –, devise specific curricula with varying levels of vocational or academic training, and set different entry rules and criteria, even within the same national system. Even if the cost of higher education stands as a key, albeit indirect, selection criterion, higher education does open more opportunities in terms of diversity than pre-tertiary education. Language skills are often one selection criterion which can constitute a specific barrier for immigrants or, on the contrary, an opportunity when international plurilingual courses have been developed so as to cater for the needs of a mix of foreign students.

The stakes related to higher education are high because on the one hand, it remains a scarce commodity, and on the other, it is a central lever of innovation and knowledge-advancement, therefore a strategic dimension of economic development. Most developed nations aim to educate further an ever-larger proportion of their population while seeking to host more international students. However, if widening participation and internationalization have become two central features of many contemporary higher education systems and institutions worldwide (inter alia Altbach, 2013; Altbach & Knight, 2007; de Wit, 2011; de Wit, Ferencz, & Rumbley, 2013; Egron-Polak & Hudson, 2014; Jones, 1998; Knight, 2004), the rationales for such processes differ widely and combine variously from one nation to the next, and from one higher education institution to the next. Widening participation, as it has evolved since the early stages of massification in the 1960s in most developed countries, generally draws on equity of opportunity rationales, as summed up for instance in the landmark Robbins report in the UK which stated that "courses of higher education should be available for all those who are qualified by ability and attainment to pursue them and who wish to do so" (Robbins, 1963, para. 31), without necessarily targeting specific under-represented sections of the population. Simultaneously, the expanding international education market has led many institutions to follow a more economic rationale, international students representing a strategic source of income at a time when public funding for higher education is dwindling dramatically, as well as a strong indicator of prestige in what has become a highly competitive market ruled by rankings and profit (e.g., Halsey & O'Brien, 2014; Shin, Toutkoushian, & Teichler, 2011; Usher & Medow, 2010). As a result, fundamental questions related to the purpose of and access to higher education are overshadowed by "pragmatic and short-sighted assumptions, largely driven by political considerations which neither benefit the participants of higher education nor society which is expected to gain from the investment" (Andres, 1999, p. 25). Such political considerations appear in visa regulation for foreign students as well as post-study work opportunities for instance.

Similarly, the opportunities to study for a higher education degree often draw on different rationales and aspirations which account for various pathways into higher education. For people on the move, access opportunities and barriers vary greatly from one country to the other and are often closely related to their socio-economic and administrative status in the host country. Whatever their previous academic background and qualifications, which remain the main criteria for access, their status as immigrants, their ability to speak the host country's main language as well as their economic situation impact on their ability to enter higher education. For students on various well-framed mobility or exchange schemes who can meet the international higher education market demands, access is often not problematic, even if certain immigration rules and visa restrictions can hinder the process: in the UK for instance, the Conservative government's wish to reduce net migration "to the tens of thousands," regardless of the status of immigrants, has led to dramatic drops in the international student intake at some middle and lower ranked universities (Morgan, 2017). For the other immigrants who either qualified from primary and/or secondary education in their host country and most likely master its main language, or are newcomers with a secondary education background from their home countries as well as various levels of proficiency in the new language, access is more problematic.

The question of access to higher education is a complex one (Andres, 1999; Altbach, 2010, p. vii), not least due to the "obvious moral and ethical implications" (Meyer et al., 2013, p. 2) it carries in trying to answer simultaneously the following questions: "What is the purpose of higher education?" and "Who is higher education for?" (Andres, 1999, p. 25). From a definitional point of view,[1] access is grounded in the two concepts of ability and opportunity: while Usher and Medow (2010, p. 1; cited by de Gayardon, 2017, p. 67) underline "the ability of people from various backgrounds to access higher education on a relatively equal basis," thereby stressing the shared responsibility of the different stakeholders in the process, the Glossary of Education (2014) puts forward a definition which focuses on the providers of access but also on completion: "In education, the term access typically refers to the ways in which educational institutions and policies ensure – or at least strive to ensure – that students have equal and equitable opportunities to take full advantage of their education." At the heart of access understood as the equal and equitable opportunity offered to students,[2] whatever their socio-economic and ethnic backgrounds, is the notion of fairness, i.e., the idea that access to higher education policies and practices should follow a social justice and equity rationale and be devised in order to provide "equality of opportunity, equality of resources, and/or equality of results" (Andres, 1999, p. 11) based on students' needs, talent and merit. The literature on access to higher education exemplifies the very complexity and multi-dimensionality of the issue: various dimensions of access have been explored such as construction of student choice (e.g., Paulsen & St John, 2002), student identity (e.g., Lopez, 2012), participation by non-traditional students in higher education (e.g., Bowl, 2001; Schuetze & Slowey, 2002), retention and attrition (e.g., Orkodashvili, 2012), lifelong learners in HE (e.g., Schütze & Slowey, 2012) and inequality in access for ethnic minorities (e.g., Atherton, 2016; Boliver, 2016; Goastellec, 2010). Some of these dimensions are tackled in the chapters of this volume, yet they are not the basis of systematic study. Instead, access to higher education is approached from a broader perspective, under the umbrella theme of inclusion, as "equal and equitable opportunities" offered to students who want to embark on higher education (Glossary of Education, 2014).

Whatever the rationale for granting access to higher education, highly-skilled migrants and the "brain circulation" they generate are increasingly perceived as an asset for modern societies, whether they contribute to the development of the knowledge society in their host countries or back home:

> The presence of high-skilled migrants and foreign students in higher education contributes to the creation of knowledge [...], and evidence shows that immigrants increase patenting activity of natives too. Networks of diaspora members contribute to the diffusion of knowledge and the presence of a more diverse workforce makes innovation more likely. (Thompson, 2014)

Their very mobility is an answer to the growing contrasts in the diverse demographics and development stages across the world: not only can migrants offer a solution to the shortage of workers with higher education qualifications in well-developed yet ageing countries – for instance, Germany and Australia are expected to experience a labour shortage of around 2.3 million each by 2020 (Boston Consulting Group; cited by Thompson, 2014) – that also face a "talent mismatch," they also contribute greatly to the development of exchanges between host and home countries – through diasporas for instance – and have been found to function as incentives for natives to pursue higher education goals (ibid.). Accordingly, various transnational organizations have begun to devise targeted policies and programmes for migrants, most particularly refugees, stretching more traditional forms of humanitarian help to encompass inclusion through higher education. The United Nations High Commissioner on Refugees (UNHCR, n.d.) notes that a mere "1 per cent of refugees attend university, compared to 34 per cent at global level," and strives to open up more higher education opportunities for this under-represented population as part of its effort to find long-term solutions: "higher education nurtures a generation of future change-makers that can take the lead in identifying solutions to refugee situations" (ibid.). Through the Albert Einstein Academic Refugee Initiative Programme (known as DAFI), created in 1992, the UNHCR has granted scholarships to allow refugees to study at universities and colleges in their host countries with a view to increasing the number of graduates returning home, thereby facilitating the transfer of skills to their countries of origin. Similarly, the International Organization for Migration's (IOM) Support for Students Programme provides scholarships to migrant students "to ensure they can take advantage of the higher education and profession opportunities" in their host countries. Another initiative is George Sampaïo's "Global Platform for Syrian Students," launched in 2013, which has supported 150 Syrian refugees in 10 countries, including Portugal. Sampaïo claims that access to higher education should be part and parcel of humanitarian aid in emergencies with a view to securing a brighter future both for the students and their countries of origin:

> [H]igher Education can maintain the hopes, help shelter and protect young men and women during crisis situations [...]. [It] can be a catalyst for change and can help the recovery and re-building of war-torn countries. Educated future leaders are necessary and we must prevent the creation of lost generations of academic graduates during wartime. (ECRE, 2016)

In keeping with this stance, this book is grounded in the idea that higher education can provide an array of answers to the chosen or unchosen experience of displacement undergone by an increasing, though still marginal, number of young adults worldwide while taking hold of the specific challenges raised by their diversity. The three intertwined thematic perspectives of access to higher education, immigration and language policies and practices are explored accordingly under the cross-cutting theme of inclusion framed as "social integration." Drawing on complexity theories such as Edgar Morin's,[3] the chosen approach is grounded in the idea that multi-faceted and complex issues should be tackled from various disciplinary perspectives so as to illuminate the various dimensions and dynamics at play. In doing so, the volume purports to interweave research perspectives which often co-exist as separate disciplinary trends (e.g., migration studies, higher education studies, comparative international higher education or language studies) but are rarely combined, as can be seen through the literature.

THEMES AND STRUCTURE OF THE BOOK

The different chapters cross disciplinary and geographical boundaries so as to explore the dynamics between these three dimensions at supra-national, national, regional and local across different continents. Different theoretical perspectives ranging from disciplinary fields such as public policy, immigration studies, education studies, sociology and ethnography, as well as various methodological tools such as qualitative research methodologies, including autobiographical narratives, field observation, instrumental case studies or Social Network Analysis (SNA), are drawn on to conceptualise and critically examine these dynamics. Rather than a systematic comparative approach of a set number of dimensions, the volume offers rich scientific material in which chapters echo each other, yet offer distinctive insights into the complex interplay between access to higher education, immigration and languages in different settings.

Part 1: Access to Higher Education and Immigration Policies and Strategies

The first part examines how higher education policies, regulations and strategies intersect with immigration rules at supra-national, national or regional levels. Depending on the specific political organization in a given region or nation, immigration policies can indeed represent different levels of constraint and/or opportunity for higher education institutions, particularly when the latter seek to intensify their internationalization strategies and increase their inflow of foreign students. Whether they set specific visa requirements or target particular groups of migrants, like refugees for instance, immigration rules can hinder or on the contrary support higher education strategies, albeit at different levels and to different extents. In an attempt to both map the complex configuration of actors and policies in Canada on the one hand, and in France, Germany and Switzerland on the other, and unveil the various struggles at play, the following chapters provide insights into the difficult political and institutional dialogue between immigration and access to higher education.

In a chapter entitled "Canada's Citizenship, Immigration, and International Education Policies: A Messy Assemblage of Actors and Priorities," Rashed Al-Haque examines the links between Canada's immigration and citizenship regulation and its higher education internationalization policies. He shows how the specific political organization in Canada, namely federalism, and the way immigration, citizenship and education mandates are mapped and related, leads to what he dubs "a messy assemblage" of actors. Indeed, the federal Canadian government recently and swiftly tightened its immigration policies, which is likely to make it more difficult for higher education institutions, under provinces' traditional educational mandate, to recruit international students, the latter being faced with scarcer prospects of transitioning into permanent residency. Drawing on Critical Policy Analysis and Actor Network Theory, the chapter studies "internationalization, citizenship, and immigration policy in a relational context" by mapping and contrasting the voice and agency of the various actors involved. The findings underline "mismatched priorities" and values at institutional, province, and federal government level: while the university chosen for the instrumental case study insists on "the academic and socio-cultural benefits of internationalization that result from a movement of ideas and peoples across borders," the federal government's international strategy follows a more economic rationale and does not take into account the potential impact of its immigration regulation on both international recruitment and retention. As a result, universities are worried that Canada may lose its attractivity on the global higher education market, and lose potential highly-skilled talents to the benefit of other nations who offer brighter post-graduation prospects on their labour markets. While the winds may change in Canada as the new liberal government seems intent on supporting the internationalization of its higher education, the methodological and theoretical framework used in this chapter provides a robust tool for exploring other, similar national and regional contexts.

At a time when increasing numbers of refugees cross borders across the world, refugees' access to higher education has become a topical issue, as visible through the various events organized by international organizations on this theme over the last couple of years. In a chapter entitled "Refugees' Access to Higher Education in Europe: Comparative Insights on a New Public Issue," Gaële Goastellec offers a timely comparative study of the way refugees' access to higher education is built as a socio-political issue in France, Germany and Switzerland. Following a cognitive approach of public policies, the author identifies the frames of reference which were developed to devise various policies and mechanisms for refugees' access to higher education; she shows that they draw on various rationales ranging from social responsibility and asylum tradition to fighting xenophobia and solidarity. Similarly, the types and configuration of institutional actors involved in refugees' access to higher education vary according to the way higher education itself is organised and managed nationally, or locally: some HEIs have put in place various mechanisms for refugees, from tailor-made non-degree programs devised as a stepping stone to degree programs which include language and financial support, to broader and fairly standard procedures for recognition of prior learning, as well as different combinations of these mechanisms. The way administrative statuses are handled also differs from one country to the next, and immigration policies sometimes interfere with access to higher education rules at various levels. The chapter sheds light on the handling of refugees' access to higher education in the three countries by analysing the complex interplay between immigration and higher education rationales against the countries' broader social and economic policy backgrounds. A central finding is that an individual's opportunity to study is sometimes weighed against more pragmatic national considerations such as labour shortages or immigration quotas.

Part 2: Access to Higher Education and Languages

The second part focuses on the different roles played by languages in access to higher education for people on the move. Language can be used indeed as a way of restricting or widening access to higher education at a supra-national, national, regional or local level: is some cases, language policies, regulations or practices are used as levers of opportunities, for instance through foreign-language taught university programs or targeted language support courses; yet language requirements can also be set as selection barriers before entry (e.g., through minimum entry thresholds in one or several languages) and therefore work as a major obstacle to inclusion into higher education and society. The three chapters in this part explore the multifaceted power of languages for different types of migrants, depending on their educational or professional aspirations, and their level in the host country language: they highlight the complex issues at play and the very context-sensitive nature of languages whereby a high level of proficiency in a target language is not always a sufficient condition for moving into higher education and being fully integrated, and the cultural and social capital it endows people on the move with is hard to build.

In her chapter entitled "When MFL Teachers Want to Move: Accessing a University Career in a Global Society," Norah Leroy focuses on highly-qualified professionals with high proficiency language skills, namely Modern Foreign Language (MFL) teachers, and the complexities for them to access mobility opportunities in Europe. Within the European Higher Education Area, where the circulation of students and teachers has been made easier by the Bologna process through various transnational mobility schemes such as Erasmus+, her chapter explores the "extent to which transnational mobility opportunities have facilitated access to a career as a HE teacher educator for secondary school teachers of MFL given the Council of Europe's commitment to continuing professional development through mobility and language learning." Through a qualitative approach based on interviews with four MFL teachers in France and in England (UK), she explores the rationales for mobility through the specific lens of professional development – not only are MFL teachers keener than other professionals to spend some time in the country where the MFL they teach is the native tongue, they also consider such mobility as part of a broader professional development project to become higher education educators and train prospective teachers in primary and secondary education. Her findings show that what drove these MFL teachers to move into higher education was not the incentives offered by transnational mobility schemes across EU countries but rather, their internal motivation and "desire to access the world of research at university in response to the issues arising from teaching and learning MFL in a global society." Her research therefore highlights the gap between European frameworks for improving the quality of modern languages teaching and learning, and the individual career paths of those who aim for both professional and geographical mobility.

In their chapter entitled "Social Inclusion and Language Support for Internationally-Educated Nurses in Canada," Nadezda Kulikova and Yuliya Miakisheva focus on foreign-educated professionals who move to Canada as economic class migrants: as the country's immigration legislation gradually shifted to a labour-oriented rationale, increasing numbers of skilled workers were brought in in an attempt to address occupational shortages, and they gradually became an asset to the Canadian labour force. However, internationally-trained professionals currently find themselves at a disadvantage, compared with their Canadian counterparts, when they try to work in government-regulated occupations such as engineering, teaching, or nursing. The chapter explores the extent to which language issues account for such inequalities in the case of internationally-educated nurses (IENs): even if they meet immigration language requirements, IENs lack fluency in academic nursing English. As a result, they face communication challenges which represent major obstacles in their attempt to become fully-qualified nurses in Canada, and more broadly, for getting socially included into society. Because IENs are given permanent resident status as part of the immigration legislation, several bridging programs with a strong linguistic component were developed across Canadian postsecondary institutions to answer their specific needs. Noting that existing research does not provide empirical support for the effectiveness of these programs, the authors review and critically examine the other programs targeting IENs in the US and Australia. Their review shows that most programs are mainly academic and only target linguistic and/or socio-cultural competences. Taking hold of the specificity of IENs' situation in Canada, the authors advocate "a more holistic approach to language instruction […] to facilitate language acquisition and, subsequently, the integration into the workforce and society" and put forward potential, context-based approaches for answering their specific, occupational language needs.

As shown in the chapter entitled "Language(s) of Power and Power of Language(s) in International Student Recruitment in French HEIs in the Context of Internationalization" by Cui Bian and Régis Malet, France remains a top, though non-English speaking, destination for mobile students. Categorized by the authors as both a "norm-maker and norm-taker" in the global landscape of higher education internationalization, the country has devised its own recruitment approach, adapted from the Anglo-American model. Against national policies which only very recently allowed the use of foreign languages in public higher education, and despite the domination of English as a lingua franca and the multiplication of English-taught higher education programs across the international higher education market, French higher education is still characterized by a specific stance regarding the role of the French language in international student recruitment. Whereas some French higher education institutions increasingly use

English as a way of enlarging their international recruitment, French still acts as the major filter for the selection of international students, and immersion in the French culture through French-taught programs is still presented as an asset to the studying experience in France. This leads the authors to conclude that the two languages exercise their power in different arenas: English is perceived as key to research in many scientific fields, and some English-taught programs have been set up in specific domains at higher study levels; yet French remains at the heart of the higher education provision, especially in social sciences and the humanities, endowed with a strong cultural and intellectual heritage. Therefore, in the global landscape of higher education internationalization, France is characterized by a distinctive approach to international student recruitment whereby English is used as a tool and represents an added value, but is not likely to replace French as the main language of instruction and passport to French culture.

Part 3: The Broader Issue of Inclusion through Access to Higher Education

The third part offers a broad perspective on social inclusion through access to higher education. It explores the close links between access to higher education and the social integration of international students and/or migrants into the civil society, the conditions under which social inclusion favours access to higher education, and vice versa. The chapters shed light on the conditions under which the synergy between the two processes benefits people on the move across different countries and cultures. Additionally, they look into the kind of inclusion that is achieved, and whether it is long-lasting enough to be considered as a long-term benefit for all parties.

Julia Carnine's chapter – "International Students' Social Inclusion and Long-term Benefits: The Case of Chinese Students in France" – looks at the patterns of integration of Chinese students in French higher education and society by exploring their personal social networks, as the latter are known to have an impact on social inclusion and long-term settlement intentions. Contemporary mobile Chinese students hold a particular interest in that they do not reproduce old migration patterns based on extended family or social relations but devise new kinds of social networks. They also contribute greatly to diasporic knowledge economies upheld by higher education academic mobility as they represent the world's largest international mobile student group. The study draws on previous comparative research which showed that institutional intervention in higher education institutions such as language help, transnational social events, and multinational housing facilities leads to a better inclusion of mobile students. On the contrary, higher education institutional settings with little or no targeted support tend to strengthen co-national segregation, which, as the chapter shows, is the case for Chinese students in France. Using Social Network Analysis and autobiographical narratives, the author maps two Chinese students' personal social networks which allow for a clear visualization and better understanding of the dynamics at play in their social and professional integration, both during their sojourn in France and upon returning to China. Mixed benefits from the time spent in France include enhanced intercultural curiosity, personal development, a new social status in the Chinese workplace as "overseas student returnees" or "sea turtles," as well as a broader and more critical vision of China's social traditions which enhance the students' social and professional situation in China. Overall, the chapter shows that both individual and institutional networks such as alumni networks can lead to long-term mutual benefits for the Sino-French knowledge diaspora circulating via mobile students from and to China and France.

In her chapter entitled "On the Margins of Inclusion: Higher Education Challenges Faced by Immigrant Tech-worker Spouses in the United States," Himabindu Timiri focuses on a specific category of immigrants, Indian tech-worker spouses, who follow their husbands to the United States and wish to fulfil higher educational goals in their host country. Under the H4 "dependent" visa rules, they find themselves under the dependence of their husbands, considered as the lead migrant in the family and holders of a separate H-1B visa: they are not allowed to work, yet the American visa legislation makes it possible for them to undertake higher education studies. The chapter explores the challenges faced by these immigrant women when they endeavour to access higher education and unveils the "web of factors" which maintain them in a "dependent" condition. It sheds light on the phenomenon of "de-skilling" which has been found to characterize many highly-skilled women and prevents them from transferring their pre-migration higher education qualifications and training to their new country of residence. Advocating "a context-specific reading" of these immigrant women's situation, the chapter presents an ethnographic study of three immigrant Indian women in the region of Atlanta. Their experiences showcase "the gamut of roadblocks that derail the educational aspirations of 'dependent' immigrant women," including family patriarchy and gender-norms which tend to value men's educational goals more than women's, overlap of family and career decisions due, for instance, to uncertainty on the duration of their stay in the US because of the project-based nature of their husbands' work in information technology, but also financial difficulties linked to high higher education fees in the US, as well as credentialing systems which do not recognize their former education. The findings uncover the various roadblocks which set these immigrant women on "tangential pathways," and the author advocates a better recognition of these obstacles in devising immigration and access to higher education policies which could better address their specific condition.

Japan has one the world's highest high school graduation rates, yet part of the population is not offered the same higher education opportunities because of a variety of factors linked to their origins. The chapter entitled "Increasing Access to Higher Education for 'Newcomer' Pupils in Japan" uncovers the reasons why some Japanese citizens are stigmatised as not being fully Japanese due to their origins or to their recent arrival in the country, and how it impacts their children's capacity and ability to access higher education. Michelle Henault Morrone focuses on a specific group of non-nationals, referred to as "newcomer pupils," whose families either came from South America and Asia when the Japanese immigration legislation was revised in 1990, then in 2009, or settled in Japan temporarily as high-skilled workers, then chose to stay. Through a qualitative approach based on autobiographical narratives, the chapter explores the roadblocks which these pupils are faced with in their aspirations for high school, then higher education. In this very rigid and selective educational system where a pupil's school results determine very early on his/her future academic and professional pathways, newcomer pupils find themselves at a distinct disadvantage in their attempts to navigate Japan's social, linguistic and academic complexities. Parents' language issues, financial constraints, insufficient information, and a general lack of familiarity with the system combine into a web of obstacles which prove difficult to overcome in a country that "prizes homogeneity and is confounded by difference." Taking stock of the issues raised by these newcomer families, the Japanese Ministry of Education recently launched various programs aiming at better including newcomer children into Japanese schools. Such programs are limited in scope though, and better prospects might come from private or individual initiatives at a time when this ageing nation needs to come to terms with welcoming more foreign workers.

In exploring the theme of inclusion through access to higher education, immigration and languages while focusing on different salient dimensions in various settings, the collection of chapters which make up this volume offers new insights into the way higher education can answer the multiple challenges raised by the increased circulation of people and knowledge worldwide. Following Edgar Morin's stance on complex thinking (2005), this cross-national and multi-thematic combination of approaches does not purport to draw a comprehensive picture but rather offers as broad a range of voices as possible so as to illuminate the relations between otherwise disconnected elements which are part of a complex and multi-faceted reality (Morin, 2005, p. 11).

I would like to thank all the contributing authors who have answered my call for chapters and trusted me with their very rich and insightful original work. I am also very grateful to all the reviewers for their valuable feedback on the chapters. Finally, my warmest thanks go to Suzanne Majhanovich for her precious help and support throughout the making of the book, and to Marie-Christine Deyrich for sowing the seeds for this volume by inviting me to a follow-up seminar on the European project INCLUDE in 2015.

NOTES

[1] For an in-depth discussion of the definitions of access, see de Gayardon (2017, pp. 67–69).

[2] Access to higher education is framed here in relation to students, but it can be analyzed at other levels which raise similar equity issues, for instance access to university title for some higher education institutions, access by scholars to publication in scientific journals (see Rumbley et al., 2015) or to global scientific networks.

[3] Edgar Morin, a French sociologist and philosopher, has defended in multiple books and articles "the need for a new paradigm of complexity capable of informing all theories, whatever their

field of application or the phenomena in question" (1992, p. 371) in an effort to account for and understand the complexity which characterises our current natural, social, economic and political environments.

REFERENCES

Altbach, P. G. (2010). Access means inequality. In G. Goastellec (Ed.), *Understanding inequalities in, through and by higher education* (pp. vii–ix). Rotterdam, The Netherlands: Sense Publishers.

Altbach, P. G. (2013). *The international imperative in higher education*. Rotterdam, The Netherlands: Sense Publishers.

Altbach, P. G., & Knight, J. (2007). The internationalization of higher education: Motivations and realities. *Journal of Studies in International Education, 11*, 290–305.

Andres, L. (Ed.). (1999). *Revisiting the issue of access to higher education in Canada* (Reader Series n°5). Winnipeg: Centre for Higher Education Research and Development & Canadian Society for the Study of Higher Education. Retrieved from http://files.eric.ed.gov/fulltext/ED456796.pdf

Appadurai, A. (2006). Disjuncture and difference in the global cultural economy. In H. Lauder, P. Brown, J. -A. Dillabough, & A. H. Halsey (Eds.), *Education, globalization & social change* (pp. 179–188). Oxford: Oxford University Press.

Atherton, G. (2016). *Access to higher education: Understanding global inequalities*. Basingstoke: Palgrave Macmillan.

Boliver, V. (2016). Exploring ethnic inequalities in admission to Russell group universities. *Sociology, 50*(2), 247–266.

Bosswick, W., & Heckmann, F. (2006). *Integration of migrants: Contribution of local and regional authorities*. European Foundation for the Improvement of Living and Working Conditions, Bamberg. Retrieved from https://www.eurofound.europa.eu/sites/default/files/ef_files/pubdocs/2006/22/en/1/ef0622en.pdf

Bowl, M. (2001). Experiencing the barriers: Non-traditional students entering higher education. *Research Papers in Education, 16*(2), 141–160.

Boyd, M. (1989). Family and personal networks in international migration: Recent developments and new agendas. *International Migration Review, 23*(3), 638–669.

Cullen, J., Bian, C., & Orlando, N. (2014). *INCLUDE network language policies and practices for active social inclusion: The state of the art*. First yearly report of the European INCLUDE project 530938-LLP-1-2012-1-IT-KA2-KA2NW.

Cummins, J. (1980). The cross-lingual dimensions of language proficiency: Implications for bilingual education and the optimal age issue. *TESOL Quarterly, 14*(2), 175–187.

de Gayardon, A. (2017). *Access in free-tuition systems: A comparative perspective of the socio-economic background of students in countries with different tuition policies* (Unpublished PhD dissertation). Boston College & Lynch School of Education, Boston, MA.

Derné, S. (2008). *Globalization on the ground: Media and the transformation of culture, class, and gender in India*. New Delhi: Sage Publications.

de Wit, H. (2011). *Trends, issues and challenges in internationalisation of higher education*. Amsterdam: Centre for Applied Research on Economics and Management.

de Wit, H., Ferencz, I., & Rumbley, L. E. (2013). International student mobility: European and US perspectives. *Perspectives: Policy and Practice in Higher Education, 17*(1), 17–23.

Downes, P. (2014). *Access to education in Europe: A framework and agenda for system change* (Lifelong Learning book series). Dordrecht: Springer.

ECRE (European Council on Refugees and Exiles). (2016). *Highlighting the need to prioritise access to higher education in humanitarian crises*. Retrieved from http://www.ecre.org/highlighting-the-need-to-prioritise-access-to-higher-education-in-humanitarian-crises/

Egron-Polak, E., & Hudson, R. (2014). *Internationalization of higher education: Growing expectations, fundamental values* (IAU 4th Global Survey). Paris: International University Association.

Fawcett, J. T. (1989). Networks, linkages, and migration systems. *International Migration Review, 23*(3), 671–680.

Glossary of Education. (2014). *Access*. Retrieved from http://edglossary.org/access/

Goastellec, G. (Ed.). (2010). *Understanding inequalities in, through and by higher education*. Rotterdam, The Netherlands: Sense Publishers.

Halsey, J., & O'Brien, K. (2014). Education markets in English and American universities. In S. Pickard (Ed.), *Higher education in the UK and the US: Converging university models in a global academic world?* (pp. 35–58). Leiden & Boston, MA: Brill.

International Organization for Migration. (2015). *World migration report, migrants and cities: New partnerships to manage mobility*. Geneva: Author. Retrieved from https://www.iom.int/world-migration-report-2015

Jones, P. W. (1998). Globalisation and internationalism: Democratic prospects for world education. *Comparative Education, 34*(2), 143–155.

Kelly, M. (2015). Challenges to multilingual language teaching: Towards a transnational approach. *European Journal of Language Policy, 7*(1), 65–83.

Knight, J. (2004). Internationalization remodeled: Definition, approaches, and rationales. *Journal of Studies in International Education, 8*(1), 5–31.

Lopez, D. (2012). Immigrant identities in transnational contexts: The figured world of a New York city English literacy and civics education classroom. In D. A. Urias (Ed.), *The immigration and education nexus: A focus on the context and consequences of schooling* (pp. 189–208). Rotterdam, The Netherlands: Sense Publishers.

Majhanovich, S. (2014). Neo-liberalism, globalization, language policy and practice issues in the Asia-Pacific region. *Asia Pacific Journal of Education, 34*(2), 168–183.

Meyer, H.-D., St John, E. P., Chankseliani, M., & Uribe, L. (Eds.). (2013). *Fairness in access to higher education: Reconciling excellence, efficiency, and justice*. Rotterdam, The Netherlands: Sense Publishers.

Morgan, J. (2017, February 23). UK's 'lower-ranked' universities take non-EU students hit. *Times Higher Education*. Retrieved from https://www.timeshighereducation.com/news/uks-lower-ranked-universities-take-non-eu-students-hit

Morin, E. (1992). From the concept of system to the paradigm of complexity. *Journal of Social and Evolutionary Systems, 15*(4), 371–385.

Morin, E. (2005). *Introduction à la pensée complexe* [An introduction to complex thinking]. Paris: Seuil.

Muñoz, F. (2006). Imperfect peace. In W. Dietrich, J. E. Alvarez, & N. Koppensteiner (Eds.), *Schlüsseltexte der friedensforschung*. Wien und Münster: LIT Verlag.

Neubauer, D. (2006). *Globalization and education: Characteristics, dynamics, implications*. EAST-WEST Center, Version of 19 September, 1–45. Retrieved from http://www.eastwestcenter.org/fileadmin/resources/education/ed2020_docs/Glob_and_Higher_Ed_2009_Seminar.doc

Orkodashvili, M. (2012). Mapping immigrant student attrition in higher education through a deictic conceptual model. In D. A. Urias (Ed.), *The immigration and education nexus: A focus on the context and consequences of schooling* (pp. 95–110). Rotterdam, The Netherlands: Sense Publishers.

Paulsen, M. B., & St. John, E. P. (2002). Social class and college costs. *The Journal of Higher Education, 73*(2), 189–236.

Räsänen, A. (2011). International classrooms, disciplinary cultures and communication conventions: A report on a workshop for content and language teachers. *Quality Assurance Review for Higher Education, 3*(2), 155–162.

Robbins, L. (1963). *Higher education: Report of the committee appointed by the prime minister under the chairmanship of Lord Robbins*. London: Her Majesty's Stationary Office.

Robertson, R. (1992). *Globalization: Social theory and global culture*. London: Sage Publications.

Rumbley, L. E., Altbach, P. G., Stanfield, D. A., Shimmi, Y., de Gayardon, A., & Chan, R. Y. (2014). *Higher education: A worldwide inventory of research centers, academic programs, and journals and publications* (3rd ed.). Boston, MA: Center for International Higher Education.

Scholten, P., Entzinger, H., Penninx, R., & Verbeek, S. (Eds.). (2015). *Integrating immigrants in Europe: Research-policy dialogues* (IMISCOE Research Series). Dordrecht: Springer. doi:10.1007/978-3-319-16256-0_11

Schröttner, B. T. (2012). The need for global consciousness: Debate on globalization, migration, and education. In D. A. Urias (Ed.), *The immigration and education nexus: A focus on the context and consequences of schooling* (pp. 21–36). Rotterdam, The Netherlands: Sense Publishers.

Schuetze, H. G., & Slowey, M. (2002). Participation and exclusion: A comparative analysis of non-traditional students and lifelong learners in higher education. *Higher Education, 44*(3), 309–327. doi:10.1023/A:1019898114335

Schütze, H. G., & Slowey, M. (Eds.). (2012). *Global perspectives on higher education and lifelong learners.* London & New York, NY: Routledge.

Shin, J. C., Toutkoushian, R. K., & Teichler, U. (Eds.). (2011). *University rankings: Theoretical basis, methodology and impacts on global higher education.* Dordrecht: Springer.

Stritikus, T., & Varhese, M. M. (2012). Global movements in education and their impact on diverse students. In D. A. Urias (Ed.), *The immigration and education nexus: A focus on the context and consequences of schooling* (pp. 37–55). Rotterdam, The Netherlands: Sense Publishers.

Thompson, L. (2014). *A world on the move: The benefits of migration.* Speech given in Brussels on September 25, 2014, on behalf of the International Organization for Migration, Brussels. Retrieved from https://www.iom.int/speeches-and-talks/world-move-benefits-migration

UNHCR. (n.d.). *Education.* Retrieved from http://www.unhcr.org/education.html

Urias, D. A. (Ed.). (2012). *The immigration and education nexus: A focus on the context and consequences of schooling.* Rotterdam, The Netherlands: Sense Publishers.

Usher, A., & Medow, J. (2010). Global higher education rankings 2010: Affordability and accessibility in comparative perspective. *Higher Education Strategy Associates* [online]. Retrieved from http://hedbib.iau-aiu.net/pdf/HESA_2010_Global_HE_Rankings.pdf

van der Linden, J. (2016). *Ensuring meaningful lifelong learning opportunities for groups at risk* (Unpublished PhD dissertation). University of Groningen, Groningen.

Marie-Agnès Détourbe
INSA Toulouse, LACES EA 7437
France

PART 1

ACCESS TO HIGHER EDUCATION AND IMMIGRATION POLICIES AND STRATEGIES

RASHED AL-HAQUE

1. CANADA'S CITIZENSHIP, IMMIGRATION, AND INTERNATIONAL EDUCATION POLICIES

A Messy Assemblage of Actors and Priorities

The internationalization of higher education is paramount to Canadian universities and until recently, to the Canadian federal government. Canada's federal international education strategy states that "international education is critical to Canada's success" and "is at the heart of [Canada's] future prosperity" (Foreign Affairs, Trade and Development Canada., 2014, p. 4). The policy seeks to create a more "prosperous, more innovative, and more competitive Canada," in a "highly competitive, knowledge-based economy" (ibid.). Around the time when its international education strategy was published, Canada, under the stewardship of the Stephen Harper's Conservative government, underwent sweeping reforms to its citizenship and immigration legislation. While citizenship and immigration regulations were tightened across the board, the changes also had a major impact on how international students studying in Canada could become permanent residents and transition into Canadian citizenship (Meurrens, 2014; Wingrove, 2014a, 2014b). As such, this chapter will explore the connections between Canada's citizenship and immigration legislation and the internationalization of higher education vis-à-vis international graduate student recruitment and retention. In particular, this chapter will identify the actors assembled around citizenship, immigration, and internationalization policies in Canada, assess how much agency and voice various actors have with respect to policy formulation and enactment, and how these polices impact both universities and international students.

SETTING THE STAGE: GLOBAL TRENDS IN TIGHTENING
IMMIGRATION CONTROL

The tightening of immigration policies is not new nor is it exclusive to Canada. It is slowly becoming a hallmark of "the age of migration" a time when there is "a massive increase in global population movement and an increase in the complexity of the types of movement – permanent and temporary, legal and undocumented, forced and voluntary, work and non-work related" (Hugo, 2004, p. 1). However, the movement of people across borders is often met with social and political resistance from receiving countries. Within our current global landscape, immigration is one

M.-A. Détourbe (Ed.), Inclusion through Access to Higher Education, 3–20.
© 2018 Sense Publishers. All rights reserved.

of the most controversial and politically charged facets of globalization. While countries are more open to international trade and financial integration, many are often against greater inflows of immigrants into a country (Malhotra, Margalit, & Mo, 2013). In European countries such as the United Kingdom, France, and Austria, Switzerland, where national security and economic hardship concerns dominate national and transnational politics, conservative political parties and their voters vie for more restrictive immigration policies to limit the numbers of dissimilar groups within their respective national spheres (Breckenridge & Moghaddam, 2012; Malhotra, Margalit, & Mo, 2013). In countries such as Norway, Sweden, Italy, and the Netherlands, skepticism towards immigration and immigrants has resulted in a growing shift away from multiculturalism and the scaling back of official and de facto multiculturalism policies. The push towards restrictive immigration policies has instead placed greater emphasis on citizenship, a push for assimilation, and greater social cohesion (Akkerman & Hagelund, 2007; de Wit, 2011a). By focusing on stricter immigration policies, conservative political parties in many Western countries introduce tensions between them and other groups who view immigration/ migration as a means to advance local economies. Thus, arguably as globalization accelerates so will the support for economic migrations and stricter rules and regulations for immigration (Breckenridge & Moghaddam, 2012).

These changes to immigration and citizenship laws are of concern to both international students and the institutions of higher education that receive them (Altbach, 2013). "As a result of the economic crisis and increased anti-immigration politics, international students and skilled immigration are...high on the political and educational agenda in [Western] countries as a potential negative issue" (de Wit, 2012, p. 431). The fear is that these restrictive immigration policies will negatively impact international student mobility and may lead to loss of talent and skill if international students are unable to transition into permanent residents in their host countries post-graduation (Altbach, 2013; Choudaha, 2011; de Wit, 2011b; de Wit, Ferencz, & Rumbley, 2013).

SETTING THE CANADIAN CONTEXT

Over the past four years, Canada has undergone some dramatic shifts in its priorities with respect to citizenship, immigration, and international education strategy. However, before we begin talking about Canada's immigration policies and its perspectives on higher education, it is important to briefly discuss the nature of Canadian federalism and how citizenship and immigration, along with higher education policy, is divided between the federal government and the provinces, respectively. Canada is a federal constitutional monarchy and a parliamentary democracy made up of three autonomous territories and ten partially self-governing provinces (Shanahan & Jones, 2007). While there is no universally accepted definition of federalism, the very nature of Canada as a federal state influences its policy towards immigration, citizenship, and higher education. "Canada has a federal system of government, which means it has a lot of governments" (Smith, 2004, p. 7). From provincial and territorial governments to local and municipal authorities, to Aboriginal and the federal government, Canadian federalism defines Canada and impacts the country's democratic life (Smith, 2004).

In Canada, the federal government controls immigration and citizenship legislation whereas individual provinces have jurisdiction over education, both K-12 and higher education. In 2014, under Stephen Harper's Conservatives, the federal government proposed changes to Canada's citizenship and immigration legislation, under *Bill C-24* that introduced changes to Canada's *Citizenship Act*. As the first update to citizenship laws in a generation, *Bill C-24* was one of the most contested Bills to make it into law as part of the 2014 *Citizenship Act* and was intended to address many of the problems facing the Canadian immigration system (Adams, Macklin, & Omidvar, 2014; The Globe and Mail, 2014; Wingrove, 2014a). However, experts warned that the revisions to the *Citizenship Act*, along with changes to Canada's *Immigration and Refugee Protection Act* would have detrimental effects on Canadian universities and international students who want to transition into permanent residency and Canadian citizenship after completing their studies (Adams, Macklin, & Omidvar, 2014). The changes include lengthening the time it takes for international students to become permanent residents and Canadian citizens, stripping away the time credit that internationals students were awarded for studying in Canadian higher education institutions when applying for citizenship, and dictating that only registered immigration consultants at universities could offer immigration advice to international students (Tamburri, 2013). Additionally, the Conservatives introduced and streamlined the use of the Express Entry system, which is a federal government-sponsored lottery system that offers immigration invitations based on the number of points a potential immigrant has.

Around the same time, the Canadian federal government released its *International Education Strategy* (Foreign Affairs, Trade and Development Canada, 2014). This was the first time that the federal government, through the Ministry of International Trade, under what is now called Global Affairs Canada, had issued a strategy on education. Historically, the federal government had limited input in educational matters, as education is a provincial mandate. With no concrete federal policy specifically governing the internationalization of Canadian universities, individual institutions are tasked with creating their own internationalization policies and had been doing so long before the federal government issued its strategy (Jones, 2009; Trilokekar, 2009). The strategy highlights the importance of international education for Canada's future economic prosperity, showcases the potential for Canada to become an educational hub, and calls for greater partnerships with actors across various levels of governance, between key stakeholders in industry, and greater cooperation between trading partners (Foreign Affairs, Trade and Development Canada, 2014). The introduction of the federal international education strategy outlines the complex relationship between the federal and provincial governments with respect to who is responsible for education. While historically, education largely fell into the jurisdiction of Canada' provinces, the

5

federal government is quickly starting to become a stronger player in the international education sphere. With the introduction of the 2014 federal international education strategy, internationalization no longer rests solely within the provincial domain but also resides within the federal policy arena.

Adding to the complexity and the political context of this research was the 2015 Canadian federal election that installed Justin Trudeau and his Liberal government in power after nine years of Conservative rule led by Stephen Harper. The policies that were ushered in under Harper in 2014 are now once again poised for review and reform, adding to the discourse around how citizenship, immigration, and international education are intrinsically tied together.

RESEARCH SITE AND METHODS

This research was conducted at Central University (pseudonym) – a public, research-intensive university in Ontario that has a strong international focus and is committed to internationalization. The university is deeply invested in research and knowledge production, markets itself as a top-Canadian institution for foreign students, and since 2014 has released a series of strategic documents that seeks to advance the university's global profile. The university prides itself as being ranked among the top 1% of the world's universities. Approximately 18% of its graduate students are international students, hailing from 95 countries.

To conduct my study, I used qualitative research methodologies and conducted an instrumental case study to understand which actors were assembled around university internationalization, federal international education, and citizenship and immigration policies (Baxter & Jack, 2008; Stake, 1995). Because case studies are extremely effective in identifying unclear boundaries between phenomena and context, and understanding how they interact (Yin, 2014), I was able to use Central University to uncover how the institution was connected to federal international education, citizenship, and immigration policies, who the key players were at the institutional and governmental levels, and how federal policies on citizenship and immigration impacted the university.

To gather data, I first analysed three sets of policies. The first set included the Central University's *Strategic Plan* and its complementary *International Action Plan* for 2014–2019. These documents gave me a sense of the university's commitment to internationalization, helped identify key players and departments at the university that are tasked with advancing its internationalization agenda, and allowed me to see if there was any connection between university policy and federal citizenship and immigration legislation. Second, I examined *Canada's International Education Strategy* that was published by the Conservative federal government in 2014. The document highlighted Canada's vision for international education. The strategy outlined Canada's goals to recruit more international students to its educational institutions, highlighted key target markets students could be recruited from, and endeavoured to make Canada a competitive destination for foreign students. Central to the strategy (and that of the Minister of International Trade) is the belief that international education is a tradable commodity that can bring economic benefits for Canada. I explored the extent to which citizenship and immigration policies are discussed in this policy document to understand if the federal government makes a link between the two. Last, I analyzed Canada's *Citizenship Act* and the recent changes to the Act proposed by the introduction of *Bill C-24*. Additionally, I also analyzed Canada's *Immigration and Refugee Protection Act* to fully understand the policies towards citizenship and immigration. In addition to the three sets of policies, I reviewed other published, archival materials that were relevant to internationalization at Central University and in Canada. I examined any archival documents that discuss Canada's citizenship and immigration policies to understand the larger discourse around how changes to Canada's citizenship and immigration policies related to the world of higher education.

In addition to analyzing policy documents, I interviewed ten mid to senior level university administrators and ten international university graduate students who expressed an interest in immigrating to Canada after graduation. All participants were given pseudonyms to maintain confidentiality and anonymity. All the interviews were conducted during the summer of 2015, were semi-structured, and lasted from 30 to 60 minutes. The interviews with administrators gave me a sense of who the central players are in enacting the university's internationalization policy, indicated how much voice and agency universities have with respect to the changes in federal citizenship and immigration legislation, as it pertains to universities, and also highlighted key actors responsible for enacting both citizenship and immigration, and internationalization policies at the federal level. Interviews with international graduate students gave me a sense of who the key players are in enacting internationalization at the university. However, seeing that this chapter is part of a larger research study, I will primarily focus on the perspectives of university administrators and how citizenship, immigration, and internationalization policies impact them and the work they do to internationalize the academy.

THEORETICAL FRAMEWORK

For this study, I used Critical Policy Analysis [CPA] (Ball, 2006; Rizvi & Lingard, 2010) and Actor Network Theory [ANT] (Edwards & Fenwick, 2015; Latour, 2005; Law, 2009) to understand internationalization, citizenship, and immigration policy in a relational context. To begin, I understand policy not just as what governments do or do not do, but rather as an "authoritative allocation of values" that is written and enacted (Rizvi & Lingard, 2010, p. 36). Therefore, policies are flexible, they change with time, and respond to the social and political milieu in which they were created (Rizvi & Lingard, 2010). Given the political nature of this research that links higher education internationalization with national/federal legislation on citizenship and immigration, it is important to look at how policies are framed and how their enactment impacts universities and ultimately international students.

While CPA seeks to uncover the unequal distribution of power, knowledge, and influence among policy actors (Ozga, 2000; Prunty, 1985; Rizvi & Lingard, 2010; Taylor, 1997), ANT explores policy in a relational context and unearths the impact of human and non-human actors assembled around policies (Law, 2009). ANT is "a disparate family of material-semiotic tools, sensibilities, and methods of analysis that treat everything in the social and natural worlds as a contentiously generated effect of the webs of relations with which they are located" (Law, 2009, p. 141). ANT's focus on the "role of matter and material in human practices" (Edwards & Fenwick, 2015, p. 1385) allows researchers to explore policies across multiple levels of governance to demonstrate how the assemblage of actors affect the network of relations to create order, meaning, and organized action (Fleetwood, 2005; Meikle, 1985; Mutch, 2002).

Unlike traditional policy analysis that often follows a linear format, CPA combined with ANT appreciates the complexities in the assemblage of actors enrolled around policies. Thus, the concept of assemblage is important to this research. Derived from the French *agencement*, the term refers to the coming together of different, heterogeneous parts to form a whole (Müller, 2015). Understanding policy as an assemblage is central not just to ANT but also to CPA and recognizes that policies involve a variety of actors that connect across people, objects, and locations (Gorur, 2011). Assemblage thinking thus seeks to understand how various actors come together around citizenship, immigration, and higher education internationalization policies and how relationally they enable and/or disable certain actors to create action and change. In the context of this study, the two complementary frameworks helped me identify the actors assembled around citizenship, immigration, and internationalization policies in Canada, how much agency and voice they have with respect to creating and enacting policies, and how federal legislation impacts university internationalization at the institutional level.

IDENTIFYING ACTORS ASSEMBLED AROUND INTERNATIONALIZATION, CITIZENSHIP, AND IMMIGRATION POLICIES

At the university level, there were several key actors assembled around internationalization. Scholars note that internationalization is a "process" that seeks to integrate an "international and intercultural dimension into the teaching, research and service functions of the institution" (Knight, 2004, pp. 9–10; Knight, 2007). Internationalizing activities include activities such as encouraging student exchanges, internationalizing the curriculum, and promoting international research collaborations (Altbach & Knight, 2007; Qiang, 2003). However, recruiting greater numbers of international students to the university is arguably one of the most prominent internationalizing activities: it is at the heart of Canada's federal *International Education Strategy* and is a key component of Central University's internationalization agenda. As such, Central University's *Strategic Plan* and its complementary *International Action Plan* served as the framework to direct and promote its internationalization vision. The *Strategic Plan* calls for the university to embody a "world-class research and scholarship culture" and engage with "international partners" including foreign research and educational institutions. Additionally, the *Strategic Plan* seeks to "increase international undergraduate student enrolment to at least 15%." Internationalization is also highlighted as one of 16 "Institutional Principles and Values" at Central University, whereby the university seeks to "embrace [its] role as an active member of the global academic community." The university's *International Action Plan* further emphasizes the goals of the *Strategic Plan*, specifically aspires to "develop a comprehensive and strategic international graduate student recruitment plan" from partner countries, and endeavors to provide more support to international graduate and undergraduate students through the university's International Office. As such a majority of administrators and many international graduate students identified the International Office, along with immigration consultants who advised students on immigration regulations, as key players in enacting the university's internationalization strategy. Other actors included the School of Graduate and Postdoctoral Studies (SGPS) in the recruitment of international graduate students and in providing them with support to file their immigration and permanent residency applications, and the Society of Graduate Students to advocate on behalf of international students. However, an overwhelming majority of administrators claimed that university leaders, including the provosts and President, were "very important" and "spokespeople" for promoting the university's international education at the federal level. Executive Director of Strategic Projects at Central University, Jessica McKinsey, claimed that the president, Dr. Anand Choudhury, was central to mobilizing the university's internationalization strategy because he "believes in it." Dr. Laura McDonald, the Vice Provost of the School of Graduate and Postdoctoral Studies, added:

> Our university president has been very active in terms of federal initiatives regarding internationalization. So I think we're probably better positioned than other universities, particularly universities in Ontario with respect to having somebody who not only has a voice but is highly regarded in that perspective. You also have an advisor to the President whose role is to be the liaison with the federal government. (personal communication, July 3, 2015)

Studies have shown that a leader's vision for international education at their institution was a driving force behind advancing internationalization on campus (Larsen & Al-Haque, 2016).

To explore the actors at the governmental levels, we have to explore the actors at both the federal and provincial levels. Provincially, in Ontario, international education lies with the Ontario Ministry of Advanced Education and Skills Development (MAESD). In 2016, MAESD published its *Developing Global Opportunities: Creating a Postsecondary International Education Strategy for*

Ontario (MAESD, 2016), where the ministry recognized the importance of internationalization to Ontario universities. As such, "the province is looking to develop a postsecondary international education strategy that not only positions Ontario as a destination and partner of choice but also showcases Ontario as a leader on the global stage" (MAESD, 2016, p. 4). However, this strategy was created after Canada's federal international education strategy, calling into question how much agency the province has with respect to international education, when compared to both individual institutions and the federal government. University administrators, however, are optimistic. Noting that other provinces such as British Columbia have a provincial international education strategy for the postsecondary sector, Central university president, Dr. Choudhury added: "I'm glad that our province, the province of Ontario is going to have one…this simply means that there will be more capacity to implement some of the ideas that we have put forth" (personal communication, July 23, 2015). Federally, Global Affairs Canada, under the portfolio of international trade, is responsible for international education. To date, the document entitled *Canada's international education strategy: Harnessing our knowledge advantage to drive innovation and prosperity* has served as Canada's federal international education strategy. It promotes an economic rationale for internationalizing education in Canada, seeks to give the country a "competitive advantage" in today's knowledge economy, and places a heavy emphasis on recruiting international students and researchers from what the strategy regards as "priority markets." These markets include Brazil, China, India, Vietnam, Mexico and most of the Middle East and North Africa. Because of neo-liberalization and the marketization of education in our global economy, it is not unusual to see market and market-like policy instruments regulating higher education and the process of internationalization (Dill, 1997; Marginson, 1999). While scholars of internationalization have critiqued the commoditization of higher education that prioritizes recruitment of international students as the sole basis of internationalizing (Knight, 2014), universities along with governmental bodies continue to view internationalization as a means to become a top, global university and remain competitive in today's global knowledge economy. As such, the educational/academic rationales of internationalization are being lost in the policy documents.

Because of the constitutional divide of responsibilities between the provincial and federal governments in Canada, the responsibility for citizenship and immigration policy lies with the federal government. As such, through an Actor-Network and socio-material lens, the Canadian Constitution can also be considered as an actor assembled around citizenship, immigration, and internationalization policy. Particularly, university administrators as well as many international graduate students noted that Citizenship and Immigration Canada (CIC; currently known as Immigration, Refugees, and Citizenship Canada) is the main player in creating, regulating, and implementing policy that is responsible for recruiting and retaining foreign students in Canada. "CIC is the decision maker" shared Jessica McKinsey (personal communication, July 14, 2015), the Executive Director of Strategic

Projects. Others opined that CIC is "definitely…leading the way" (Eric Doherty, Registered Immigration Consultant and Student Advisor, personal communication, July 3, 2015) and that the department "has a huge impact in terms of visa processing," (Mark Brown, Administrative Director of Entry-Level Language Program, personal communication, June 26, 2015). Other actors at the federal level include upper levels of the government, including the Prime Minister's Office and Employment and Social Development Canada (ESDC) that regulates employment regulations allowing international students to seek jobs in Canada post-graduation (MacDonald, 2016).

A key actor that was mentioned over and over again during the interviews was the Canadian Bureau of International Education (CBIE). As a special interest group, (SIG), CBIE has been instrumental in promoting international education in Canada. CBIE supports both MAESD and university presidents to promote "a grassroots, build-it-up approach so that we can find common ground about the best ways to promote Canada and have a considered internationalization strategy" (Christina Forrester, director of Central University's International Office, personal communication, September 11, 2015). Studies have shown that SIGS have been crucial to advancing the interests of their partners (Grossmann, 2012). These studies also highlight that by linking with key stakeholders across various political spheres, SIGs such as CBIE influence public policy (Richardson, 2000) and promote international education in Canada (Viczko & Tascón, 2016). The Vice-Provost International for Central University, Dr. Joelle McLean highlights the role of special interest groups such as CBIE and Universities Canada by saying:

> So I should mention those as well. So Universities Canada is a lobbying body to the federal government. And it continuously, I mean that sort of a standing item for them, is continuously lobbying the government on behalf of universities in Canada with respect to these matters. And the other body is the Canadian Bureau of International Education. And they lobby the Canadian government and CIC with respect of these matters as well. (personal communication, August 4, 2015)

CBIE's physical proximity to Ottawa means that "they have the ear of the government" to champion universities' concerns to the various levels of the federal government. University administrators felt that CBIE worked as a "unified lobbying force for universities in Canada" (Joelle McLean, Vice-Provost International, personal communication, August 4, 2015). A prime example of CBIE's lobbying power and influence over immigration and citizenship legislation was their successful efforts to reduce the amount of training university immigration consultants needed to support international students. Before the 2014 changes to Canada's citizenship and immigration laws, university student advisors could support international students by answering their immigration-related questions. However, after changes to Canada's *Immigration and Refugee Protection Act*, only trained and licensed immigration consultants were able to offer advice. Dr. McLean shared a key example of CBIE's lobbying capacity and how the Bureau worked on behalf of universities:

> So, CBIE just as an example, they actually, with respect to the certification of our staff to be able to give advice on immigration matters…So it used to be that in the first iteration of the legislation, we would have to have our staff member go through the entire immigration professionalization status. Now it seems that within the next few months, we're going to be able to just have a special component that will deal with students. So they were able to successfully lobby the government to make that change…So that's one example of how there has been successful lobbying done. (personal communication, August 4, 2015)

According to Samantha Kobe, the Director of Internationalization and Simulation at Central University's Medical School:

> CBIE is developing a course specifically for International Student Advisors whereas in the past the advisors who have been certified, who are now registered, they had to do the full program. So they didn't just have to know about the international student advising piece but also business immigrants, refugees, areas that have absolutely nothing to do with their area.

It is clear that SIGs, such as CBIE, have a great deal of influence over the federal government and present a unified voice to champion the needs and concerns of Canadian higher education.

ASSESSING AGENCY, VOICE, AND INFLUENCE OVER CITIZENSHIP, IMMIGRATION, AND INTERNATIONALIZATION POLICIES

Individual institutions of higher education in Canada have the greatest amount of agency in devising and enacting internationalization policy. Unlike other countries like the United States, Australia, and the United Kingdom, Canada is relatively new to having a federal strategy on international education (Jones, 2009; Trilokekar, 2009), leaving individual institutions with the task and flexibility to design internationalization strategies that fit them best. As such, some university administrators interviewed in the study felt that there were mismatched priorities between the federal international education strategy and that of Central University, and that universities had been internationalizing long before the federal government published its international education policy in 2014 (Dr. Donald Johnson, Vice-Dean of Basic Medical Science, personal communication, July 20, 2015). According to Johnson, this is primarily because of lack of communication between the federal government and the universities, and the difficulties of having a "one-size-fits-all" international education policy. Administrators felt that only through concerted and effective dialogue can all actors involved – universities, the provincial government, and their ministries responsible for higher education – have a voice in championing international education in Canada. Until then, it seems as though they have all been competing against each other to dictate what values are championed in internationalizing higher education. While the federal strategy places greater emphasis on the economic rationales for international education, Central University's internationalization policy highlights the academic and socio-cultural benefits of internationalization that result from a movement of ideas and peoples across borders. As such, in the context of internationalization, universities have the greatest say.

Universities however lack a voice and influence over Canada's citizenship and immigration legislation and are expected to abide by the country's federal laws. This includes abiding with regulations around international student recruitment and the ability to support international students with advice on immigration matters. Additionally, international students have to follow Canada's immigration laws and are subject to government-sponsored pathways to immigration via the Express Entry system. Most of the university administrators interviewed for the study felt that the university lacked the ability to voice concerns to the federal government on laws that directly influenced international student recruitment and retention. "I just think the federal government hasn't really been consulting with universities with respect to immigration policies" said Dr. Laura McDonald, the Vice-Provost of SGPS (personal communication, July 3, 2015), while Dr. Donald Johnson, the Vice Dean of Basic Medical Science, thought that "influence of the universities on immigration and citizenship part of the government is fairly limited" (personal communication, July 20, 2015). Throughout the interviews, many administrators were critical of the federal government's disregard for universities' concerns and thought that there was a lack of cooperation between the two. Even the university president felt that the federal government and universities lacked harmony and cooperation when it came to citizenship and immigration policies, adding: "they do whatever they do, and you know, from time to time, they will reach out to us. Most of the time they don't. And then we react to those changes" (Dr. Anand Choudhury, Central University President, personal communication, July 23, 2015). According to the university president, universities merely react and try to adapt to changes, as they have "very marginal" influence over national policy discourses that directly affect universities.

At least one of the participants, Dr. Donald Johnson, felt that this disconnect was heightened by the Conservative Party of Canada, who were in power in 2014 when citizenship and immigration policy changes took place. He felt that the Conservative government "[didn't] tend to listen well, regardless of what you're coming forward with." He described the Conservative government as "a closed shop," explaining that the government was "not particularly...sensitive to some of the feelings of some of the constituents over some of these issues," and that it was "far more closed-minded," which resulted in the passing of stringent laws on immigration and citizenship that clashed with the aspirations of universities (personal communication, July 20, 2015). The Conservative government's lack of "sensibility" is what silenced universities from voicing their concerns.

Specifically within the federal government and with respect to citizenship and immigration policies, Citizenship and Immigration Canada (CIC) is the most important player. Citizenship and Immigration Canada has the greatest say in regulating laws that allow people to come in and out of the country, and also facilitates the transition of international students to permanent residents. However, some participants, including Eric Doherty who is Registered Immigration Consultant and Student Advisor at Central University, felt that CIC "do whatever they want" when it comes to creating and enacting citizenship and immigration laws, irrespective of how it may impact universities. When asked about the amount of communication that universities have with CIC and about a reciprocal consultative process between the federal body and universities, Doherty shared that "it is piss-poor communication, as far as [he knows] …But in terms of direct communication from the universities to the CIC, I don't think it happens…[it] is one way communication" (personal communication, July 3, 2015). In this regard, CIC, and through extension the federal government, is didactic in its approach to citizenship and immigration policy development and enactment. "Anyone who thinks that post-secondary institutions have power is really misguided. They could but they are not well organized…" shared Doherty in a rebuke of both the federal government and also universities' abilities to approach the federal government (personal communication, July 3, 2015).

Part of this disconnect seems to be because universities are not seen as key actors in policy discourses around citizenship and immigration in Canada. University president Dr. Anand Choudhury shared that "the opportunities are very minimal" for universities to voice their opinions and concerns, "because [universities] are not seen as stakeholders, serious stakeholders in that sort of conversations." He added that the "government still doesn't see the universities" and opined that "when [universities] explain to [the federal government], they see it. But in general they don't see us as institutions that are instrumental to their immigration policy" (personal communication, July 23, 2015). Therefore, universities are largely absent from policy discourses at the federal level, even though they are impacted when federal policies around citizenship and immigration are enacted.

How do these policies affect Canadian higher education institutions and international students? As part of this chapter, I want to highlight three impacts mismatched policies, lack of effective consultations between universities and the federal government, and restrictive immigration and citizenship laws have on both universities and internationals students. First, these policies may make it harder for universities to recruit international students and discourage highly skilled international students from remaining in Canada after graduation. Second, these mismatched policies negatively impact universities and their ability to internationalize. Third, these policies negatively impact international graduate students as they study in Canada and seek to transition into permanent residents post-graduation.

We must remember that in our globalized and interconnected world, more and more international students cross borders to seek an education. Countries around the world, including Canada, are competing against each other to attract highly skilled individuals who often come in as international students. Even though Europe and North America are top destinations for mobile students, other non-traditional countries are rising as destinations for tertiary education (de Wit, 2012; de Wit, Ferencz, & Rumbley, 2013). However, scholars warn that restrictive immigration policies will impact skilled labour recruitment in Western countries and ultimately impact international student mobility and recruitment: "As a result of the economic crisis and increased anti-immigration politics, international students and skilled immigration are...high on the political and educational agenda in [Western] countries as a potential negative issue" (de Wit, 2012, p. 431). Administrators from Central University echoed these concerns in the interviews and shared that if Canada was making it more difficult for international students to remain in Canada post-graduation, then the university may have a harder time attracting future international students, promoting Canada as a study destination, and retaining international talent that Canadian universities have nurtured. Mark Brown, an administrative director for Central University's entry-level language program, warned that "for people with higher education degrees, there is a tremendous amount of competition globally for talent." He explained that "[Canada] cannot rest on [its] laurels! We have a great country...but we can't rest on our laurels," adding that "if we don't leave the welcome mat out, they are not going to stay; they can easily leave to somewhere else" as "there are all kinds of countries that want educated people" (personal communication, June 26, 2015). International students view their study experiences in Canada as an investment and want tangible outcomes and payoffs. A mismatch between international students' expectations and experiences may lead to dissatisfaction and also poor retention (Ortiz & Choudaha, 2014), thus disrupting Canada's aspirations to advance its economy and society.

Recall that international student recruitment is such a key component of Central University's internationalization strategy. Because Canada is trying to market itself as a prime study destination, mismatched policies that seem to penalize international students and limit how universities can support them will only hinder universities' internationalization efforts. If federal policy changes without notice and without proper consultation across various levels of governance, universities are often caught off-guard. When asked how citizenship and immigration policy changes impact universities, the Vice Provost International of Central University shared that "the short answer [was] that it [didn't] help too much." She added that when policy changed, universities "[had] to comply...[making] it challenging for [them]" to operate. Many administrators shared the sentiment that they were "troubleshooting" as "matters come up" instead of focusing on the university's internationalization agenda (Joelle McLean, personal communication, August 4, 2015). One prime example of how abrupt policy changes to the federal government negatively impact the university's ability to internationalize and support international students comes from the federal government's amendment to Canada's *Immigration and Refugee Protection Act*, along with changing who can offer immigration advice to international students at Canadian universities. Samantha Kobe, the Director of Internationalization and Simulation at Central University Medical School explained how universities are not engaged in discussion with the federal government about how universities can and should support international students about immigration issues. Kobe stated:

> The student advising change maybe is an example where I really don't think the government realized the implications of making that change of requiring someone to be a registered legal consultant. Another one is a recent change with immigration, is the temporary foreign workers…Universities across Canada invite all kinds of international visiting scholars and post-docs and short term visitors. And with these recent changes at CIC, they are now deemed as workers. They have to apply for a work permit. And there is a cost associated with it. And you basically have to prove that this person isn't taking away a position from a Canadian. So it's jumping through hoops. And again, all of this was released… in February of this year. And it completely caught all of the university off-guard. And I know that organizations like the [CBIE], which advocates on behalf of universities wasn't apprised either of this neither was [Association of Universities and Colleges of Canada]. So, based on my own experience, no. The response to your question is no. I don't think that universities are actively engaged in the discussions. (personal communication, August 19, 2015)

Kobe's explanation is an explicit example of what happens when sweeping policy changes happen at the federal level and how a lack of consultation on policy issues across multiple levels of governance (federal, provincial, and institutional) impacts universities. Her explanation also highlights the limits of organizations such as CBIE that work on behalf of universities. Even organizations based in Ottawa and physically closer to the federal government in comparison to universities are often not made aware of policy changes and are left to adapt instead of having an active role in the consultative process. Some senior level administrators shared that as a result of the change, the university had to hire new immigration consultants, which itself had a financial cost to the university and ultimately made it more difficult for the university to internationalize.

Ultimately, those who are the most affected by these policy changes are international students. For international students, federal policy changes meant that some were unable to access timely immigration advice from university advisors and were caught off-guard by immigration and citizenship polices deemed strict and restrictive. International students had the least amount of say in Canada's internationalization, citizenship and immigration policies, even though it affects them and their future career goals. Initial data from the interviews with international graduate students at Central University reveal that these policies placed huge stresses on international graduate students, particularly those who are at the end of their degree programs. Both university administrators and international graduate students shared that restrictive immigration policies may hinder both the recruitment and retention of international students and make Canada seem like an unfavourable country to study in. "Restrictions in immigration and greater barriers for access to higher education for national and foreign students will make Europe less attractive for international students" warned de Wit (2011a, p. 31), who saw similar trends emerging in Europe. Arguably, Canada's citizenship and immigration reforms may have the same effect as these policies place systemic barriers to integration into Canadian society vis-à-vis immigration and make students feel unwelcome.

CONCLUSIONS, IMPLICATIONS, AND FUTURE PROSPECTS

As mentioned earlier, this chapter is part of a larger study that explores the relationships between citizenship and immigration policies and the internationalization of higher education in Canada. Unlike other research on internationalization and international student mobility, this study looks at policies in a relational context. Using Actor Network Theory and Critical Policy Analysis, this study uses a critical sociomaterial lens to investigate the human and non-human actors assembled around citizenship, immigration, and internationalization polices. From the data, we can clearly see that there are a variety of competing actors assembled around citizenship, immigration, and internationalization policies in Canada. This assemblage is complex, and includes both human actors such as presidents and ministers and non-human actors such as the Canadian constitution and federal departments. The complexity of this assemblage helps reveal the unevenness of agency and voice in policy discourses, in how policies are enacted, and the misalignment of values between the government and the university.

Because the changes to Canada's citizenship and immigrant polices are still relatively new, it will take some time to fully understand how they will affect higher education, student mobility, and Canada's image as a welcoming country for future transnational students. One of the most challenging aspects of this research has been the rapid changes to federal immigration and citizenship policy. Just as university administrators and international students struggle to cope and adapt to policy changes, as a researcher, it has been difficult for me to track policy changes from 2014 to 2016. The ascent of the Liberal government in Canada after the 2015 elections has brought new hope. The Liberal government has made it explicitly clear that it sees international students as an asset to Canada and is in the process of reviewing federal citizenship and immigration policies along with the Express Entry system to see how it may impact international students (McCallum, 2016). University leaders are optimistic that the Liberal government's interest in international education will serve as a boon to both universities and their international students. As of November 19, 2016, the Liberal government changed the Express Entry scoring system to help rebalance the points awarded to applicants applying for permanent residency. Under the revised Express Entry system, applicants who do not have a job offer from a Canadian employer, such as new international graduates, will have a higher chance of being invited for permanent residency. Additionally, under the new scoring system, international students with a Canadian university and/or college degree will be awarded 30 points, increasing the likelihood that international graduates and highly skilled foreign workers can become permanent residents (Zilio, 2016).

17

Because the federal government's review process is still in its early stages, we will have to wait and see how the Liberal government's reforms will affect universities. Time will tell if and how federal immigration and citizenship polices, governed by Citizenship and Immigration Canada, will reflect the internationalization strategy of Global Affairs Canada, and if both will reflect the internationalization aspirations of Canadian institutions of higher learning.

While this research is still in its early stages, the implications and methods used in the study are significant and can be replicated in other national contexts that are hubs for international higher education and foreign students. At a time when internationalizing higher education is important across the world (Larsen, 2016), it is imperative that we study the enactment of internationalization policy at the university and how internationalization policy works in relationship to a country's citizenship and immigration laws. Only then will we be able to appreciate how national and/or federal legislation connects with the internationalizing aspirations of the university, where policies align, and where they are misaligned. Future studies that examine citizenship, immigration, and internationalization policies need to explore how these policies impact universities' relationships with national governments, how nation/federal policies affect international students, and how policies across various levels of governance impact higher education in an age of increased global mobility, transnationalism, and internationalization.

REFERENCES

Adams, M., Macklin, A., & Omidvar, R. (2014, May 21). Citizenship act will create two classes of Canadians. *The Globe and Mail.* Retrieved from http://www.theglobeandmail.com/globe-debate/citizenship-act-will-create-two-classes-of-canadians/article18778296/

Akkerman, T., & Hagelund, A. (2007). Women and children first! Anti-immigration parties and gender in Norway and the Netherlands. *Patterns of Prejudice, 41*(2), 197–214.

Altbach, P. G. (2013). *The international imperative in higher education.* Rotterdam, The Netherlands: Sense Publishers.

Altbach, P. G., & Knight, J. (2007). The internationalization of higher education: Motivations and realities. *Journal of Studies in International Education, 11,* 290–305.

Ball, S. J. (2006). *Education policy and social class: The selected works of Stephen J. Ball.* New York, NY: Routledge.

Baxter, P., & Jack, S. (2008). Qualitative case study methodology: Study design and implementation for novice researchers. *The Qualitative Report, 13*(4), 544–559.

Breckenridge, J. N., & Moghaddam, F. M. (2012). Globalization and a conservative dilemma: Economic openness and retributive policies. *Journal of Social Issues, 68*(3), 559–570.

Choudaha, R. (2011, October 2). The future of international student mobility. *University World News.* Retrieved from http://www.universityworldnews.com

de Wit, H. (2011a). International students and immigration: The Netherlands case in a European context. *Lifelong Learning in Europe, 16*(1), 30–34.

de Wit, H. (2011b). *Trends, issues and challenges in internationalization of higher education.* Amsterdam: Centre for Applied Research on Economics and Management, Hogeschool van Amsterdam.

de Wit, H. (2012). Student mobility between Europe and the rest of the world: Trends, issues and challenges. In A. Curaj, P. Scott, L. Vlasceanu, & L. Wilson (Eds.), *European higher education at the crossroads* (pp. 431–439). Dordrecht: Springer.

de Wit, H., Ferencz, I., & Rumbley, L. E. (2013). International student mobility: European and US perspectives. *Perspectives: Policy and Practice in Higher Education, 17*(1), 17–23.

Dill, D. D. (1997). Higher education markets and public policy. *Higher Education Policy, 10*(3), 167–185.

Edwards, R., & Fenwick, T. (2015). Critique and politics: A socio-materialist intervention. *Educational Philosophy and Theory, 47*(13–14), 1385–1404.

Fleetwood, S. (2005). Ontology in organization and management studies: A critical realist perspective. *Organization, 12*(2), 197–222.

Foreign Affairs, Trade and Development Canada. (2014). *Canada's international education strategy: Harnessing our knowledge advantage to drive innovation and prosperity* (Catalogue No.: FR5-86/2014). Ottawa: DFATD. Retrieved from http://international.gc.ca/global-markets-marches-mondiaux/assets/pdfs/overview-apercu-eng.pdf

Gorur, R. (2011). Policy as assemblage. *European Educational Research Journal, 10*(4), 611–622.

Grossmann, M. (2012). Interest group influence on US policy change: An assessment based on policy history. *Interest Groups & Advocacy, 1*(2), 171–192.

Hugo, G. (2004). *A new paradigm of international migration: Implications for migration policy and planning for Australia* (Research paper No. 10). Canberra: Department of Parliamentary Services.

Jones, G. A. (2009). Internationalization and higher education policy in Canada: Three challenges. In R. Trilokekar, G. Jones, & A. Shubert (Eds.), *Canada's universities go global* (pp. 355–369). Toronto: James Lorimer and Company (CAUT Series).

Knight, J. (2004). Internationalization remodeled: Definition, approaches, and rationales. *Journal of Studies in International Education, 8*(1), 5–31.

Knight, J. (2007). Internationalization: Concepts, complexities and challenges. In J. Forest & P. Altbach (Eds.), *International handbook of higher education* (pp. 207–227). Dordrecht: Springer.

Knight, J. (2014). Is internationalisation of higher education having an identity crisis? In A. Maldonado-Maldonado & R. M. Bassett (Eds.), *The forefront of international higher education* (Vol. 42, pp. 75–87). Dordrecht: Springer.

Larsen, M. (2016). *Internationalization of higher education: An analysis through spatial, network, and motilities theories.* New York, NY: Palgrave Macmillan.

Larsen, M., & Al-Haque, R. (2016). Higher education leadership and the internationalization imaginary: Where personal biography meets the socio-historical. In L. Shultz & M. Vizcko (Eds.), *Democracy, social justice and leadership in higher education* (pp. 403–423). New York, NY: Palgrave Macmillan.

Latour, B. (2005). *Reassembling the social: An introduction to actor-network-theory.* Oxford: Oxford University Press.

Law, J. (2009). Actor network theory and material semiotics. In B. Turner (Ed.), *The new Blackwell companion to social theory* (pp. 141–158). Singapore: Blackwell Publishing Ltd.

MacDonald, M. (2016, May 10). Canadian government signals renewed openness to international students. *University Affairs* (News section). Retrieved from http://www.universityaffairs.ca/news/news-article/canadian-government-signals-renewed-openness-international-students/

MAESD. (2016). *Developing global opportunities: Creating a postsecondary international education strategy for Ontario.* Toronto: Ministry of Training, Colleges and Universities. Retrieved from http://www.tcu.gov.on.ca/pepg/consultations/PSIDDiscussionPaperEN.pdf

Malhotra, N., Margalit, Y., & Mo, C. H. (2013). Economic explanations for opposition to immigration: Distinguishing between prevalence and conditional impact. *American Journal of Political Science, 57*(2), 391–410.

Marginson, S. (1999). After globalization: Emerging politics of education. *Journal of Education Policy, 14*(1), 19–31.

McCallum, J. (2016, June 14). *Speaking notes for John McCallum, minister of immigration, refugees and citizenship at a luncheon hosted by the Canadian club of Ottawa.* Retrieved from http://news.gc.ca/web/article-en.do?nid=1086189

Meikle, S. (1985). *Essentialism in the thought of Karl Marx.* London: Duckworth.

Meurrens, S. (2014, August 03). Bill c-24 is now law: Canadian citizenship is harder to get, easier to lose. *The Times of India.* Retrieved from http://timesofindia.indiatimes.com/world/new-to-canada/Bill-C-24-is-now-law-Canadian-citizenship-is-harder-to-get-easier-to-lose/articleshow/38975551.cms

Müller, M. (2015). Assemblages and actor-networks: Rethinking socio-material power, politics and space. *Geography Compass, 9*(1), 27–41.

Mutch, A. (2002). Actors and networks or agents and structures: Towards a realist view of information systems. *Organization, 9*(3), 477–496.

Ortiz, A., & Choudaha, R. (2014, May 1). Attracting and retaining international students in Canada. *World Education Services (WES) Research & Advisory Services.* Retrieved from https://wenr.wes.org/2014/05/attracting-and-retaining-international-students-in-canada

Ozga, J. (2000). *Policy research in educational settings: Contested terrain.* Buckingham: Open University Press.

Prunty, J. J. (1985). Signposts for a critical educational policy analysis. *Australian Journal of Education, 24*(2), 133–140.

Qiang, Z. (2003). Internationalization of higher education: Towards a conceptual framework. *Policy Futures in Education, 1*, 248–270.

Richardson, J. (2000). Government, interest groups and policy change. *Political Studies, 48*(5), 1006–1025.

Rizvi, F., & Lingard, B. (2010). *Globalizing educational policy.* London: Routledge.

Shanahan, T., & Jones, G. A. (2007). Shifting roles and approaches: Government co-ordination of post-secondary education in Canada, 1995–2006. *Higher Education Research & Development, 26*(1), 31–43.

Smith, J. (2004). *Federalism.* Vancouver: University of British Columbia Press.

Stake, R. E. (1995). *The art of case study research.* Thousand Oaks, CA: Sage Publications.

Tamburri, R. (2013, August 7). University staff face new restrictions on how they advise foreign students. *University Affairs.* Retrieved from http://www.universityaffairs.ca/news/news-article/university-staff-face-new-restrictions-on-how-they-advise-foreign-students/

Taylor, S. (1997). Critical policy analysis: Exploring contexts, texts and consequences. *Discourse: Studies in the Cultural Politics of Education, 18*(1), 23–35.

The Globe and Mail. (2014, February 6). Chris Alexander's flawed overhaul of citizenship law. *The Globe and Mail.* Retrieved from http://www.theglobeandmail.com/globe-debate/editorials/chris-alexanders-flawed-overhaul-of-citizenship-law/article16732791/

Trilokekar, R. D. (2009). The Departments of Foreign Affairs and International Trade (DFAIT), Canada: Providing leadership in the internationalization of Canadian higher education? In R. Trilokekar, G. Jones, & A. Shubert (Eds.), *Canada's universities go global* (pp. 98–118). Toronto: James Lorimer and Company (CAUT Series).

Viczko, M., & Tascón, C. I. (2016). Performing internationalization of higher education in Canadian national policy. *Canadian Journal of Higher Education, 46*(2), 1–18.

Wingrove, J. (2014a, June 12). Minister Chris Alexander under fire as citizenship bill poised to pass. *The Globe and Mail.* Retrieved from http://www.theglobeandmail.com/news/politics/minister-chris-alexander-under-fire-as-citizenship-bill-poised-to-pass/article19151131/

Wingrove, J. (2014b, February 6). Ten ways Ottawa is changing how to become a Canadian citizen. *The Globe and Mail.* Retrieved from http://www.theglobeandmail.com/news/politics/ten-ways-ottawa-is-changing-how-to-become-a-canadian-citizen/article16724611/

Yin, R. K. (2014). *Case study research: Design and methods* (5th ed.). Thousand Oaks, CA: Sage Publication, Inc.

Zilio, M. (2016, November 14). Ottawa to ease path to permanent residency for skilled workers, students. *The Globe and Mail.* Retrieved from http://www.theglobeandmail.com/news/politics/ottawa-to-ease-path-to-permanent-residency-for-skilled-workers-students/article32846606/?cmpid=PM1116

Rashed Al-Haque
Faculty of Education
Western University
Canada

GAËLE GOASTELLEC

2. REFUGEES' ACCESS TO HIGHER EDUCATION IN EUROPE

Comparative Insights on a New Public Issue

INTRODUCTION

Asylum seekers and refugees' access to higher education (HE) has become a topical issue in the agenda of European higher education institutions since 2015, as testified by the flourishing number of position statements at European, national, and institutional higher education levels, through various media such as websites, press releases, journals or conferences. The United Nations hosted several conferences[1] on the topic, organised by the Council of Europe, the British Council, the League of Arab States, etc., as did the British Council.[2] In June 2016, the European Association for International Education (EAIE) ran a seminar[3] and the European University Association (EUA, online) even developed a website, the "refugees welcome map," centralising information on policies set up by higher education institutions in Europe. This relatively new political issue can be analysed as the product of a specific context. First, refugees' access to higher education remains scarce: 1% of all refugees access higher education (Sampaio, 2016), while around 32% of the world student-age population does (The Economist, 2015). Second, in the European Union, influxes of refugees have almost tripled within six years, from 215,000 asylum seekers in 2008 to 626,000 in 2014 (Eurostat, 2015). Access thus potentially concerns an increasing number of individuals. Furthermore, 29% of all asylum seekers are less than 18 years' old and 53% of them are between 18 and 34 years' old (Eurostat, 2015), meaning that a large majority potentially belongs to the main student age group. Lastly, an increasing proportion of refugees come from countries where education and higher education systems are well developed, for example Syria, which accounted for 20% of the refugees in 2015 (Eurostat, 2015), Iraq and the Kurdish areas (de Wit & Altbach, 2016), and are thus educationally prepared for studying at a higher level, or were already studying before they had to leave their country.

Nevertheless, little information is available about the extent to which refugees access higher education, who does and how, both at a European and national level. "Refugee" is understood here in a broad sense as comprehending the different administrative categories used by the states to classify people seeking asylum. It includes those eventually recognised and categorised as refugees by the state

M.-A. Détourbe (Ed.), Inclusion through Access to Higher Education, 21–38.

(individuals who obtained a residence permit, at least temporarily), individuals in the process of seeking asylum or "asylum seekers," and individuals willing to but not entitled to apply for asylum (such as those for whom the Dublin regulation applies which allows European states to send people back to the country of Europe they first entered to have their asylum application processed). These three general categories are crossed by a variety of administrative statuses, which entitle people to different types of social rights depending on the host country. The term "refugee" therefore encapsulates a variety of administrative situations that can impinge on access to higher education, an issue which does not appear to have been addressed by researchers yet.

Existing research mainly focuses on the effects of local policies in some specific national contexts (e.g., Hek, 2005; Mestan, 2008) or on the resources, aspirations and barriers of refugees in access (Gateley, 2015; Morrice, 2009; Stevenson & Willott, 2007). While one can hypothesise that the management of the issue varies strongly depending on the specificity of the national context, no research appears to address the building up of refugees' access to higher education as a specific political issue by comparing which policies and mechanisms have been set up in different national settings.

This chapter aims at filling part of this gap by adopting a cognitive approach of public policies (Hassenteufel, 2008; Muller, 2000): it explores the way in which refugees' access has been built as a social issue and put on the political agenda in three European countries (France, Germany, and Switzerland) by looking in turn at the frame of reference which has been set for handling the issue of access, the arenas and key actors (mediators) involved, the policies and mechanisms that have been set up, as well as their effects.

This approach thus considers the formulation of public policies as including a cognitive dimension, which, following Muller (2014), we shall refer to as the frame of reference of the policy. In order to unveil the specific frame of reference at play in the three countries under study regarding refugees' access to HE, we adopted the following method: we first identified online written public statements by HE governing bodies regarding refugees' access and conducted research using keywords in French, German, and English. This led us to identify the HE actors taking a public position in the different national contexts, both through their own websites and press articles, as well as others identified in those statements as active in the issue. Then, we checked if the actors identified in a specific national setting had counterparts in the others by researching related websites. This two-entry research method made it possible to identify precisely the actors involved in the production of public written statements as well as in the implementation of access policies for refugees.

Once the frame of reference and the main actors were identified, we isolated the policies implemented in these three European and neighbouring countries. Comparing the frame of reference, the public policies actors and their implementation in these three countries has made it possible to document the extent to which the question is raised as a social issue and by whom, the characteristics of the targeted population as well as the implemented policies (type of admission criteria and processes, access programs and funding programs, administrative student status category used, etc.). In order to enhance the secondary data analysis, we conducted formal and informal interviews as well as participant observation in one Swiss HEI setting both with senior administrators and refugee students. The fieldwork consisted in observations during meetings at a Swiss HEI, as well as interviews with administrative and academic actors involved in refugees' access, refugee students and student candidates. This fieldwork was designed as action-research, aimed at identifying the configuration of actors involved and their rationale, as well as current barriers to access, with the explicit goal of influencing local policies in the management of access. Additionally, two meetings were organised with a junior academic from another HEI who initiated an admission program for refugees to obtain comparable information on another HEI. This fieldwork was used in the methodological process to inform the interpretation of the public statements and their translations into policies and processes, and not as a case study per se.

Finally, we confronted these new public policies with pre-existing structures (organisation of the HE sector, regulation of immigration) which appear to be weighing on the development of access policies for refugees and to account for how they are linked in settings that facilitate or impinge on their development. Those structures reflect a normative dimension of the frame of reference, as they participate in the legitimation of what is or should be done, i.e., the general principle of action.

A first section of the chapter focuses on the public statements and the frame of reference they unveil, the policies that were implemented, and the actor configurations that characterise the three contexts, underlying the variability of the political agenda. A second section discusses this variability with regard to HE organisation and immigration regulation that appear to have an impact on this political agenda, and thus participate to the definition of the frame of reference.

FRAMES OF REFERENCE, ACTORS AND POLICIES IN THREE NATIONAL CONTEXTS

The analysis of public statements is a particularly appropriate means to identify the frame of reference developed to build refugees' access to HE as a social issue, the actors involved in their definition and the implemented policies: first, because it provides information on the type of rationales disclosed by political and higher education institutions' actors in different national settings; second, because besides the various rationales presented in the discourses that reformulate the refugees' access issue by translating it into a national context, these discourses also contain information on which actors are identified by policy makers as being key actors of access; and, third, because the extent to which access policies and instruments are publicised on the Internet also accounts for the states' and HEIs' will to indeed support refugees' access. Accessible information is a key issue and the Internet has become an important source of information for refugees (Maitland, 2015). Some states are very keen on publicising information on access policies and resources – sometimes in a dozen languages spoken by the refugees – while others appear to remain more cautious and display limited information targeting only those who have already mastered English or the national language(s).

A Range of Frames of Reference Expressed in National Governing Bodies' Statements

In the three national contexts, HEIs' national governing bodies – *Conférence des présidents d'université* (CPU) in France, the Hochschul Rektoren Konferenz (HRK) in Germany, and Swiss Universities in Switzerland – published statements regarding refugees' access more or less over the same period (September 2015, earlier for Germany).

In France, the CPU statements (2015a) underline the social responsibility issue as well as the integration issue: "Refugees and their children are part of the country." This rationale is referred to as an "asylum tradition," which has already been implemented previously, a recent example being the post-earthquake situation in Haiti. More generally, the CPU, along with its partners in France and abroad, wants to "take part in political citizenship and social actions aimed at facilitating the integration of refugees in the whole territory" (CPU, 2015b, our translation). In Germany, more than a sole statement, it is a whole campaign aimed at "fostering an open mindset at universities and opposing xenophobia" (Technical University of Munich, 2015) that has been implemented, including the development of a survey aimed at documenting how German HEIs tackle the refugees' access issue, leading to a press release entitled "HRK survey reveals: universities are committed to education and training for refugees" (HRK, 2015). In Switzerland, a statement entitled "For an adapted access of refugees to HEI" (Swiss Universities, 2015) questions the social responsibility and the solidarity principle of HEIs in building up access processes for qualified refugees, and presents the importance of helping refugees return to their countries and participate in national reconstruction.

An initial tension thus appears between the rationales regarding the need to support access, from social and political citizenship responsibility, solidarity, to integration in the host society or potential return to the home country. In these statements, as well as on these national HE organizations' websites, this general discourse is accompanied by the presentation of different policies supporting access as well as the identification of further important actors in dealing with the access implementation.

Actors and Policies

Identifying the involved actors serves two goals: setting a backdrop for the various types of people who play a part in access, and comparing national configurations, the responsibility of access being borne by different actors depending on the context.

They can be grouped along four dimensions: higher education actors, external actors, academic actors, and social services actors. The actors identified are equipped with different tools and admission policies (admission policies being the instruments through which access is organised). In sum, a strong will to facilitate access appears through a large number of actors within and outside universities as well as several tools and admission processes that deal with academic standards as much as the economic and social needs of refugees. Additionally, different configurations of actors apply, in the sense that the political organisation of public higher education has an impact on the bearing of access responsibility.

In France: HEIs' responsibility with support from national and local organisms. In France, the CPU has produced guidelines for HEIs that identify the actors who should work together in order to facilitate refugees' access. These include higher education actors who are related to the academic dimension – HEIs' European and International relation services, student associations, student peers, academics – and are in charge of developing adapted admission processes, tutorials, mentoring, etc., as well as social services both within and outside HEIs – the CROUS (*Centre régional des oeuvres universitaires et scolaires*) and the HEIs' own social services such as health services – that deal with access to housing, and financial support. Besides, the COMUE (*Communauté d'universités et d'établissements*), the administrative structure gathering universities in a city, is in charge of coordinating regional and local authorities (*rectorat, préfecture, et municipalité*), and ministries – both the Ministry of National Education, Higher Education and Research (MENESR) and the Ministry of Foreign Affairs and International Development (MAEDI). University websites echo the CPU discourse and underline the importance of one additional type of actor: local volunteers, within and outside the university (such as neighbourhood inhabitants), who support not only student access but more generally student refugees' needs.

The instruments which are used to build policies facilitating access thus take into account both financial issues and academic issues: considering that not all students are able to provide evidence of their former education, specific admission processes ("pragmatic" ones, as underlined in the guidelines) that include testing (which do not exist in the French universities' context for access) are called upon, and the language issue is tackled by the Faculties of French as a Foreign Language to facilitate the acquisition of language skills; the waiving of tuition fees is supported along with the provision of social emergency aid. Access programs mostly consist of ad hoc non-degree programs, as a way to provide access before being able to join a standard degree program of study. These access programs are often presented on websites not only in French or English but also in the main languages spoken by the refugee population (e.g., Arabic).

In Switzerland: HEIs' responsibility within a double – national and cantonal – political framework. Although Swiss Universities publicly support the principle of refugees' access, their website does not directly tackle the issue, but indicates that refugees should directly contact HEIs without actually providing additional information, either about the actors who should be involved, or the admission processes that should be developed. Instead, the central issue concerns the recognition of refugees' prior degrees, a process that does not imply major state funding and can facilitate the economic integration of the refugees. Swiss Universities propose to provide "recommendation of recognition of diplomas in non-regulated professions." A translation of their degrees is required, and if no evidence can be provided, it can be replaced by a description of their studies. Some adaptation has thus been introduced in the pre-existing framework.

On universities' webpages, the actors identified overlap with the ones presented at the French national level, with an additional distinction reflecting the political organisation between federal and cantonal levels: outside universities, they include the Federal Office of Migrations, the Population Cantonal Office for Foreign Students (distinct from the one for European students), and the Swiss Consular Authorities. At university level, those referred to are the student services for studies and careers, the offices for social affairs and student mobility (where the waiving of fees and scholarships can be obtained) or faculties where student mentoring already exists. In this case, existing admission processes for local students are presented as tools for the access of refugees.

In very few universities, specific admission programs have been developed for refugees, providing a non-degree program with an ad hoc curriculum to prepare the refugees to gain access to general degree programs. The type of admission process depends on the Cantonal context: HEIs are under Canton rules, and the HE tradition varies strongly from one Canton to the next. As a result, in one of the HEIs under study, interviews with senior administrators revealed that the difficulty to develop ad hoc access programs for refugees was linked to the fact that only a small share of the cantonal population accesses HE. The statement can be summed up as follows: "how can we publicly advocate an enlarged access for refugees when most of the population does not have access to HE?" Conversely, in another Canton characterised by broader access to HE, a specific admission program for refugees was developed through a bottom-up process: it was placed on the HE agenda by a junior academic and it involved identifying potential allies within and outside the university. This signals the importance of integrating local contexts, and considering various levels of political territories as well as the ways of designing policies.

In Germany: A national political responsibility implemented by HEIs. The management of the issue in Germany is national. The Federal Ministry of Education and Research has developed a program to facilitate refugees' access, and 4/5 of all universities have asked to be part of it. The program is managed by the German Academic Exchange Service which deals with international students and mobility, along with the BAföG (*Bundesausbildungsförderungsgesetz*), a structure of the Federal Ministry for Education and Research (Bundesministerium für Bildung und

Forschung) that deals with German students' applications for fellowships and has extended to refugees.

Access policies include funding for both HEIs (the federal government offers specific extra funding to prepare students) and students (no tuition fees, scholarships as well as financial support for living costs). If students are, as everywhere else, expected to meet some academic standards, specific access processes have been developed to meet the distinctive refugees' needs. Those who cannot provide former diploma papers are invited to take tests and interviews. Those who are not qualified for access can register in a foundation course (2,500 additional places specifically provided). Moreover, structural support is offered to speed up the learning of German. And finally, post-study rights are presented, that entitle the students to an 18-month post-study period to look for and find a job adapted to their level of qualification and to obtain a permanent residence permit.

Access as a Public Policy for Whom? Targeted Population and Funding Policies

The comparison of access policies between countries and institutions underlines the importance of specific admission programmes to facilitate access. Academic criteria come first, but the level of expectation varies between countries and HEIs, as illustrated by the different types of admission processes and programs: when no specific admission programme exists, refugees are expected to fit in the existing system, which limits access to a small elite. Conversely, specific admission processes provide opportunities for a larger and more diverse group of students.

The targeted population is, in all three countries, the one that is deemed academically fit for studies in HE. This leads political actors to identify some countries of origin as an indicator of a possible preparedness for studies, due to differences in educational systems. In France, the CPU explicitly mentions "Syrians, Iraqis and Eritreans" as populations for which access to higher education should be eased, and more generally "refugees from countries with conflicts." In Germany as well, the HRK identifies Syrians and Iraqis as populations for which access is particularly an issue.

Besides academic characteristics, the second issue at stake is the administrative status of the person. This is particularly apparent and complex in the Swiss case. Indeed, at the national level, Swiss Universities (2016) stipulates that, in order to recognize prior degrees without proof, benefiting from an F Permit (temporary admission, expulsion decision not applicable due to the country of origin situation), or a B Permit (5 years' residence authorization, renewable) is compulsory.

Taking one HEI website as an example of how the issue is dealt with at a university level, it appears that the registration process is specific for students who are from countries for which a student visa is required to go to Switzerland. The choice of the study program has to be made up front and they must be able to prove that they have sufficient financial resources to cover their needs (estimated at a minimum 2,100 CHF per month). In addition, age and former studies must be compatible with the targeted studies.

Furthermore, a specific webpage presented in the two languages in which study programs exist provides further explanations regarding application by refugees. It describes the existing access procedures (specific exam for those who do not hold the required high school diploma), the possibility to attend courses freely, and points to the university student service for studies and careers as a key actor for refugees seeking to study, along with the office for social affairs and student mobility. The webpage also provides a link to information regarding study and life costs in Switzerland. In sum, in this case, no specific access program was developed. First, the access process starts by targeting individuals who are eligible for a student permit, willing and able to join existing study programs, whether they are refugees or not, meaning that these students are capable of obtaining an administrative status before they come to Switzerland and thus prove their economic capacity to support themselves as well as to provide evidence on the degrees they hold. This implies anticipating a stay in Switzerland and possessing economic resources. Second, refugees who already hold a stay permit to live in Switzerland are welcome to apply by using the standard admission processes. In this case, the university management, when interviewed, mentioned that the asylum status is not a reason for denying access to university, adding that they have not really experienced demands from asylum seekers. In some other HEIs, where specific programs have been implemented, often by local students and academics, the asylum status issue is addressed more straightforwardly in the public depiction of the program, explaining that the type of asylum status or stage in the asylum seeking process do not interfere with access and these programs target both refugees and asylum seekers. There thus seems to be a trade-off between the national framework, its local translation and its legitimacy in the public cantonal sphere.

In France, the CPU (2015a) proposes to "freely host student refugees who registered with the OFPRA (*Office français de protection des réfugiés et apatrides*) and applied for access to HE." Depending on the HEI, non-academic criteria for accessing specific programs for refugees can include an age limit (28 years' old), a place of residence (in the administrative region where the university is located), as well as an identity paper or a document attesting to the administrative situation – an official asylum application form, an official decision by OFPRA, an appeal to the National Court of Asylum rights (*Cour nationale du droit d'asile*, CNDA), or an official decision by CNDA. If the administrative situation regarding the asylum application process must be documented, the refugee status does not seem to be absolutely required to gain access to HE.

In Germany, not only is the access of refugees encouraged, but asylum seekers are also explicitly welcome. As explained by Morris-Lange and Brands (2016, p. 10):

Technically, access to HE is less restricted in Germany than in many other European countries. Already today, asylum seekers would not have to wait to enrol in one of the tuition-free study programs at German universities. As of August, none of the country's 16 states (Länder) prevents its universities from admitting asylum seekers who have yet to receive protected status. Nevertheless, only a handful of newcomers can be found in lecture halls across the country. This is in part due to the residency requirements imposed during the asylum process.

The German framework thus appears more favourable for supporting asylum seekers' and refugees' access but the administrative and political implementation of asylum is limited.

The targeted population and the level of public acknowledgement of the issue come with varying program sizes (in terms of available places) and different funding commitments. In France, the CPU (2015a) estimates that each HEI can host 20 to 50 refugee students while the National Centre for Students (CROUS) is estimated to fund around 500 scholarships per year for student refugees. Moreover, the French state provides financial guarantees to facilitate students' access to accommodation. In Switzerland, university websites present specific programs with a maximum of 20 refugee students in each university. Scholarships are to be applied for at cantonal level (for Swiss students, C permit, i.e., residence permit with no time limit for refugees). A university website details the rights to scholarships depending on the residence permit type: to apply for a bursary at the Social Affairs and Student Mobility Service, the student needs to be registered, and if (s)he holds a short-term residence permit (B or L), (s)he must first obtain 60 bachelor credits or 30 masters credits to be entitled to apply for financial help. The same type of limitation applies to asylum seekers studying in the French as a Foreign Language faculty: some financial help can be obtained for a maximum of two semesters. For B permit holders studying in a degree-granting French as a Foreign Language program, 60 credits must be obtained before applying for funding. In Germany, according to the German Academic Exchange Service (O'Malley, 2016), the number of potential refugee students is estimated to be between 30,000 and 50,000 and 100 million euros are to be spent over the course of 4 years on providing access.

In the three countries under study, HEIs thus develop access policies that take into account the national administrative categorisation for asylum seekers and the rights associated with their different statuses. By doing so, they pursue one of the university's traditions that caters to hosting foreign scholars threatened by a political situation in their home countries, and more broadly the academic freedom of students defined as the freedom to study "without unreasonable interference or restriction from law, institutional regulations or public pressure" ("Academic freedom", 2017).

Still, the institutional management of the issue varies. The administrative categorisation of "refugees" seems to influence differently the possibility of access in the three countries. For example, the asylum seeker category implies that potential students are entitled to seek asylum, which seems somehow to exclude those to which the "Dublin" agreement applies, as they are not entitled to apply for asylum in certain countries. HEIs' room to manoeuvre for supporting academic freedom must be understood in the broader context of political organisation in which HEIs are embedded.

The effort to support refugees' access appears to vary from one country to the other, as shown by the existing policies, i.e., the number of specific access programs, the number of available study places, the existence and scope of specific funding programs and the level and modes of communication aimed at facilitating refugees' access. While it is a national goal endowed with significant national funds in Germany, where access is largely publicised, the French context is characterised by local arrangements with no specific national funding, and the public funding of refugees' access to HE appears even scarcer in Switzerland.

The configuration of actors involved at different political levels, and the access and admission processes which were implemented suggest that access to student status (whether it be in non-degree or degree programs) and its associated rights (in particular funding entitlements and rights not only to study but to validate a degree) are tightly linked to both the HE system organisation and the administrative asylum seeker status in the three countries. In other words, the access issue appears to be embedded in two broader social policy sectors: education and immigration, the latter being linked to the social rights which different types of refugees are granted.

EXPLAINING DIFFERENCES IN PUBLIC POLICIES BY HE ORGANISATION AND IMMIGRATION REGULATION

The frame of reference underlying refugees' access policies and the various actors they involve show that other, broader structures play a significant role too. These structures must be understood in relation to the values and legitimation principles of what is done or should be done in terms of public policies, the role of the state and of HE in different national settings, as well as the political processing of immigration with regard to economic and social benefits in the three countries.

How the Very Structure of Higher Education Influences Refugees' Access

Numbers and gatekeepers. What are the HE organisational characteristics which facilitate the development of refugees' access policies? As noted previously, the public discourse of HE actors on access is more developed in Germany and France compared to Switzerland, suggesting a more central public issue in the former.

This could first be related to the size of the HE sector: there are nearly 2.8 million tertiary education students in Germany, around 2.3 million in France, and a mere 280,000 students in Switzerland (Eurostat, 2013). Beyond numbers, the countries differ with regard to the share of people qualified to access tertiary academic education. Indeed, while the proportion of the population reaching at least upper secondary education is quite similar in the three countries – in 2012, 83% of the 25 to 34 year-old age group in France, compared with 87% in Germany and 89% in Switzerland (OECD, 2014d) –, the picture is quite different when the type of HE program is taken into consideration: in Germany, about half of the students follow a vocational track and a general diploma (Abitur) is required to access universities. In France, 43% of upper secondary students choose a vocational path, but the type of high school diploma, vocational or general, does not limit university access. The share of students qualified to pursue university studies is thus higher and the legitimacy of widening access bigger. Conversely, in Switzerland, two thirds of students register in the vocational track. In fact, Switzerland stands out as one of the countries with the smallest share (31%) of young people graduating from tertiary type A programs, i.e., programs which grant access to higher education, in comparison with the OECD average (39%) (OECD, 2014a, 2014b, 2014c).

The degree of Malthusianism (restriction of access) in secondary general education, in which general high school diplomas are considered as a gatekeeper for access to HE or on the contrary, a common good, sheds light on the role allocated to higher education in different societal contexts, with various consequences on refugees' access. This probably explains why, when debates were organised on a Swiss university campus to tackle refugee issues, some posters appeared on the campus walls asking what the point was about "worrying about visible minorities and not about the Swiss invisible majority" (observation, April, 2016). The majority of the Swiss population does not access university, or the broader higher education system. In this context, facilitating refugees' access does not appear as a central public issue

Internationalisation of the student body. Another dimension that appears to influence how the refugee access issue is tackled relates to the degree of internationalisation of the higher education student body. Here again, the relation is not straightforward. Indeed, at first glance, Switzerland appears to have the highest share[4] of international HE students (16%), not only compared to Germany (11.5%) and France (12%), but also to the OECD countries, this rate being the highest after Australia, Luxembourg and the UK.

At least two dimensions should be taken into account to understand this degree of internationalisation: the geographical origin of international students, and the level of studies for which they migrate. The link between these two dimensions explains why in some countries, admission processes targeting non-European students were already in place before the refugee issue had to be dealt with, facilitating the reactiveness in addressing the issue, while in others the profile of the students, mainly European (thus benefiting from the Bologna process diploma recognition and credit transferability) and at advanced levels of study (and thus not implying the development of undergraduates' admission processes) did not require such tools.

It is especially the case in Switzerland where half of all international students come from neighbouring countries, and half of them are registered in advanced research programmes (OECD, 2014a). In Germany, around half of the students come from non-European countries (China, Russia, India...) and 60% are enrolled in bachelor's and master's degree programs (Make it in Germany, 2015). In France, a large share of international students come from former colonies (Morocco, Algeria, and Tunisia) and, as in Germany, 60% enrol in bachelor's and master's degree programs (European Migration Network, 2012).

What can be inferred from these data? Switzerland has the highest share of international students in its student body, but it is also characterised by an elitist process of internationalisation. Elitism thus characterises the accessibility of the HE sector for both national and international students, whereas in France and Germany the sector is much more widely open internally and externally.

The demand for HE. Academic requirements come first in the regulation of access, for refugees as well as for all potential students. Differences in the way refugees' access is handled within various political and societal organisations may thus be looked at first and foremost in terms of answering various demands from refugees. As noted previously, depending on their country of origin, the probability that refugees had access to higher education or to studies preparing them for higher education in their home country can vary. But in all three countries under study, asylum is most frequently granted to the same national group (Syrians) (Eurostat, 2015). Therefore it does not explain variations in HE access.

If the qualitative characteristics of the refugee population do not explain the variability of the political management of their access to HE, numbers may well be influential. Here again, the broader picture of asylum demand does not support such a hypothesis: indeed, the asylum seekers' demands per 1,000 inhabitants in 2014 show that Switzerland is the country where it reaches its highest level, with 2.9 demands compared with 2.5 in Germany and 1 in France, as well as where the highest level of positive answers is to be found (70% compared with respectively 41.7% and 21.7%) (Eurostat, 2015). The proportion of refugees is thus at least as high in Switzerland as in France and Germany, although, here again, in absolute numbers it concerns fewer people.

But these trends must be nuanced, as the ability to apply for asylum is not shared by all incoming refugees. Regarding the use of the Dublin Regulation, Switzerland appears as the country where the number of migrants sent back to the European countries they first set foot on is the highest with 4,673 people in 2012 (same in 2016), whereas there were around 3,000 in Germany (Amnesty, 2016). This signals a stronger filtering of those accepted as refugees, confirming the hypothesis that what counts eventually is not so much the number of refugees, nor their educational characteristics, but the state specification of the refugee influxes through filtering processes based on economic adequacy criteria.

If the refugee population shares similarities in the three countries, one can therefore link the demand for HE with existing admission processes and available information. German and French HEIs communicate largely and in different languages on their access policies while Swiss HEIs remain more discreet. In the Swiss university under study, little information was available for potential applicants and at the same time receiving little demand was mentioned by the administrators as a reason for not developing specific admission processes (observation, 2016).

Beyond HE: The Political Processing of Economic Needs or Refugees as Immigrants

Neither the national economic wealth nor the level of unemployment appear to explain the variability of the political treatment of the HE access issue, Switzerland having the highest level of wealth and the lowest level of unemployment. Still, comparing Switzerland with Germany underlines diverse ways of catering for the lack of professionals in specific economic sectors: bringing in qualified workers has become an important way of meeting such labour needs, in a context where the relative elitism of the HE sector leads to shortcuts in the training of some professional categories. Brain drain thus appears as a tool for the Swiss economic sector. Immigration rules frame this organisation by making getting a job and owning specific professional characteristics the main assets to get a residence permit. Indeed, data on new Swiss immigrants in 2014 show that 48.9% of them came for professional reasons, 32% for family grouping, 10.6% for training and 1.2% as refugees. The share of migrants coming for professional activity has more than doubled since 1990 (when it represented 20% of all migrants). Additionally, they largely came from non-European countries (more than half of them) at that time while today, those from the European Union make up two thirds of this population. Immigration regulation is thus increasingly used as a way to identify missing types of professionals. As a result, migrant workers do not compete with national workers as they complement the characteristics of the local population, especially as they have higher levels of education (Müller-Jentsch, 2008) in activity sectors characterised by labour shortage in Switzerland (e.g., health, catering, the academic profession), thereby allowing the state to save money on education (Le Temps, 2014). The reasons for migrating are differently weighed in Germany, which introduced a "Blue Card" in 2012 to make it easier for skilled-worker immigrants from non-European countries to settle, and where in 2013 only 18% of the non-European migrants came for professional reasons (RT, 2015). At the same time, unfilled positions reached more than a half million (589,000) in July 2015, and unfilled apprenticeships were close to 40,000 (Dettmer, Katschak, & Ruppert, 2016).

Demography and economic needs in terms of manpower can thus provide a more or less facilitating frame for refugees' access to HE, but the broader regulation of immigration for both work and studies appears to be of central importance: in Switzerland, non-EU students must prove their economic solvability before obtaining a student permit; for refugees, economic autonomy is prioritised over education, which is the case for the national population. This is not so much the case in Germany and France. While Germany also targets highly qualified workers in its immigration plans, it largely funds educational training simultaneously.

Thus in Germany over the last years, policies favouring immigration are the consequence of another political rationale: in a context of demographic crisis, welcoming refugees and providing them with financial support to help them settle, both in terms of social benefits and with regard to their education and training, is presented by public actors as an investment (with around 400,000 refugees being eligible for social benefits) as a lot of newspaper articles underline (e.g., Groden, 2015). But in all cases, the management of refugees' access issue appears, although to different extents, constrained by broader immigration public policies, and thus at the intersection between human rights related policies and economic ones.

OPEN-ENDED CONCLUSION

Researching refugees' access to higher education through a cognitive approach of public policies from a comparative perspective shows the variety of frames of reference, political agendas, configurations of actors as well as the structures influencing the extent and modalities of building refugee access to HE as a political issue. Germany, over the period of time under study (2014–2016), is characterised by its openness towards refugees with discourses being translated into reactive and proactive policies managed at the national level. Those policies are both educational and social, students being sustained in the admission process as well as everyday life costs. Their implementation follows the frame previously developed to attract international students as a tool to answer the large needs of the national employment market, lacking highly educated professionals. The economic market needs as well as pre-existing structures facilitate the openness of access.[5]

In Switzerland, over a similar period of time, the access issue developed more slowly, and the political organisation of the Confederation as well as of the HE sector contributes to Cantonal variation on if and how the refugees' HE access is addressed. Mirroring this, there have been national attempts to organise access to vocational education and training for refugees: the employment market needs identified by policy makers are more related to professionals with lower skills, as the country already welcomes large numbers of highly educated foreigners to balance a small share of university degree holders in the national population.

In France, looser ties between the employment market and the education system, along with growing numbers of HE students, have eased the development of refugees' admission processes backed up by official discourse on human rights, but resources are generally scarce and local actors work on a shoestring.

Besides identifying national differences, which calls for further research over a longer time-span to analyse how different traditions of policy making affect access, the cognitive approach more generally sheds light on a transversal issue: the tension between individuals' human rights, national economic and labour market needs and above all, regulation with regard to immigration and the dynamics of human capital.

At an individual level, refugees' socio-economic backgrounds appear to weigh on their access to HE to various degrees, depending on the administrative categories applied by the states, and the access rights to non-degree HE studies they offer: for example, the administrative status of asylum seekers makes it possible to embark on HE studies in Germany but the refugee status is necessary to graduate, while this is rarely the case in Switzerland. Citizenship thus operates as an instrument of social stratification (Heidenheimer, 1981), but to different extents depending on the country and the categorisation of refugees by the state.

This also underlines individual and administrative temporality conflicts. The temporality of asylum processes in different national settings is at odds with individuals' temporal needs in access. Preliminary research on students' academic trajectories in Switzerland suggests that those who follow the traditional university curriculum straight away have family that had already settled in Switzerland, or came with a student visa. This highlights the importance of individual resources, such as networks, local family ties and economic assets, in the ability to transfer a higher education study project from the country of origin to the country of settlement. All the more so when refugee policies include the assignation to a specific territory and limit geographical mobility: accessing HE thus depends on its availability in the region of constrained residence or the ability to anticipate by asking asylum in a specific canton, land or region. These individual resources appear, unsurprisingly, all the more important in countries where higher education is an elitist sector.

This exploratory research suggests that understanding the various ways in which refugees' access to HE is built as a political issue implies a need to analyse the education, economic and social policy fields simultaneously so as to identify the global frame of reference in which a refugee's access is embedded. A country's administrative and political handling of asylum, including language issues, higher education and more broadly social policies, affects how asylum seekers and refugees are considered. This emphasizes the need to develop a research program that crosses traditional research field lines by bringing together educational studies and social policies studies as well as linguistic studies (Zeiter-Grau & Goastellec, 2017). Understanding refugee access to HE depending on national contexts requires identifying what comes first in national settings, access to education or economic autonomy, and the type of national project and social state it nurtures, depending on how and if education is fully included in the Welfare State frame or addressed separately. More broadly, it calls into question the extent to which economic actors rule education, and immigration rules frame asylum. In this respect, refugees' access to higher education appears as a useful tool to reconsider more broadly the place allocated to education in different national settings and how it impacts individuals' opportunities to study. Simultaneously, it leads to analysing asylum with regard to immigration and thus to interrogate the economicisation of a human rights frame of reference.

NOTES

[1] For example, the "International conference on higher education in Emergencies" in Brussels, December 2014, organised by the Council of Europe, the British Council, the League of Arab States, the Institute of International Education and the Global Platform for Syrian Students (Council of Europe, 2014).

[2] It organised a conference for leaders of international education entitled "Higher education in emergency environments" in June 2015, attended by 70 country representatives amongst which 130 university presidents and government ministers (British Council, 2015).

[3] Conference on "integrating refugees into higher education: solutions for a generation on the run." Held in Amsterdam (EAIE, 2016).

[4] This trend is relative as this higher share concerns smaller numbers of students due to the smaller size of the country.

[5] Of course this says nothing about the outcome, i.e., the extent to which this political openness allows large numbers of refugee students to access HE and succeed in their studies. The difficulties of access also lie in the administrative organisation of asylum as well as in the specific needs of the refugees (for example academic, language, and psychological support).

REFERENCES

Academic freedom. (2017). In *Encyclopædia Britannica Online*. Retrieved from https://www.britannica.com/topic/academic-freedom

Amnesty. (2016). *Asile La Suisse fait preuve de formalisme excessif dans les renvois Dublin*. Retrieved from https://www.amnesty.ch/fr/pays/europe-asie-centrale/suisse/docs/2016/la-suisse-fait-preuve-de-formalisme-excessif-dans-les-renvois-dublin-1

British Council. (2015, June). *Higher education in emergency environments*. Conference for Leaders of International Education, Brussels. Retrieved from https://www.britishcouncil.org/going-global/programme/conference-sessions/higher-education-emergency-environments

Conférence des Présidents d'Université. (2015a). *Les institutions universitaires françaises s'engagent pour l'accueil des réfugiés* [Press release]. Retrieved from http://www.cpu.fr/actualite/les-institutions-universitaires-francaises-sengagent-pour-laccueil-des-refugies/

Conférence des Présidents d'Université. (2015b). *Accueil des réfugiés dans les universités* [Press release]. Retrieved from http://www.cpu.fr/actualite/accueil-des-refugies-dans-les-universites/

Council of Europe. (2014, December). *International Conference on Higher Education in Emergencies, Brussels*. Retrieved from http://globalplatformforsyrianstudents.org/index.php/news-room/international-conference-on-higher-education-in-emergencies-1/496-international-conference-on-higher-education-in-emergencies-1

Destatis, Statistisches Bundesamt. *Social benefits accessible to asylum seekers*. Retrieved from https://www.destatis.de/EN/FactsFigures/SocietyState/SocialStatistics/SocialBenefits/BenefitsAsylumSeekers/BenefitsAsylumSeekers.html;jsessionid=D8E0550D8F8D79A9A10EFB0319521777.cae4

Dettmer, M., Katschak, C., & Ruppert, G. (2016). German companies see refugees as an opportunity. *Spiegel*. Retrieved from http://www.spiegel.de/international/germany/refugees-are-an-opportunity-for-the-german-economy-a-1050102.html

de Wit, H., & Altbach, P. (2016). The Syrian refugee crisis and higher education. *International Higher Education, 84*, 9–10.

European Association for International Education. (2016, June). *Integrating refugees into higher education: Solutions for a generation on the run*. Seminar held in Amsterdam. Retrieved from http://www.eaie.org/spotlight-seminar

European Migration Network. (2012, September). *Immigration of international students to France*. Paris: European Commission, Ministère de l'Intérieur.

European University Association. (n.d.). *Refugees welcome map*. Retrieved from http://www.eua.be/activities-services/eua-campaigns/refugees-welcome-map

Eurostat. (2013). *Students in tertiary education.* Retrieved from http://ec.europa.eu/eurostat/statistics-explained/index.php/File:Number_of_tertiary_education_students_by_level_and_sex,_2013_(thousands)_YB16-fr.png

Eurostat. (2015). *Demandes d'asile dans l'UE. Le nombre de demandeurs d'asile dans l'UE a bondi en 2014 à plus de 625000 personnes. 20% étaient Syriens* [Press release 53/2015].

Gateley, D. E. (2015). A policy of vulnerability or agency? Refugee young people's opportunities in accessing further and higher education in the UK. *Compare: A Journal of Comparative and International Education, 45*(1), 26–46.

Groden, C. (2015, September 8). Here's why Germany is welcoming migrants with open arms. *Fortune.* Retrieved from http://fortune.com/2015/09/08/germany-migrant-crisis/

Hassenteufel, P. (2008). *Sociologie politique: L'action publique.* Paris: Armand Colin.

Heidenheimer, A. J. (1981). Education and social security entitlements in Europe and America. In P. Flora & A. J. Heidenheimer (Ed.), *The development of welfare states in Europe and America* (pp. 269–304). New Brunswick, NJ: Transaction, Inc.

Hek, R. (2005). The role of education in the settlement of young refugees in the UK: The experiences of young refugees. *Practice: Social Work in Action, 17*(3), 157–171.

HRK. (2015). *HRK survey reveals: Universities are committed to education and training for refugees* [Press Release]. Retrieved from https://www.letemps.ch/suisse/2016/03/17/aide-sociale-travail-defi-suisse-face-aux-refugies

Le Temps. (2014, January 12). L'eldorado migratoire Suisse. *Le Temps.* Retrieved from https://www.letemps.ch/no-section/2014/01/12/eldorado-migratoire-suisse

Maitland, C. (2015, September). *Internet and mobile phone use by refugees: The case of Za'Atari Syrian refugee camp.* Paper presented at the TPRC43, The Research conference on communication, information and Internet, George Mason University School of Law, Arlington, VA.

Make it in Germany. (2015). *New record 2014: Number of international students continues to increase* [Press release]. Retrieved from http://www.make-it-in-germany.com/en/for-qualified-professionals/about-the-portal/news/detail/new-record-2014-number-of-international-students-in-germany-continues-to-increase

Mestan, K. (2008). *Given the chance: An evaluation of an employment and education pathways program for refugees.* Fitzroy: Brotherhood of St Laurence. Retrieved from http://library.bsl.org.au/jspui/bitstream/1/6127/1/Mestan_GivenTheChance_evaluation.pdf

Morrice, L. (2009). Journeys into higher education: The case of refugees in the UK. *Teaching in Higher Education, 14*(6), 661–672.

Morris-Lange, S., & Brands, F. (2016). German universities open doors to refugees: Access barriers remain. *International Higher Education, 84*, 11–12.

Muller, P. (2000). L'analyse cognitive des politiques publiques: Vers une sociologie politique de l'action publique. *Revue Française de Science Politique, 2*, 189–208.

Muller, P. (2014). Référentiel. In L. Boussaguet, S. Jacquot, & P. Ravinet (Eds.), *Dictionnaire des politiques publiques* (pp. 555–562). Paris: Presses de Sciences Po.

Müller-Jentsch, D. (2008). *La nouvelle immigration: La Suisse entre l'accueil des cerveaux et la peur de l'étranger.* Zurich: NZZ libro.

O'Malley, B. (2016, March 12). Most universities have applied to take on refugees. *University World News.* Retrieved from http://www.universityworldnews.com/article.php?story=20160312030638812

OECD. (2014a). *France, country note. Education at a glance 2014.* Paris: OECD Publishing. Retrieved from http://www.oecd.org/edu/education-at-a-glance-2014-country-notes.htm

OECD. (2014b). *Germany, country note. Education at a glance 2014.* Germany: OECD Publishing. Retrieved from http://www.oecd.org/edu/education-at-a-glance-2014-country-notes.htm

OECD. (2014c). *Switzerland, country note. Education at a glance 2014.* Switzerland: OECD Publishing. Retrieved from http://www.oecd.org/edu/education-at-a-glance-2014-country-notes.htm

OECD. (2014d). *Education at a glance 2014: OECD indicators. Table A.1.2A. Percentage of adults that have attained at least upper secondary education by age group (2012).* Paris: OECD Publishing. Retrieved from http://dx.doi.org/eag-2014-en

37

RT. (2015, March 28). Germany needs 500,000 migrants a year until 2050 – study. *RT*. Retrieved from https://www.rt.com/news/244873-germany-economy-immigrant-workforce/

Sampaio, J. (2016, May 22). Higher education should be a priority in humanitarian Crises. *University World News*. Retrieved from http://www.universityworldnews.com/article.php?story=20160513152443253

Stevenson, J., & Willott, J. (2007). The aspiration and access to higher education of teenage refugees in the UK. *Compare: A Journal of Comparative and International Education, 37*(5), 671–687.

Swiss Universities. (2015). *Swiss universities s'engage pour un accès adapté des réfugiés aux hautes écoles* [Press release]. Retrieved from https://www.swissuniversities.ch/fr/publications/communiques-de-presse/

Swiss Universities. (2016). *Description du diplôme pour réfugiés avec documents incomplets* [Press release]. Retrieved from https://www.swissuniversities.ch/fr/services/reconnaissanceswiss-enic/

Technical University of Munich. (2015, November 25). TUM supports German rector's conference initiative. *Campus News*. Retrieved from https://www.tum.de/en/about-tum/news/press-releases/short/article/32761/

The Economist. (2015, March 28). The world is going to university. *The Economist*. Retrieved from http://www.economist.com/news/leaders/21647285-more-and-more-money-being-spent-higher-education-too-little-known-about-whether-it

Zeiter-Grau, A.-C., & Goastellec, G. (2017). Cartographie de l'enseignement-apprentissage du français aux requérants d'asile: Des enjeux en tension pour l'individu et la société. *Babylonia, 2017*(1), 75–78.

Gaële Goastellec
University of Lausanne
Switzerland

PART 2

ACCESS TO HIGHER EDUCATION
AND LANGUAGES

NORAH LEROY

3. WHEN MFL TEACHERS WANT TO MOVE

Accessing a University Career in a Global Society

INTRODUCTION

Patterns of globalisation and policies of internationalisation have led to a focus on efficiency, standards and performance in the competition for international students. In this context, transnational mobility schemes are flourishing and consequently Modern Foreign Language (MFL) learning is higher on the agenda than ever before. The Council of the European Union (EU) considers that transnational mobility opportunities improve the quality of school education in the EU overall and that such opportunities maintain the attractiveness of the teaching profession and contribute to professional development. The question of transnational mobility cannot be addressed without referring to the Bologna process, viewed as "revolutionary in the development of EU higher education" (Katsarova, 2015, p. 9) and was initiated by education ministers from France, Italy, the United Kingdom and Germany in 1998. This European cooperation process was intended to make it easier to move from one country to another for the purpose of further study or employment within the European Higher Education Area (EHEA) through the introduction of various tools and mechanisms: common three-cycle degree system for undergraduate and postgraduate studies; European Credit Transfer and Accumulation System; as well as the recognition of qualifications. The Bologna Declaration, this intergovernmental initiative of voluntary policy convergence towards a common higher education structure, was signed by 30 countries in 1999. Today the number of countries which are part of the EHEA stands at 47.

One reason for this intergovernmental initiative and schemes such as Erasmus+ is that access to different education systems is considered beneficial for teachers: it allows teachers the opportunity to compare their own teaching approaches and methodologies with those of their colleagues abroad and therefore helps them develop better skills and more innovative ways of teaching. Moreover, when teachers visit a country whose main language is not their mother tongue, the time spent studying or working in the foreign context is likely to help them develop their language skills. It goes without saying that this is of particular importance to MFL students or teachers as a means of maintaining their MFL skills. Consequently, the Council encourages transnational mobility amongst all teachers with a "view to making periods of learning abroad – both within Europe and the wider world – the rule rather than the exception."

M.-A. Détourbe (Ed.), Inclusion through Access to Higher Education, 41–61.

The TALIS 2013 report (OECD, 2014) defines transnational mobility as a physical mobility for professional purposes to a country other than the country of residence (either during the initial teacher education or as a teacher). Private mobility – such as travels abroad during holidays for nonprofessional purposes – is not taken into account. It restricts this definition to stays abroad of a week or more at an educational institution or a school and does not take into consideration journeys abroad to attend a conference or a workshop. The 2012 Bologna process implementation report identified three main categories of obstacles which impeded mobility: language knowledge, legal issues and personal situation. In addition, The Eurydice Report, *The Teaching Profession in Europe* (European Commission, 2015b) compiled three years later found that the EU secondary teachers most likely to be internationally mobile are MFL teachers. On the grounds that MFL secondary teachers can exploit mobility experiences to the full given their linguistic skills and are more likely than teachers of other subjects to experience it, they are at a vantage point as far as professional development is concerned. Kelly (2015) also makes the point that language teachers are central to the success of policies of multilingualism in the classroom which necessarily involve mobility. He proposes the notion of a "transnational language teacher" (p. 78) who promotes multilingualism through cooperation and collaboration with teaching associations and professional bodies, embassies and cultural institutes across borders for the benefit of early language learners to university students.

Accordingly, this chapter examines the extent to which the European cooperation process and mobility programmes such as Erasmus+ have had an impact on the professional development of a small sample of secondary school teachers of MFL who have moved into university teaching as higher education teacher educators.

This chapter first focuses on a brief overview of teacher recruitment procedures in France and England at secondary level and then at university level to trace the real-life educational and career options available to MFL secondary teachers who access a career in higher education as a teacher educator. Following this, I examine the consequences of promoting English as a global lingua franca in the EU and its impact on language teaching and learning. Finally the chapter moves on to a consideration of teacher mobility, its purposes and the potential of EU cooperation schemes such as Erasmus+ for promoting quality language learning. Qualitative research data drawn through the lens of a small sample of HE MFL teacher trainers working in two EU countries, France and the UK (England), attempt to identify whether access to a career in higher education for secondary school teachers of MFL was indeed determined by EU policy measures regarding transnational mobility or by other factors.

TWO WORLDS: FROM CLASSROOM TEACHER TO TEACHER TRAINER

Aiming High – Accessing a University Career

Moving from school teaching to higher education teaching is, in general, considered a challenge because the qualifications required to teach at university not only differ significantly from the professional teacher training qualification for teaching at secondary level but they are more demanding. Universities generally recruit staff with higher academic qualifications such as a Master or a PhD degree. Consequently, secondary education teachers who wish to access a university career are required to take up doctoral studies. In the past, secondary teachers who became teacher educators were not systematically required to have a PhD. Indeed, the most important requirement was to be an experienced and skilled teaching professional with recognised pedagogical expertise; however, presently there is an increased focus on research on initial teacher training courses and so this is becoming less common. Mass education has increased the number of students in higher education institutions (HEIs) in Europe whilst policies of internationalisation have made mobility and the teaching and learning of MFL a priority in HEIs. In this context, those secondary MFL teachers who wish to teach at university may feel more optimistic about being recruited given their language competence and teaching skills and therefore ready to take up or continue with doctoral studies either in their own time or on part-time study leave. For teachers in a full-time teaching position, this demands a high level of commitment and determination.

Entering the Teaching Profession: France and England

The European Qualifications Framework (EQF) is a tool to improve "the transparency, comparability, and portability" of Member State citizens' qualifications in the EU (European Parliament & European Council, 2008, p. 2). The aim of this tool is to avoid people having to repeat their learning if they move from one country to another. The EQF consists of eight reference levels which describe what a learner knows, understands and is able to do – learning outcomes. National qualifications are placed at one of the reference levels which range from basic (Level 1) to advanced (Level 8). In England and France, the qualification level required to teach is level 7. Qualified teacher status (QTS) is required to be employed as a teacher and is attained on successful completion of this teacher training programme which takes into account subject knowledge. In France, secondary teacher students of MFL specialise in one language whereas in England, they are advised to specialise in two languages to maximize their curriculum vitae when applying for teaching positions. For the primary teachers, the situation is a little different. In England, students can select a major subject specialism in English, Mathematics, and Modern Languages or Science primary maths or be a generalist. Only those teachers who have passed a subject specialism in MFL teach the subject. For those who wish to qualify as a Modern Languages Specialist, their MFL linguistic and pedagogy skills come under close scrutiny of both the HE MFL teacher educator, mentor and subject tutors when recommending QTS. In contrast, French primary teachers are all expected to teach MFL to their pupils from the age of 6 upwards as a consequence of legislation which aimed to improve MFL proficiency – *la loi n° 2013–595 du 8 juillet 2013 d'orientation et de programmation pour la refondation de l'école et de la République.*

Consequently, the French government made it mandatory for all students sitting the Master's degree in Primary Education – *Métiers de l'enseignement, de l'éducation et de la formation 1er degré* (Master MEEF 1er degré) – to achieve a minimum B2 attainment according to the Common European Framework of Reference for Languages: Learning, teaching, assessment (CEFRL) criteria (Council of Europe, 2001). The *Certificat de Compétences en Langues de l'Enseignement Supérieur* (CLES) exam is an exam which is accredited by the French government and attests the communication skills (oral comprehension, written comprehension, written production, oral production and oral interaction) of students enrolled in any type of higher education institution at any point in their university career as long as they are not specialists in the CLES certification language that they want to take. For instance, a student sitting an English degree is allowed to sit the CLES exam in any other language but English. There are two CLES exams: CLES 1 and CLES 2. The former attests level B1 CEFRL whilst the latter attests level B2 CEFRL. However, the CLES (*Certificat de compétences en langues de l'enseignement supérieur*) exam results in 2013–2014 indicated that only 34% of Master MEEF students reach the B2 level. This key difference between the two countries results in a lower teacher/student ratio in England than in France and leads to a higher number of HE MFL teacher educators who are recruited in French universities than in English ones. Consequently, there is a greater chance of being recruited as a teacher educator in France than in England as a direct consequence of EU language policy measures being implemented.

There are various routes to gaining QTS for primary and secondary school teachers in England. It is necessary to hold an undergraduate degree awarded by a UK higher education provider, or a recognised equivalent qualification. There are some undergraduate degree qualifications leading to QTS, such as the Bachelor of Education. It is also required to have passed a set of professional skills tests which are done online. The professional skills tests for prospective teachers assess the core skills that teachers need to fulfil their professional role in schools rather than the subject knowledge needed for teaching to ensure all teachers are competent in numeracy and literacy, regardless of their specialism. The Postgraduate Certificate of Education (PGCE) and the Postgraduate Diploma of Education (PGDE) are run by colleges and universities throughout the UK. They are one-year training programmes which include a minimum of 120 days in school amongst blocks of study at their chosen provider. The two training programmes do not provide access to higher education positions as they are restricted to prospective primary and prospective secondary school teachers. Graduates can also enter a School Direct programme: this teacher training programme is school-led. School Direct is non-salaried and is run by a school or group of schools who work closely with a university or a School-Centred Initial Teacher Training (SCITT) consortium who certify successful trainees. Once qualified, students apply to the schools to obtain a position as a newly qualified teacher (NQT).

To enter the teaching profession in France, the Master's degree is required as a level 7 qualification. As a general rule, intending teachers sit the two-year Master

MEEF *1er degré* (primary pathway) or 2nd *degré* (secondary pathway) at an ESPE (*Ecole Supérieure du Professorat et de l'Education*). ESPEs are Institutes of Education within universities but there is only one ESPE per *académie*, which means that there are 32 ESPEs nationally. At the end of the first year (M1), students sit a competitive civil service entry examination known as a *concours*. As long as the students pass the first year of the Master's, they can enter into the second year (M2) even if they have failed the *concours*. Those who succeed the *concours* are required to teach in a school part-time and are paid as probationary teachers. They are recruited permanently at the end of the M2 year if they meet the academic and professional requirements. This chapter focuses on those *concours* that MFL students are most likely to pass in order to enter a teaching career. The first is the *Certificat d'aptitude au professorat de l'enseignement du second degré* (CAPES) and the *Agrégation*, a more highly selective exam which was created in 1766. Successful candidates who pass the CAPES are known as *professeurs certifiés* (PRCE) and those that pass the *Agrégation* as *professeurs agrégés* (PRAG). Finally, it is also possible for MFL students to pass the *Concours de recrutement de professeur des écoles* (CRPE) to teach at primary level and then move on into MFL secondary teaching through internal promotion.

Teacher Educators between Two Worlds

In France, certain teaching positions at university are reserved for PRCE and PRAG teachers. These teachers are not required to conduct any research but teach twice as many hours as lecturers, senior lecturers or professors. Positions are advertised each year online through a national centralised portal between mid-September and the end of October. Candidates apply for the job openings and up to ten short-listed candidates are then invited for an interview which lasts around 20–30 minutes. The candidates are then ranked and the one ranked first then decides whether or not to accept the job. Should this candidate refuse the job, the candidate in second position is then offered the position. Given the competitive nature of this recruitment process, candidates with the *Agrégation* as well as a PhD are clearly in a more favourable position particularly for teacher educator positions. However, although a PGCE is not systematically required to teach in England, it is highly recommended for those who want to move on to a Master's degree later on in their careers. As a general rule, this qualification is considered an asset for those who wish to apply for positions as HE teacher educators given that university teacher educators guide their students through the complex learning process of professional development and practice.

Teacher educators find themselves between two worlds: not only do they play a key role in the teaching and training of student teachers in the field of innovative pedagogical practice in the primary or secondary classroom but given the university context, their work also concerns research into teaching and learning theory. Yet, they juggle the two roles and assert their unique professional identity as teacher educators. In a similar fashion, MFL teachers juggle between languages and cultures both within the classroom and outside when they organise school trips abroad, use foreign literature with their pupils, watch films in a foreign language at the local cinema, keep up with news from the BBC or the Guardian on their smart phones and go on holiday abroad to places where they can speak with the locals. Students and teachers of MFL enjoy learning languages and discovering other cultures; they find it natural to participate in mobility as a means of consolidating and maintaining MFL proficiency for academic, professional, recreational, and cultural purposes. Transnational mobility is part of their world. HE teacher educators who specialise in MFL are likely therefore to have demonstrated that not only are they experienced skilled teaching professionals but that they have probably also experienced transnational mobility either in a professional or personal capacity. To what extent have their transnational mobility opportunities had an impact on their professional development and facilitated their access to a career in higher education as teacher educators or not? The first step towards answering this question is to examine the reasons why languages hold such a central place in EU policy particularly in the face of global economic ambitions given that teacher educators of MFL are at the forefront of language education policy measures.

MULTILINGUALISM IN EUROPE OR ENGLISH AS LINGUA FRANCA

All for One or One for All?

The concept of the European Union (EU) was inspired by a vision of sustainable peace, justice and solidarity in the aftermath of two horrific World Wars. A process of co-operation between the countries of Europe was set in motion in 1950 to prevent future military conflict and ensure economic and social progress for all. The key to creating a society promoting ideals of democracy, prospects for peace and a more integrated Europe was the endorsement of multilingualism and intercultural understanding. This endorsement is expressed in Article 22 of the Charter of Fundamental Rights of the EU approved by the European Parliament and the European Council and Commission in December 2000 which commits the EU to respect linguistic diversity.

However, Androulla Vassiliou, Commissioner for Education, Culture, Multilingualism and Youth suggests in her talk at Harvard University in 2014 that the rich linguistic and cultural diversity that exists within Europe also represents a challenge to the "European project" because it presents a potential barrier to creating unity and common purpose:

> Language serves as a useful measure of our diversity. Today, the European Union functions with 24 official languages, more than 60 regional and minority languages and more than 120 migrant languages. Since I am also the

Commissioner responsible for multilingualism, allow me to say, with some pride, that the Tower of Babel still stands tall in 2014. But of course all of this presents a challenge, and it lies in striking the right balance between the respect for cultural diversity and the construction of a shared European identity – an identity that does not replace the sense of national belonging, but adds a new layer to the multiple identities of our citizens. The search for this balance is part of what we call intercultural dialogue. It is an integral part of the European project, and it has been so right from the start. (Vassiliou, 2014)

On the one hand, the Council insists that multilingualism and diversity "should be encouraged in teaching and research throughout the higher education curriculum" (European Commission, 2013, para. 2.1), whereas on the other that in order to "attract talent which would otherwise not come to Europe" and "widen career prospects" for European Union students, "proficiency in English is de facto part of any internationalisation strategy for learners, teachers and institutions" (para. 2.2). It seems increasingly the case that the rationale for the EU promoting English as a lingua franca or a lingua academica is linked to the global economy. This can be understood in the context of the Lisbon agreement to make Europe a leading knowledge-based economy in the world: not only is it desirable for young people to acquire proficiency in English but it is also considered necessary for future employment. Despite the EU promoting multilingualism, English is being reinforced in the EHEA at the expense of other EU languages. It would appear therefore that in terms of language policy, conflicting forces are at play.

For Phillipson (2003), the EU multilingual policies relate to "projects" or "future goals" rather than something real that exists in Europe (p. 95). He believes that multilingualism can only be achieved "if the experience of grassroots and elite multilingualism worldwide is related to the global economic, political, and cultural trends that determine whether languages thrive or perish" (ibid., p. 64). He considers this difficult because there are structural and ideological factors in place such as the "substantial investment in the teaching of English in EU education systems or a popular demand for English that is strongly connected to a language that is projected in advertising and the media as connoting success, influence, consumerism, and hedonism" (ibid., p. 65), which are responsible for the advance of English as a 'common' EU language:

There is now a common market, a common commercial policy, and a common defence and security policy. There is a common agricultural policy of long standing (…). Are we moving towards a common language policy? And if so, does this mean that a single language will be given a special status? (ibid., pp. 12–13)

English is considered the language of the market and a high level of English proficiency is valued as human capital. Students with excellent language skills acquired through a privileged background where parents have financed private

47

language tuition are likely to have the competitive edge when aiming to get into the better schools and universities whereas those who do not have access to such learning opportunities tend to fail in climbing up the socio-economic ladder. Majhanovich (2014, p. 169) points out that this situation bears consequences for the Global South in which "millions of non-English speakers" are under pressure to "acquire sufficient English proficiency in the language for participation in the globalized world." In this context, English is perceived as the key to securing a future which is economically promising yet in reality is inaccessible to the vast majority.

English as a lingua franca also presents a problem for English native speakers in the Global North. The All-Party Parliamentary Group on Modern Languages (APPG on Modern Languages) lobbies for improving the linguistic skills base of the UK and published its manifesto for languages in July 2014. The manifesto makes clear its position concerning English as a global language for English native speakers:

> [T]he latest cutting-edge research shows that, in the 21st century, speaking *only* English is as much of a disadvantage as speaking *no* English. Knowledge of other languages – and of other cultures – is important for education and skills, the economy, international engagement, defence and security and community relations. (APPG on Modern Languages, 2014, p. 1)

English as lingua franca also has an impact on the type of English that universities promote. Underdal (2010, p. 50), a former vice-chancellor, proposes that in the case of the "supply of graduates exceeding the demand for expertise in the labour market," practical measures should be adopted when planning and organising university courses to increase 'employability' such as:

> more emphasis on 'Business English' (rather than, say, the English language in 19th Century literature), case-work focusing on current problems or opportunities of a particular industry or community, or practical training in a particular type of activity (such as memo-writing for decision-makers).

The above is an example of how English skills for the purpose of business and market logic are considered more valuable than the knowledge acquired through studying English language in 19th century literature. English is valued as a commodity in the knowledge economy and culture is disregarded. The dichotomy between linguistic skills versus cultural content illustrates that from a neo-liberal perspective, cultural knowledge is no longer understood as an end in itself but is instead legitimated in society only by its utility in the global economy. Cummins (1981) explains that the Cognitive Academic Language Proficiency (CALP) skills in English such as those required to study 19th century literature take much longer to develop (at least five years) than those necessary for basic communication in English – Basic Interpersonal Communication Skills (BICS) – which only need on average "one to two years of language exposure" (Cummins, 1981; Hakuta, Butler, & Witt, 2000; Thomas & Collier, 2002; cited in Jang, Cummins, Wagner, Stille, & Dunlop, 2015, p. 92). In a context where time is money, investment into more culturally charged language learning may therefore take second place particularly when foreign languages are purposely learnt to promote corporate, military or political interests rather than to acquire a greater understanding of other cultures and societies (Kramsch, 2006). To this end, Lyotard explains:

> The transmission of knowledge is no longer destined to train an elite capable of guiding the nation towards its emancipation, but to supply the system with players capable of acceptably fulfilling their roles at the pragmatic posts required by the institution. (Lyotard, 1984, p. 48; cited in Jarvis, 1996, p. 181)

MFL learning at primary level has been an official European Union priority since 1997 (Grin, 2005) when the Council passed a Resolution on the early teaching of European Union languages. When the European Council met in Barcelona in March 2002, it renewed its commitment to languages and agreed on improving the mastery of basic language skills with special regard to the teaching of at least two foreign languages from a very early age. However, the publication in 2012 by the European Commission of the findings of the first European Survey on Language Competences (ESLC) indicated that pupils at the end of compulsory schooling in England and France continued to demonstrate poor levels of proficiency in their first MFL (Jones, 2012). Decades earlier, Stern (1983) had insisted on the necessity of language policy decisions being based on grounded research:

> Theorists and practitioners alike want to improve language learning, and they must decide for themselves what to do about it. The question is whether the decisions made individually or collectively are well thought out, informed, based on theoretical foundations, and are as effective as they can be expected to be, or whether they are patently naïve, uninformed, ill-founded, and inconsistent. (Stern, 1983, p. 2)

These results were problematic for policy-makers but hold very little surprise for language researchers. Bearing in mind Stern's words above, it can be understood why the ESLC results were so disappointing given that most primary children have less than two hours a week of MFL learning in the classroom: "one or two hours a week will not produce advanced second language speakers, no matter how young they were when they began" (Lightbown & Spada, 2006, p. 74).

Unlike in France where pupils study one or more modern foreign languages to the age of 18 for their *baccalauréat* exam, pupils in England have the option of dropping MFL at the age of 14 which over time has resulted in a considerable MFL primary and secondary teacher linguistic skills deficit on a national scale. The consequences of this deficit are outlined in the report, "The Language Trends Survey 2014/2015" carried out under the joint management of the CfBT Education Trust and the British Council:

> However, many differences remain in key aspects such as the amount of curriculum time dedicated each week to the learning of a language, the level of linguistic competence of class teachers, who are still the majority source

of language teaching for Key Stage 2 pupils, and the degree to which primary teachers are able to achieve a consistency of provision and achievement in pupil learning to meet the needs of Key Stage 3 teachers receiving pupils into Year 7. Primary teachers report that their biggest challenges are finding sufficient curriculum time for languages and boosting staff confidence and linguistic proficiency to teach reading, writing and grammatical understanding. (Board & Tinsley, 2015, p. 135)

There are four crucial issues identified in this report concerning the teaching and learning of MFL nationally: weak MFL linguistic and pedagogy skills; poor transition from primary to secondary; MFL learning becoming more elitist and finally difficulty in achieving a high grade in MFL A-level compared with other subjects such as maths and science subjects.

To make things more complicated, there is a long-standing belief that a language can be learnt rapidly. This is a throwback to American wartime language programmes, initiated between 1941 and 1943 when, according to Stern (1983), the approach to language teaching in the USA changed radically. Although research has shown the limits of the American 'Army Method', this method has continued to influence post-war thinking about language learning in the USA and globally ever since:

The Armed Forces' foreign language learning training programmes demonstrated that language training does not necessarily have to be done in the conventional school-type language course [and] made earlier approaches in school and university appear almost irrelevant and ineffectual, [...] that languages can be taught to much larger populations of ordinary learners, servicemen, and much more quickly than had previously been thought possible. And they demonstrated the possible advantages of intensive language training and of an oral emphasis. (Stern, 1983, p. 102)

The study of MFL remains the preserve of the elite despite efforts to increase access through strategies such as the "Languages for All: Languages for Life" (Department for Education and Skills, 2002) in England and *"Apprendre les langues – Apprendre le monde"* (Halimi, 2012) in France. This is revealed by recent studies such as the one published by the British Council which reports that access to quality MFL learning is still directed towards those with more privileged backgrounds compared to the rest of the population:

Opportunities to learn more than one language are in decline in the state sector. It is far more common for the independent sector to offer pupils the opportunity to study two languages than it is in the state sector. More than 90 per cent of independent schools offer all pupils the opportunity to learn more than one language at Key Stage 3, whereas only 35 per cent of state schools do so. (Board & Tinsley, 2015, p. 134)

Consequently, despite MFL skills being perceived as providing increased opportunities in a global world, the best educational opportunities regarding MFL learning are, to a large extent, restricted to those pupils who belong to the elite of society who attend independent schools or whose families can afford private tuition, linguistic summer schools and gap year experiences. In addition, French and English students who display good levels of MFL skills are more likely than ever to be attracted towards higher status professions involving mobility and successful career prospects, and be snapped up by employers who demand these skills. In the next section, I first focus on why mobility is valued educationally and economically before moving on to an overview of the reasons why transnational mobility opportunities are foundering from an MFL learning perspective.

TRANSNATIONAL MOBILITY: IMPROVING EDUCATION OR THE ECONOMY?

EU Ambitions

The Council of the European Union considers that mobility opportunities for teachers improve the quality of school education in the EU overall, maintain the attractiveness of the teaching profession and also contribute towards continuing professional development (CPD):

> [T]he experience represents first-hand contact with a different education system in which approaches to teaching, as well as its methodologies and organisation, may differ. It is a unique opportunity for teachers to reflect on their own ways of teaching and exchange views about their experience with colleagues abroad. Transnational mobility may also help them overcome scepticism regarding other teaching methods, by providing them with an opportunity to observe their use directly and their impact on students. This experience may in turn motivate them to gain fresh skills for more innovative approaches of their own. Conversely it may be an opportunity too, for them to discuss their own approaches with teachers at their host institution, thereby developing a greater sense of empowerment and professional recognition. Finally, working visits by teachers to a country whose main language is not their mother tongue is likely to help them develop their language skills, an asset of special importance to those whose subject is modern foreign languages. (European Commission, 2015b, p. 85)

As part of its design to make the European Union a "world-leading knowledge economy" (European Council, 2009, p. 2), and to achieve "sustainable economic prosperity and employability" (ibid.) for its citizens, the Council of Europe stated its intention to invest in "human capital" (ibid.) and ensure the "provision of excellent and attractive education, training and research opportunities" (ibid.) according to the principle of 'lifelong learning" (ibid., p. 3). By providing greater opportunities for transnational mobility to learners, teachers and teacher trainers, it hopes to enhance "employability and adaptability" (ibid., p. 2) for Europeans because school education is improved:

> Strengthening the intensity and scale of the mobility of school staff is necessary to improve the quality of school education in the Union, as stated in the new Erasmus+ Programme, the EU programme for education, training, youth and sport (2014–2020). (European Commission, 2015b, p. 85)

The Council recommended that work be pursued on language learning as part of its strategy to improve the quality and efficiency of education and training (Council of the European Union, 2011). Therefore, mobility and the learning of foreign languages seem to be a priority for the European Union:

> To enable citizens to communicate in two languages in addition to their mother tongue, promote language teaching, where relevant, in VET (Vocational education and training) and for adult learners, and provide migrants with opportunities to learn the language of the host country. (Council of the European Union, 2011, para. 7)

Mobility is also perceived positively in a neo-liberal world in which workers are expected to take up new jobs and relocate to new places according to the fluctuating demands of the workplace. Jones (1998, p. 241) explains that "[w]hat made the globalisation agendas feasible were, of course, the communications and information revolutions, combined with an increased mobility of persons, services and goods." Park (2015, p. 4) suggests that neoliberalism encourages workers to consider mobility as a "new, exciting opportunity" to "reinvent oneself by learning new skills, taking up new jobs, and relocating to new places" when faced with "corporate downsizing," "irregular employment" and "dwindling pay." This new economy demands that work be organized in terms of "flexible teams that form and disband depending on needs of production" which involves "communication with other workers inside and outside one's team, often across hierarchical and professional boundaries" (Iedema & Scheeres, 2003; cited in Park, 2015, p. 4).

Communication across the EU requires good language skills and this is the crux of the problem in relation to mobility. A close reading of the Bologna Process Implementation Report (European Commission, 2015a) reveals on the one hand that "a lack of funding" and a "lack of information and encouragement" (ibid., p. 245) pose obstacles to mobility; however, "linguistic barriers represent the greatest obstacle to mobility" in the EU. There are multiple references to the language difficulties experienced by the non-MFL secondary teachers who experienced transnational EU mobility schemes: "language–related barriers"; "[l]anguage obstacles concerning ingoing mobility"; "need to extend the overall duration of studies due to recognition, curriculum and language problems"; "[t]he most relevant obstacles to degree mobility appear to be lack of funding and languages"; "due to recognition, curriculum and language problems" (ibid.). The European Commission suggests therefore that "language considerations should be a focus of attention at both national and institutional levels (through a comprehensive language policy, for example)" (ibid., p. 253). Given the inherent value of mobility for language learning and the difficulties faced by non-MFL secondary teachers, it would be reasonable to expect the EU to encourage mobility among modern foreign language (MFL) teachers, especially as transnational mobility represents a professional need for teachers of MFL "more than those of other subjects" (European Commission, 2015b, p. 88):

> Modern foreign language teachers obviously need to train and practice the language they teach. They also need to experience close contact with one of the countries which national language corresponds to the language they teach, in order to gain a deeper cultural insight to transmit to their students.

Although, the Eurydice report (European Commission, 2015b) points to the fact that among all teachers, "modern foreign language teachers are the most transnationally mobile" (p. 13), the same report indicates that up to 40% of MFL teachers surveyed had not experienced any transnational mobility. The European Commission implied that this non-negligible percentage of MFL teachers lacking mobility opportunities might bear down on the standard of MFL taught in the classrooms of Europe: "a finding possibly relevant to *the quality teaching of foreign languages*" (ibid., p. 89) [bold characters mine]. So in the long-term, improving mobility opportunities for MFL students and teachers may indeed be the first step to improving the quality of modern foreign languages in Europe. Yet, it may also be legitimate to question why the EU has not targeted MFL secondary teachers at an earlier stage and whether there has not been a temptation to "shift from the cultural to the economic agenda" (Tomusk, 2011, para. 25) and promote a utilitarian approach to the teaching and learning of English as a lingua franca devoid of cultural content instead of a multilingual agenda. From this perspective, mobility and language learning are not intended to serve the future generations of children from all walks of life but rather a group of international students, a global elite who can combine:

> studies and pleasure, travel in Europe and collect study credits from various universities in different countries. The credit transfer system and the unquestionable recognition of the credits throughout the EHEA would allow the student checking out and collecting the degree at the final university on the travel list. Such would have been the proverbial *cafeteria university of Europe*. (ibid., para. 53)

Ballatore (2006) highlights that the Erasmus programme serves to accentuate inequalities rather than eradicate them:

> Looking at the skills and the migratory capital already acquired by students and at the selection practices in the departments or faculties, it is obvious that this program tends to consecrate young people whose educational trajectories are, if not brilliant, at least fast and/or atypical. Moreover, the European commission's data show that reciprocity of exchanges is rarely achieved. Hence,

this program seems to reinforce the pre-existing supremacy (of languages and of some institutions in particular) and the growing diversification of students' trajectories. (Ballatore, 2006, p. 2)

Economic reasons are therefore influencing educational convergence in Europe and reveals that the education systems of France and England are more susceptible than they have ever been to the market forces at play within the context of globalisation despite both countries having very different academic, institutional and ideological traditions in educational provision (Broadfoot, 1985, p. 56; Malet, 2009). Now my attention will focus on the extent to which the international frame has shaped the career of the teacher educators participating in this study.

METHODOLOGY

As a reminder, the overall objective is to identify the extent to which transnational mobility opportunities have facilitated access to a career as a HE teacher educator for secondary school teachers of MFL given the Council of Europe's commitment to continuing professional development through mobility and language learning. This study draws on semi-directive interview data and contextualises the findings through a critical analysis of EU policy and its implementation in the two contrasting education systems of UK-England and France. Each of the participants in this study is identified by a pseudonym. The participants are graduates, have QTS and have taught as qualified secondary education teachers in their respective domestic education systems after graduating. They all went on to doctoral studies after a career spanning at least fifteen years as a school teacher. Two of the HE teacher educators in this study work in the French higher education system (Isabelle and Catherine) and two in the UK-English system (Helen and Susan). The themes covered during interview related to the reasons why the teachers were interested in MFL learning or teaching, why they wanted to teach and become teacher educators, how they set about it and the impact EU policies concerning mobility and MFL teaching and learning had had on their decision to access higher education and become a teacher educator. The teachers were free to add any comments concerning obstacles or issues that were not necessarily related to the themes but had some bearing on the overall subject. Although the semi-structured interview format guided the participants, narrative was encouraged allowing each teacher to elaborate on their responses to trace the 'real life' options available at various points of their academic and professional career in relation to the context. This formed a basis for comparing the factors which influenced the decisions taken by each HE teacher educator in relation to the French and English education systems within the wider EU context. When undertaking a comparative study of education systems it is important to compare countries which share enough similar characteristics to be comparable and yet present specific individual profiles to elucidate points of convergence and divergence. In the present study, interviewees share a common sociolinguistic and sociocultural heritage which is reflected by English being the first foreign language studied in France and French in UK-England. In addition, their history as colonial powers has resulted in both French and English having the status as a lingua franca although in the context of the internationalisation of higher education in Europe, English is quickly establishing itself as the dominant lingua academica.

QUALITATIVE ANALYSIS OF DATA

Interest in MFL

Helen and Susan both confirmed that they had been fortunate enough to have had early childhood experiences abroad in France. They studied French at school and obtained good O-Level and A-Level grades in French and German. Similarly, Isabelle and Catherine found English to be their best subject at school. Catherine's mother was an English teacher so she had been immersed in English culture since childhood. In contrast, Isabelle's first contact with the English speaking world was through music and to a lesser extent literature. She explains that the differences between French and English culture caught her attention and were a major source of motivation: "I wanted to understand why there was such a difference." In the same way, Helen explains that she had always been intrigued by languages and describes her relationship with languages as being associated with both "wonderment" and "curiosity." Susan points to the "human dimension" of language learning which made it stand out for her: "languages are a bit different and sit outside the rest of the curriculum (…) not like geography or it's not like history or PE – it's totally different because it's so closely bound up with your identity and your being, you know."

The four teacher educators recognise that their expertise is linked, on the one hand, to hard work: "language is a motor skill – practice is necessary" (Helen), "English is hard, it's hard work – I spent hours and hours on learning vocabulary and grammar rules" (Catherine) and using the language in its context: "it's hard to get the point if you've never visited the country or a country where the language is spoken" (Susan) and "my experience as a language assistant was a turning point – everything I had studied and learnt became real." The comments reveal that language learning for the teacher educators is enjoyable and a source of pleasure and pride not only because it represents an investment of time and effort but also because languages provide insights into other cultures through communication with people in context and through the study of literature. Languages stand apart from other school subjects because they are so closely linked with identity. The study of languages also promotes metalinguistic awareness. It would seem that because it has a human dimension, these teachers do not consider language learning can be restricted to a practical functional purpose.

Entering the Teaching Profession

Helen entered the teaching profession because she loved the subject and wanted to "inspire kids." She explains that she wanted her pupils to not only speak the languages she taught but to reflect on "what languages are for." She entered teaching later on in life after having had other life experiences so that she could bring all this with her into the classroom for the benefit of the children. Susan cares deeply about children's learning being "as broad an experience" as possible and she finds that language teaching introduces "creativity" and "opportunities for pupils to express themselves." Isabelle decided to be a teacher because this was a career she had always wanted to follow: "I wanted to teach and I happened to be good at languages." As for Catherine, she explained that at the time you had to be good at English, very motivated and hard-working because the CAPES exam was so difficult. Only people who "really wanted to teach" who "loved English culture could make it because in those days you had to study Shakespeare, Dickens, British or US civilisation topics, you had to be good at translating and writing, you had to know everything about lesson planning and teaching theory and speak perfectly without a French accent. It's not the same today – the topics are more general, broader."

The teachers in this study entered the profession because they wanted to teach and because they wanted to teach languages. Children's learning is at the forefront and from these comments there is a real sense of vocation concerning the choice of career. They are all communicators who convey how important languages are for a child's educational growth. All four participants love languages and have done so since their first contact with MFL whether that was at home, at school or through a medium such as music or literature. Teaching was a natural career choice and they experienced many years of classroom teaching before moving on to higher education. The MFL they promote with their pupils and their students is one which is strongly associated with culture, human experience and intercultural understanding. This vision seems to be in line with the vision of Europe that respects linguistic diversity. Enjoyment, creativity and sensitivity are important but just as important is the notion that expertise comes with hard work and practice on a regular basis.

Becoming a Teacher Educator

In the French context, Isabelle and Catherine had already been singled out by inspectors, county advisors and head teachers for their expertise as effective classroom teachers. They had demonstrated their potential to access a post as a teacher educator in higher education. In addition because they had already obtained a PhD which involved teaching and learning MFL, they were at a distinct advantage given the competition for posts. Despite this, Catherine also points out "there is a huge demand for teacher educators in France who can teach English so it isn't that much of a challenge to obtain a post – most primary teachers are required to teach English at school and they need training. Sometimes we can't find anyone at all." Isabelle signals that a PhD is "valued by the university" and that those teachers who wish to do a research degree are entitled to paid study leave. However, she also states that "having a PhD is not necessary, you know most of the work at the School of Education involves language teaching because so many students who are going to teach English cannot speak it." Susan also refers to the poor proficiency levels of English primary teachers: "Well that's the issue that we have in the UK – that we have a lot of primary school teachers that have the pedagogy but don't have the language skills." Helen also refers to this issue at high school when MFL secondary teachers try to rectify the pronunciation errors acquired at primary school: "we have very persistent things in our system in secondary where kids who are very attached to their primary peripatetic French teacher will pronounce certain words wrong for five years." Helen decided to live in Germany for ten months and used this time to carry out research in both Germany and France for her MPhil. She explained that she wished to develop German as her second language with the objective of becoming head of department. She was halfway through her PhD when she applied for a post at university as a teacher educator. She feels she was lucky because the introduction of "languages for all" and the National Curriculum resulted in "a huge shortage of language teachers." However things have changed "because kids were able to drop languages at high school after primary and now we haven't got enough language graduates coming through the system." Helen believes that entering HE as a teacher educator today would be "fairly impossible" because "so much teacher education has been taken out of HE and given to the schools instead." Like Helen, Susan also feels that School Direct has had "a big impact and some university departments have shrunk to almost nothing." She complains that: "it's been a shambles really in teacher education – you know we used to have a system of places being allocated so every university would have maybe 50 places and … we would have 20 places and … that shrunk to three a couple of years ago."

These comments suggest that EU policy targeting early language learning at primary school indirectly led to the teacher educators in this study gaining access to a career in higher education as a consequence of a recruitment drive in the past but that things have now changed. In France, there continues to be a demand for primary MFL teacher educators given that all primary teachers are expected to teach modern languages in the primary classroom. This is not the case in England as only specialist MFL primary teachers teach languages. Taking into account the fact that there are less places on university courses in England as a result of government cuts and fewer applicants choosing to specialise in primary MFL, the recruitment opportunities which existed in the past seem to have dwindled. The contexts are very different but the resultant problems for MFL learning and teaching appear to have motivated both the French and English teachers to address these concerns through research and collaboration. They have all actively invested in their professional and academic development through research and expressed a sense of delight to collaborate with colleagues who share the same outlook as they do. For instance, Helen describes how "coming to university was great" because there was "so much more intellectual stimulation" than she had experienced in the school environment. She was now able to "talk to other people who were interested in theory." Helen explains that there was no formal training to be a teacher educator but considers that her desire to understand why there were problems in language learning coupled with the carrying out of action research in her classroom gave her the insight and the reflexivity to develop as an effective teacher educator. Clearly their idea of 'quality' does not seem tally with policymakers who they accuse of not understanding what language teaching is all about. Professional relationships are valued but it seems that in England teacher educators are more isolated than ever because conferences are no longer funded which saddens both Helen and Susan particularly because these occasions provided an opportunity for professional development. It would appear that they chose to move to HE because they wanted to be more involved in the world of research because it was stimulating intellectually but also because it was a means of addressing the concerns they met in their professional capacity as language teachers as a consequence of the implementation of EU language policy.

Mobility Opportunities

Helen's year abroad provided her with an insight into quality French teaching: "I've seen that age group in France with really expert teachers who'd been teaching for ages and they would be getting their kids to be talking a lot" and it also provided her with the opportunity to improve her language skills whilst undertaking research. However, the other three participants did not have the experience of studying teaching methods because their experience of mobility involved conversation classes with small groups of school children as a language assistant in the third year of their four-year degree courses in a school abroad. None of the participants have ever received funding for any EU transnational mobility scheme and the only experience of mobility during their career as HE teacher educators involved international conferences and the occasional opportunity to visit students on teaching practice abroad. Catherine says: "No, I started teaching before Erasmus came in and never got the chance. It's a great idea but I don't know anyone who has experienced Erasmus. I think it is probably more for the younger ones. When I go abroad it is to check on my students who are on teaching practice in an English school but I never speak to any university teachers when I'm over – only the primary teacher who has welcomed the student into his or her classroom." Isabelle makes the point that: "there is a lot of competition for Erasmus at this university – we are not a priority. It's a pity because we need this experience abroad for so many reasons and our students do too but I'm afraid primary teachers are not big business." Helen thinks that part of the problem is that Europe is "looking at outcomes and the idea of teaching as a mechanistic activity…that if you go through a certain set of motions – then the learners will learn and then they will get what their parents are paying for or what the state is paying for." She suggests that this is: "a lack of joined up thinking – people with the power and the money are not thinking – what do we need to do to bring quality?" She then points out that there are too many who "have some simplistic idea of understanding what language teaching is and don't realise that it is, you know, the hardest thing to teach at schools but could be incredibly useful if it's taught the right way in terms of opening up and has incredible global use in terms of intercultural understanding." These final comments present an insight to the consequences of considering languages from a utilitarian perspective for language learning and the market economy. They present the case that policy-makers are missing the point: quality language learning at school taught in the right conditions will reap benefits for the whole of society not in terms of capital gains but in terms of intercultural tolerance, cultural and intellectual growth, equitable social integration and a profound respect for diversity.

CONCLUSION

This small-scale study was exploratory in nature. It provides a snapshot of the challenges facing HE teacher educators in France and UK-England and information concerning their careers. Results indicate that access to a career in higher education as a secondary school teacher was more influenced by a love of teaching, a drive to convey a love of languages to pupils, concerns raised by language policy and its impact on the primary and secondary classroom as well as the need to carry out research to tackle these concerns. Despite the obvious advantages that EU transnational mobility experiences provide for teachers, the teacher educators in this study did not experience any mobility schemes such as Erasmus before accessing HE. They do, however, consider such schemes as valuable but do not feel that policy-makers target them. It could be suggested that, on the contrary, MFL teachers and HE MFL students should be at the top of the list because improving mobility opportunities for MFL teachers may indeed be the first step to improving the quality of modern foreign languages in Europe, in line with Kelly's recommendations (2015, p. 70) for providing "access to appropriate forms of professional recognition across a range of countries." Given the lack of mobility opportunities, the overriding factor which determined the career paths of these teachers was the desire to access the world of research at university in response to the issues arising from teaching and learning MFL in a global society.

REFERENCES

Apple, M. W. (2001). Comparing neo-liberal projects and inequality in education. *Comparative Education, 37*(4), 409–423.

Ballatore, M. (2006). Le programme erasmus en France, en Italie et en Angleterre: Sélection des étudiants et compétences migratoires. *Cahiers de la Recherche sur l'Education et les Savoirs, 5*, 215–239.

Broadfoot, P. (1985). Changing patterns of educational accountability in England and France. *Comparative Education, 21*(3), 273–286.

Council of Europe (COE). (2001). *A common European framework of reference for languages: Learning, teaching, assessment*. Cambridge: Cambridge University Press.

Cummins, J. (1981). The role of primary language development in promoting educational success for language minority students. In C. F. Leyba (Ed.), *Schooling and language minority students: A theoretical framework* (pp. 3–49). Los Angeles, CA: National Dissemination and Assessment Center & California State Department of Education.

Department for Education and Skills. (2002). *Languages for all: Languages for life: A strategy for England*. London: Department for Education and Skills. Retrieved from http://dera.ioe.ac.uk/6364/7/DfESLanguagesStrategy_Redacted.pdf

Détourbe, M.-A. (2014). *Les enjeux de l'évaluation dans l'enseignement supérieur: Le cas des universités britanniques*. Toulouse: Presses Universitaires du Mirail.

European Commission. (2013). *European higher education in the world*. Communication from the Commission to the European Parliament, the Council, the European Economic and Social Committee and the Committee of the Regions, Brussels. Retrieved from http://eur-lex.europa.eu/LexUriServ/LexUriServ.do?uri=COM:2013:0499:FIN:en:PDF

European Commission/EACEA/Eurydice. (2015a). *The European higher education area in 2015: Bologna process implementation report*. Luxembourg: Publications Office of the European Union.

European Commission/EACEA/Eurydice. (2015b). *The teaching profession in Europe: Practices, perceptions, and policies* (Eurydice Report). Luxembourg: Publications Office of the European Union.

European Council. (2009). *Council conclusions of 12 May 2009 on a strategic framework for European cooperation in education and training ('ET 2020')*. Retrieved from https://www.consilium.europa.eu/uedocs/cms_data/docs/pressdata/en/educ/107622.pdf

European Parliament and European Council. (2008, May 6). Recommendation of the European parliament and of the council of 23 april 2008 on the establishment of the European qualifications framework for lifelong learning. *Official Journal of the European Union, 51*(C 111), 1–7.

Grin, F. (2005). *L'enseignement des langues étrangères comme politique publique* (Report No. 19). Paris: Haut Conseil de l'Evaluation de l'Ecole.

Hakuta, K., Butler, Y. G., & Witt, D. (2000). *How long does it take English learners to attain proficiency?* (Report 2000–2001). Santa Barbara, CA: University of California Linguistic Minority Research Institute Policy.

Halimi, S. (2012). *Apprendre les langues, apprendre le monde*. Rapport du comité stratégique des langues, Ministère de l'éducation nationale, de la jeunesse et de la vie associative. Retrieved from http://cache.media.education.gouv.fr/file/02_Fevrier/91/5/Apprendre-les-langues-Apprendre-le-monde_206915.pdf

Iedema, R., & Scheeres, H. (2003). From doing work to talking work: Renegotiating knowing, doing, and identity. *Applied Linguistics, 24*(3), 316–337. doi:10.1093/applin/24.3.316

Jang, E. E., Cummins, J., Wagner, M., Stille, S., & Dunlop, M. (2015). Investigating the homogeneity and distinguishability of STEP proficiency descriptors in assessing English language learners in Ontario schools. *Language Assessment Quarterly, 12*(1), 87–109.

Jang, E. E., Stille, S., Wagner, M., Lui, M., & Cummins, J. (2010). *Investigating the quality of STEP proficiency descriptors using teachers' ratings*. Final research report presented to the Ministry of Education, Modern Language Centre, OISE, Toronto.

Jarvis, P. (1996). Continuing education in a late-modern or global society: Towards a theoretical framework for comparative analysis. *Comparative Education, 32*(2), 233–244.

Jones, N. (2012). Europe: SurveyLang, l'enquête européenne sur les compétences langagières. *Revue Internationale d'Éducation de Sèvres, 60*, 18–21.

Jones, P. W. (1998). Globalisation and internationalism: Democratic prospects for world education. *Comparative Education, 34*(2), 143–155.

Katsarova, I. (2015). *Higher education in the EU: Approaches, issues and trends*. Brussels: European Parliamentary Research Service, European Union.

Kelly, M. (2015). Challenges to multilingual language teaching: Towards a transnational approach. *European Journal of Language Policy, 7*(1), 65–83.

Kramsch, C. (2006). The traffic in meaning. *Asia Pacific Journal of Education, 26*(1), 99–104.

Lightbown, P. M., & Spada, N. (2006). *How languages are learned*. Oxford: Oxford University Press.

Lyotard, J. F. (1984). *The postmodern condition: A report on knowledge* (Theory and History of Literature, Vol. 10). Minneapolis, MN: University of Minnesota Press.

Majhanovich, S. (2014). Neo-liberalism, globalization, language policy, and practice issues in the Asia-Pacific region. *Asia Pacific Journal of Education, 34*(2), 168–183.

Malet, R. (2009). Former, réformer, transformer la main-d'œuvre enseignante? Politiques comparées et expériences croisées anglo-américaines. *Éducation et Sociétés, 21*(1), 91–122.

OECD. (2014). *TALIS 2013 results: An international perspective on teaching and learning*. Paris: Author.

Park, J. S. Y. (2015). Language as pure potential. *Journal of Multilingual and Multicultural Development, 37*(5), 453–466.

Phillipson, R. (2003). *English-only Europe? Challenging language policy*. London: Routledge.

Stern, H. H. (1983). *Fundamental concepts of language teaching: Historical and interdisciplinary perspectives on applied linguistic research.* Oxford: Oxford University Press.

Thomas, W. P., & Collier, V. P. (2002). *A national study of school effectiveness for language minority students' long-term academic achievement.* Santa Cruz, CA: Center for Research on Education, Diversity and Excellence, and University of California-Santa Cruz.

Tomusk, V. (2011). The garbage of the garbage. *Cahiers de la Recherche sur l'Education et les Savoirs, 3,* 21–41.

Underdal, A. (2010). Implications of the change from elite to mass or multi-purpose institutions. In J. E. Fenstad & E. De Corte (Eds.), *From information to knowledge; from knowledge to wisdom* (pp. 45–51). Portland, OR: Portland Press.

WEB REFERENCES

All-Party Parliamentary Group on Modern Languages. (2014). Retrieved from http://www.all-languages.org.uk/uploads/files/Press%20Releases/APPGManifestoforLangs-EmbargoTo14July.pdf

Board, K., & Tinsley, T. (2015). *Language trends 2014/2015: The state of language learning in primary and secondary schools in England.* London: British Council & CfBT Education Trust. Retrieved from https://www.britishcouncil.org/sites/default/files/language_trends_survey_2015.pdf

Certificat de compétences en langues de l'enseignement supérieur (CLES). Retrieved from http://www.certification-cles.fr/medias/fichier/bilan-national-de-la-passation-du-cles-2013-2014_1432199026151-pdf

European Convention. (2000). *Charter of fundamental rights of the European Union.* Retrieved from http://www.europarl.europa.eu/charter/pdf/text_en.pdf

European Commission. (2016). *Communication from the commission to the European parliament, the council, the European economic and social committee and the committee of the regions.* Retrieved from http://eur-lex.europa.eu/legal-content/EN/ALL/?uri=CELEX:52013DC0499

Council of the European Union. (2011). *Council conclusions on language competences to enhance mobility.* Retrieved from http://eur-lex.europa.eu/legal-content/EN/TXT/PDF/?uri=OJ:C:2011:372:FULL&from=en

European Qualifications Framework in the UK and Ireland. Retrieved from http://www.qaa.ac.uk/en/Publications/Documents/qualifications-can-cross-boundaries.pdf

European Qualifications Framework in France. Retrieved from https://ec.europa.eu/ploteus/sites/eac-eqf/files/Rapport-FR-NQF-EQF-VF.pdf

European Parliament. (2008). *Mobility of school teachers in the European union: Study.* Retrieved from http://www.europarl.europa.eu/RegData/etudes/etudes/join/2008/408964/IPOL-CULT_ET(2008)408964_EN.pdf

Universities and Colleges Admissions Service (UCAS). Retrieved from https://www.ucas.com/ucas/teacher-training/getting-started/teacher-training-programmes/programmes-explained-%E2%80%93-0

Vassiliou, A. (2014). *Cultural diversity, global politics and the role of Europe* [Press release]. Retrieved from http://europa.eu/rapid/press-release_SPEECH-14-165_en.htm?locale=en

Norah Leroy
ESPE d'Aquitaine
University of Bordeaux
France

NADEZDA KULIKOVA AND YULIYA MIAKISHEVA

4. SOCIAL INCLUSION AND LANGUAGE SUPPORT FOR INTERNATIONALLY-EDUCATED NURSES IN CANADA

INTRODUCTION

For decades, Canada has welcomed millions of economic class immigrants, many of whom are internationally-trained professionals who become an important asset to the Canadian labour force. However, many recent immigrants to Canada have difficulty finding employment in their trained professions and their earnings have been declining in the last three decades. While existing research offers no single explanation of this phenomenon, Picot and Sweetman (2012) argued that insufficient language skills are among the contributing factors to this decline. Immigrants who seek employment in government-regulated occupations such as engineering, medicine, nursing, and teaching are particularly at a disadvantage. Foreign-educated professionals in these fields are less likely to work in the profession for which they were trained than their Canadian counterparts. There is a substantial discrepancy in the total number of people with a degree in a field of study which would typically lead to a job in a government-regulated occupation and the number of people actually employed in these occupations among internationally-trained professionals and their Canadian-born counterparts. For instance, in 2006 only 56% of internationally-trained nurses worked in their field of study compared to 73% of nurses born and educated in Canada (Zietsma, 2010). In government-regulated occupations like nursing, the impact of poor language skills on the successful integration of immigrants into the new society is particularly crucial. Many internationally-trained professionals often struggle with completing the licensure process: thus, occupation-specific language skills are identified as the key determinant of success (Covell, Neiterman, & Bourgeault, 2014).

To address the communicative challenges faced by internationally-educated professionals who aspire to become nurses in Canada and to highlight the need for internationally-educated nurses (IENs) to develop language competencies in order to respond to those challenges, this chapter provides a historical overview of the immigration policies in Canada, discusses the unique characteristics of nurses who immigrated to Canada, outlines the communication challenges these nurses face in their professional fields, and examines several language support programs available to immigrant nurses from the communicative competence perspective.

M.-A. Détourbe (Ed.), Inclusion through Access to Higher Education, 63–82.

IMMIGRATION TO CANADA: OVERVIEW

For hundreds of years, Canada has welcomed millions of immigrants, who have played and continue to play a critical role in the nation's growth and prosperity. The country relied on immigrants in its early years as one of the means of nation building, and it continues to rely on immigrants nowadays to sustain population growth and economic development (Pang, 2013).

Immigration to Canada was encouraged during its early years mainly to promote growth in industrial and agricultural sectors as well as for colonial expansion (Marsden, 2011). Starting in the sixteenth century, the eastern part of what is now Canada experienced a wave of settler migration from France, England and other western European countries. Over the years, more immigrants from southern and eastern Europe, Asia, and the United States arrived in Canada. People were drawn to Canada by opportunities to start a new life and in some cases to escape hardships they experienced in their own countries. For many, however, immigration to Canada was a challenge. Early Canadian immigration legislation was often governed by racial or ethnic background preferences. Such documents as the Chinese Immigration Act, issued in 1885, and the Act to Amend the Immigration Act, issued in 1908, specifically aimed to restrict or discourage immigrants from China or South East Asia from migrating to Canada. Furthermore, several immigration acts that followed in 1910 and in 1952 gave the Canadian government the freedom to discriminate against immigrants of certain nationalities, ethnicities, or cultural backgrounds (Marsden, 2011).

Later, the views of Canada on immigration focused mainly on the person's skills rather than their ethnic background or place of origin (Van Dyk, 2016). In 1971, Canada introduced multiculturalism as an official policy (Government of Canada, 2012). The Immigration Act of 1976 brought in a point system of immigration to Canada which allowed newcomers to adjust to the new environment by joining the Canadian labour force in the areas of their former professional experience and to contribute to the Canadian economy (Van Dyk, 2016). These reforms in immigration policy significantly redefined the profile of immigrants to Canada and introduced a new category of immigrants who were driven by economic motivations. These immigrants, referred to as skilled workers, became an important asset to the Canadian labour force.

Although the present immigration system has its own challenges, Canada continues to welcome thousands of internationally-trained professionals in the skilled worker category in an attempt to fulfil multiple short-term and long-term economic goals and to fill in the gaps in the labour market to benefit the Canadian economy. According to the immigration plan for 2017, almost 60% of immigrants are expected to arrive in Canada through the economic immigration category and further growth is projected (Government of Canada, 2016). Many of these economic immigrants are brought into the country to address a number of occupational shortages, particularly in the health care professions, such as nursing.

INTERNATIONALLY-EDUCATED NURSES IN CANADA

In Canada, nursing is a government-regulated occupation. There are three regulated nursing professions: registered nurses (which include nurse practitioners), licensed practical nurses, and registered psychiatric nurses. Registered nurses (RNs) "coordinate health care, deliver direct services and support clients in their self-care decisions and actions in health, illness, injury and disability in all stages of life" (Canadian Institute for Health Information [CIHE], n.d., para. 3). Nurse practitioners (NPs) are "RNs with additional educational preparation and experience. NPs may order and interpret diagnostic tests, prescribe pharmaceuticals, medical devices and other therapies and perform procedures" (CIHE, n.d., para. 4). Licensed practical nurses (LPNs) "assess clients and work in health promotion and illness prevention. They assess, plan, implement and evaluate care for clients" (CIHE, n.d., para. 5). Registered psychiatric nurses, or RPNs, "coordinate health care and provide client-centered services to individuals, families, groups and communities" (CIHE, n.d., para. 6). All these groups of nurses work both individually and in collaboration with other health care providers.

Forecasts show that Canada will need an additional 60,000 nurses by 2022 (Tomblin-Murphy et al., 2009). As a result, Canada has been actively involved in the recruitment of international nurses for whom English is an additional language to address the nursing shortage in the country as well as to improve healthcare in Canada (Coffey, 2006). Canada is indeed one of the leading host countries for internationally-educated nurses (IENs), who can be defined as "registered nurses who obtained their basic nursing education outside the hosting countries where they are working or intend to work" (Xu & He, 2012, p. 216).

However, in contrast to other recruiting countries, such as Australia, the UK, or the US, where IENs are contracted health care providers on work visas, most IENs in Canada are landed immigrants with permanent resident status. Some IENs enter the country through the Live-in-Caregiver program with the goal to become residents and to join the nursing workforce later (Xu & He, 2012).

According to the Canadian Association of the Schools of Nursing (CASN, n.d.), registered nurses, nurse practitioners, and licensed practical nurses with credentials from other countries are not being successfully integrated into the nursing workforce in Canada to the extent they could be. In 2010, the proportion of IENs in the Canadian nurse workforce employed as registered nurses was only 8.6% or 23,076 nurses (Canadian Nurses Association [CNA], 2012a). The percentage of employed internationally-educated nurse practitioners was even lower, 4.2% or 102 nurses (CNA, 2012b). From 2008–2012, the number of IENs employed as registered nurses in Canada grew only marginally from 21,980 to only 22,144 (less than a 1% increase). Almost half of these IENs, 49%, were employed in the province of Ontario (CIHE, n.d.). The number of applications for the Canadian Registered Nurse Examination (CRNE) from IENs in Ontario dropped from 1,011 in 2006 to 683 in 2015, and the share of IEN applications for the CRNE decreased from

28.4% to 12.2% (College of Nurses of Ontario [CNO], 2016). The gap between the licensure examination passing rates of IENs and their Canadian counterparts is almost twice as large (Atack, Cruz, Maher, & Murthy, 2012). In 2015, the pass rate for IEN applicants was 40.4%, which was a 3.6 percentage-point decrease compared to the exam pass rate in 2011. At the same time, the total number of test-takers decreased almost three-fold, from 1,124 to 396 in the same time frame. In the same year, only 35.9% of IENs who took CRNE passed the exam after the first attempt. After the third attempt, 62% of the test takers still could not pass the exam (CNO, 2016). Certainly, low passing rates and failure to complete the licensure process affect successful integration of IENs into the new society and profession (Covell, Neiterman, & Bourgeault, 2014).

THE COMMUNICATIVE LANGUAGE ABILITY PERSPECTIVE

Cummins (1980) distinguished between basic interpersonal communicative skills (BICS), such as accent, oral fluency, or socio-linguistic competence and cognitive/ academic language proficiency (CALP) which is related to the advancement of literacy skills and scholastic success in general. While basic interpersonal communication skills can be acquired in 2–3 years, it may take up to 7 years for students to acquire formal academic English, as many years of intensive exposure to academic texts and materials are required (Abriam-Yago, Yoder, & Kataoka-Yahiro, 1999; Hansen & Beaver, 2012). Successful continuing professional development of nurses educated abroad largely depends on their fluency in academic nursing English (Terry, Carr, & Williams, 2013). Many IENs often lack this fluency, or take their time to develop it, so attending clinical nursing courses and passing professional exams present more challenges for them than for domestic students (Carter & Xu, 2007). Developing language ability, and particularly the competence in occupation-specific language skills, is one of the key determinants of success in completing the nursing licensure process in Canada (Covell, Neiterman, & Bourgeault, 2014).

The multidimensional nature of the communicative language ability is reflected in the different models of communicative competence (Centre for Canadian Language Benchmarks [CCLB], 2012). These models developed by Hymes (1972), Canale and Swain (1980), Canale (1983), Moirand (1992), Bachman (1990), Celce-Murcia, Dörnyei, and Thurrell (1995), and Bachman and Palmer (1996, 2010) served as a guiding tool for Pawlikowska-Smith's model of communicative proficiency (as cited in CCLB, 2012). The model of communicative proficiency consisted of five components, namely linguistic (or grammatical) competence, textual competence, functional competence, socio-cultural competence, and strategic competence (Pawlikowska-Smith, 2002).

Linguistic competence includes the knowledge of the language itself, its rules and patterns. Effective language users are expected to produce language that is grammatically accurate, so their linguistic competence includes grammatical knowledge, which, in turn, consists of knowledge of vocabulary, syntax, phonology, and graphology. Language users need grammatical knowledge to determine how words are pronounced and written. They can accurately identify and use different parts of speech, determine the meanings of words, and know how to use words correctly in sentences. They can construct sentences that are grammatically accurate. However, linguistic competence alone may not be enough for effective communication. Language users should have knowledge of discourse and know how to link ideas and utterances accurately and effectively based on a given context. This area is governed by textual knowledge, which refers to the ability to make language logically connected and coherent, to know how information is organized in context, and to react accurately to prompts in a conversation. Functional competence helps language users to choose accurate utterances suitable for each communicative situation. A language user possessing functional competence would correctly identify and choose communicative devices, for example, to greet someone or to ask for directions. Socio-cultural competence is the one that non-native speakers of language may find most challenging, as it refers to using the language appropriately in a social situation, which includes the accurate and effective choice of linguistic devices, such as genres, dialect, register, idiomatic expressions, or cultural references. This competence allows language users to express their ideas effectively when speaking or writing to their peers or superiors, when speaking at a meeting, or at a party, or in public, or in other social situations. Strategic competence unites all other competencies to equip language users with tools for effective communicative language performance. It allows a language user to assess a communicative situation accurately and evaluate whether they can deal with it effectively based on their language abilities. A strategically competent language user can identify the appropriate language tasks in each situation, plan the steps to achieve the tasks, and implement the plan effectively (Pawlikowska-Smith, 2002).

ASSESSING LANGUAGE PROFICIENCY

Canada is the only country that has developed an occupation-specific language assessment tool to assess the English language proficiency of IENs (Xu & He, 2012). The development of the Canadian English Language Benchmarks Assessment for Nurses (CELBAN) was a government-funded initiative which aimed to address the projected nursing shortage in Canada and to facilitate the entry and integration of IENs who sought employment opportunities in Canadian nursing contexts (Touchstone Institute, 2015a).

CELBAN was developed in 2004 by Red River College in Manitoba under contract with the Centre for Canadian Language Benchmarks and allows IENs to demonstrate their English language proficiency within a professionally-relevant context (Touchstone Institute, 2015a). The test is based on the Canadian Language Benchmarks framework, which is "a descriptive scale of language ability in English as a Second Language (ESL) written as 12 benchmarks or reference points along a continuum from basic to advanced" (CCLB, 2012, p. v). The Canadian Language Benchmarks can be described as:

- a set of descriptive statements about successive levels on the continuum of language ability,
- a description of communicative competencies and performance tasks through which learners demonstrate application of language knowledge (i.e., competence) and skill (i.e., ability),
- a national standard for planning curricula for language instruction in a variety of contexts,
- a framework of reference for learning, teaching, programming and assessing adult ESL in Canada (CCLB, 2012, p. v).

The Canadian Language Benchmarks are founded on several theoretical principles, including the principle of communicative language ability, which consists of the five components discussed by Pawlikowska-Smith in her communicative proficiency model (CCLB, 2012). The 12 benchmarks are organized into three stages: basic, which represents simple tasks in non-demanding contexts and includes Benchmarks 1–4, intermediate, which represents moderately complex tasks in moderately-demanding contexts and includes Benchmarks 5–8, and advanced, which represents complex tasks in demanding contexts and includes Benchmarks 9–12. Each stage consists of four levels which reflect a learner's language ability (initial, developing, adequate, and fluent) in simple, moderately complex and complex tasks in non-demanding, moderately-demanding, and demanding contexts (CCLB, 2012). The benchmarks are used to assess all four language skills: listening, speaking, reading, and writing.

There are three versions of the CELBAN test (Touchstone Institute, 2015a). Candidates are allowed to retake parts of the test if they do not meet the regulator-required cut scores, but these attempts are limited to three. Currently, there are seven locations in the country which administer the test, located in the provinces of Alberta, British Columbia, Manitoba, Ontario, and Saskatchewan (Touchstone Institute, 2015b). From 2004 to 2014, over 4,500 candidates from 109 different countries took the test. Most candidates identified themselves as female (85%) and came from the Philippines (60%), India (24%), and China (3%).

The CELBAN scores are reported as CLB levels or benchmarks. Originally, to be eligible to enter their profession, nurses were expected to achieve the following benchmarks: listening – CLB 9, speaking and reading – CLB 8, and writing – CLB 7 (CCLB, 2012). In 2011, the benchmark for listening was increased to CBL 10 (Touchstone Institute, 2015a).

There exists an unofficial version of the CELBAN, the Institutional CELBAN, which replicates the high stakes testing environment of the official CELBAN and is seen as an effective tool in determining the level of readiness of IENs for the official test and conducting pre- and post-testing assessment of bridging programs (Touchstone Institute, 2015b). The Institutional CELBAN is used to:

- Determine CELBAN test readiness in IENs
- Conduct pre/post testing for bridging programs
- Provide diagnostic assessments for curricular purposes
- Determine readiness for pre-clinical and experiential placements
- Build test inoculation (CELBAN Centre, 2015, para. 3).

Only not-for-profit organizations, public post-secondary institutions and school boards working with internationally-educated health professionals, including nurses, are allowed to purchase and administer the Institutional CELBAN (CELBAN Centre, 2015).

BRIDGING PROGRAMS IN CANADA

Due to the status of IENs in Canada as landed immigrants, the Canadian government focuses its efforts on helping IENs to address gaps in education and professional experiences and pass the CRNE through participation in various learning programs. These programs can be defined as "any program designed to address gaps and/or differences in education and competencies, so that an internationally-educated nurse may become registered to practice in Canada, and successfully integrate into the Canadian healthcare system" (CASN, 2012, p. 2) and are generally government-funded or government-supported (Baumann & Blythe, 2009). In the literature different terms are used to describe these programs, such as adaptation program, bridging/upgrading program, orientation program, and integration program, which are often used interchangeably (Xu & He, 2012). Baumann and Blythe (2009) distinguished between bridging programs and adaptation programs, stating that the former "are intended to provide students with the skills, competencies or formal criteria necessary for registration exam eligibility," and the latter "are intended to help candidates pass their examination and achieve success in the workforce by familiarizing them with the Canadian health care system and culture, as well as enhancing their language and practice skills" (p. 20).

Bridging programs can be offered by postsecondary institutions, such as community colleges and schools of nursing, as well as various immigrant support organizations and employers. In 2012, there were 35 bridging programs available for nurses in Canada; 19 of these programs were designated for registered nurses, ten programs were developed for nurse practitioners and another ten for licensed practical nurses, and six programs included all categories of nurses. Ontario had the highest number of bridging programs, 12, followed by Alberta and British Columbia, which had five bridging programs. Each of these bridging programs differed substantially in the scope, content, and method of delivery, but across different programs there was an agreement that language proficiency is a determinant to student success (CASN, 2012). Overall, language proficiency is viewed as an essential component of a bridging program, with the focus on the development of professional communication in all courses, not just basic language training (CASN, 2012). While different bridging programs are offered to IENs in Canada, Covell et al. (2014) noted that the literature for the most part provides only the descriptions of the programs and does not provide empirical support for their effectiveness.

LANGUAGE SUPPORT PROGRAMS

It is well documented in the literature that high-income countries actively recruit IENs to address the nursing shortage in their labour force, but adaptation and integration of IENs into the western workforce is challenged by several factors, including the difficulty in meeting English language requirements (O'Neill, 2011). Language is consistently mentioned as one of the key areas of concern, if not the single most significant obstacle, for IENs as they transition to professional practice (Choi, 2005; Malecha, Tart, & Junious, 2012; Olson, 2012; Xu, 2010). Immigrants with sufficient language skills convert their education into earnings more successfully than those who do not possess such skills (Picot & Sweetman, 2012), so the literature is consistent in maintaining that language support for IENs is vital. However, empirical research on language support programs designed to improve communicative competence of IENs is limited. In addition, research predominantly focuses on two of the five competencies discussed by Pawlikowska-Smith (2002), specifically the linguistic competence and/or the socio-cultural competence.

Programs Addressing the Linguistic Competence

According to the Centre for Canadian Language Benchmarks, the linguistic or grammatical competence as one of the components of communicative competence "enables the building and recognition of well-formed (grammatically accurate) utterances or sentences, according to the rules of syntax, semantics, morphology, phonology or graphology. It is the knowledge of grammar, vocabulary and pronunciation or graphology at a sentence level" (Holmes, Kingwell, Pettis, & Pidlaski, 2001, p. 3). Several intervention programs with the major focus on developing the linguistic competence of IENs were identified in the literature. All of them were implemented either in the USA or Australia.

Student success program. The Student Success Program (SSP) was a five-semester program offered to students at Texas Women University – Houston Center in the USA as an alternative placement for a regular four-semester nursing program (Symes, Tart, Travis, & Toombs, 2002). SSP used Ertmer and Newby's discussion of the concept of expert learners who are self-directed, goal-oriented, and are aware of their strengths and weaknesses as a theoretical basis for the program (as cited in Symes et al., 2002). SSP aimed to increase retention of nursing students by assessing, diagnosing, planning, implementing, and evaluating their learning needs. It specifically targeted students who were identified as at-risk for academic difficulties.

At-risk students who received less than 55% on the reading comprehension part of the Nurse Entrance Test, which was a test required by the institution for advisement purposes, were placed in the SSP. In addition to the general nursing curriculum, SSP students were required to take a two-semester sequence of three-credit courses, Skills for Success 1 and Skills for Success 2. ESL learners admitted as SSP students were also required to take 15 hours of accent modification. Symes et al. reported increased student retention as a result of the SSP placement, and positive evaluation of SSP students by the nursing faculty. The faculty members noted increased oral communication skills of students who participated in the program.

Individual tutoring approach. The University of Akron in Ohio developed a support program for students in its nursing program who came from ESL backgrounds. The purpose of this support program was to help students who were struggling with the course load to improve their English language skills in all skill areas (listening, speaking, reading, and writing) and to increase the ESL student retention rates in the university nursing program (Guhde, 2003). Participation in the tutoring sessions was organized on a referral basis, when faculty members or nurse tutors would encourage students who were struggling with their coursework to participate in the sessions. The support program consisted of regular one-hour individual or group tutoring sessions provided by nurse tutors, who developed session activities based on students' medical and health assessment courses. Before each tutoring session, the students received study materials consisting of a vocabulary list on a given topic and a selection of listening and reading materials on the same topic. The session consisted of four separate exercises to allow them to practice each language skill separately. The activities included but were not limited to reading the provided vocabulary words for correct pronunciation and explaining their meanings, listening to materials from the nursing field, writing nursing notes and editing them for grammar, syntax, and vocabulary (Guhde, 2003).

Guhde (2003) discussed the results of a single case study of a student who participated in the tutoring support program for 10 weeks. The student's listening and note taking abilities as well as her understanding of culturally bound vocabulary substantially improved. The accuracy of the recorded information increased from 25% in the beginning of the tutoring sessions to 40% at the end of the support program. In addition to improved linguistic competence, the student reported more confidence in participating in the study groups with non-ESL students which positively impacted her communication skills and socialization with other students. Even though this tutoring support system led to positive results and was easy to implement in a variety of academic settings, Guhde noted potential challenges as funding for such support programs might not be easily available.

The Integrated Skills Reinforcement (ISR) model. Guttman (2004) described the ISR model which was developed at La Guardia Community College in the USA in the late 1970s and used as a form of developmental education to improve the

71

writing, reading, listening, and speaking skills of students with second language deficiencies. The model gave such students an opportunity to practice all four skills while learning the course contents. The IRS model consisted of learning and teaching guides and three types of strategies – assessment strategies, implementation strategies, and evaluation strategies. Learning guides were distributed to students in addition to the course outline as a tool to help them navigate the course contents and contained specific guidelines as well as samples of assignments. Teaching guides for faculty included various strategies for assessment, implementation, and evaluation. Assessment strategies were used to establish the baseline of students' basic writing, reading, listening, and speaking competencies using a variety of assessment methods, such as tests and holistic scoring. Then the implementation strategies targeting each of the four basic skills were introduced using the content of what students learned in class. Reading implementation strategies included readings assignments using guiding questions, developing vocabulary lists, and providing definitions of unknown words. The writing strategies required students to complete brief writing exercises, prewrite and write drafts as well as complete peer-evaluation of drafts before submitting papers for grading. The speaking strategies included oral presentations which were evaluated by the faculty as well as peer-reviewed for content, form, clarity, and listener response. The listening strategies consisted of taking notes and summarizing the most important concepts learned during the class. Finally, evaluation strategies were used to investigate both quantitatively and qualitatively the effect of the implementation strategies on students' skills improvement. Guttman argued that the ISR model could be used to address language challenges of registered nurses educated abroad for whom English was an additional language and mentioned conference presentations on the use of the IRS model to improve linguistic competencies of minority nursing students. No details of how exactly the model impacted the linguistic competencies of these nurses were provided.

The Teaching and Learning Enhancement Scheme (TALES) program. The TALES program at the Victorian campus of Australian Catholic University (ACU) National was designed to provide support to the international nursing students enrolled in its accelerated Bachelor of Nursing program (Seibold, Rolls, & Campbell, 2007). The program participants were 20 international nursing students who participated in group sessions with three mentors twice a month during the first semester, and in group and team meetings during the second semester of the program. During the first semester, the focus of the support initiative was mostly on improving the students' linguistic competence. The mentoring sessions provided the participants with opportunities to practice reflective writing and learn nursing jargon and idiomatic expressions. The students also participated in creating individual portfolios. In addition to providing language support, the mentoring session during the second semester focused on professional skills in the nursing field including resume writing and participating in simulated occupational situations. Seibold et al. noted that the attendance of the sessions during the first semester was much greater compared to the sessions during the second semester. As part of the program, the students developed professional portfolios enabling them to showcase their professional experiences from various perspectives as well as demonstrate their skills in reflective writing, resume writing, and clinical reports writing. When the students joined the program, they completed a questionnaire which was later used for program evaluation purposes. The students were also asked to fill out a course completion survey consisting of a few statements about the quality of the program. While the entry questionnaire was distributed exclusively to the international student participants, the end-of-program survey was sent to all students enrolled in the Bachelor of Nursing program. In addition, a follow-up survey was mailed to the students three months after the program ended to collect data on their career experiences; however, very few students responded to this form of evaluation. Another form of evaluation was a focus group interview, in which participants had to comment of the strengths and weaknesses of the program and the level of their preparedness to join the nursing work force in the country. The participants of the TALES program described their overall experience as positive. They praised the opportunities they were given to form friendships and build support networks. However, the students did not feel that the tools they were provided with to increase their linguistic competence as well as the program acculturation activities were enough to ease their adjustment to the academic environment (Seibold et al., 2007).

The Culturally and Linguistically Diverse (CALD) program. In 2008, the University of Sydney introduced a program targeting the needs of its culturally and linguistically diverse nursing students in the accelerated Master of Nursing program at the Faculty of Nursing and Midwifery (Boughton, Halliday, & Brown, 2010). The program was implemented during the first semester of their studies and was designed to help participants achieve better academic success at the university as well as empower them with solid foundation for their future careers in the nursing field. The program consisted of a series of academic workshops designed to improve the students' overall experience in the program. The purpose of the workshops was to encourage students' participation in their courses, to improve their overall academic achievement, to increase student retention in the program, to reduce stress levels associated with the students' professional prospects, and to prepare them better for clinical placements. The contents of the workshops included but were not limited to academic research process and strategies, critical reading, academic honesty and plagiarism, exam preparation, and Australian nursing jargon and colloquial expressions. The workshops also aimed at encouraging participants to build their social and professional networks. Participation in the program was on a volunteer basis. The program focused mainly on encouraging student participation in the course by improving their communication skills in role play situations. During the program, the participants formed small study groups and shared their study materials. By studying together in these small groups, the participants demonstrated better understanding of the course materials and improved communication skills. They also demonstrated higher levels of confidence, better academic writing skills, and better participation in their tutorials.

Overall, the participants evaluated the program as an extremely positive experience. The program components helped students feel more confident and participate more in their courses as well as be more prepared for their clinical placements. They indicated they were better equipped with linguistic tools to tackle the challenges of the nursing profession, and they felt less stressed about the clinical placement as they had a better understanding of the requirements and expectations of the field. Boughton et al. noted that the CALD program successfully provided its participants with the tools necessary to increase their linguistic competence and academic success as well as encourage much needed social inclusion and better adjustment to the rigors of the nursing profession.

Academic writing intervention strategy. Weaver and Jackson (2011) emphasized the importance of developing strategies to support the academic writing skills of IENs. To address the need for such support, a four-day Academic Writing Intervention Strategy workshop was developed for first-year ESL nursing students in Australia. Weaver and Jackson provided instruction on general academic and subject-specific writing to 28 participating nurses. The participants were provided with individual feedback on grammar, structure, clarity of expression, and referencing in one-on-one sessions. The findings suggested two problematic areas for students taking the workshop, namely understanding course content in English and expressing their understanding of the content. Individual feedback was reported as the most helpful aspect of the whole program. However, Weaver and Jackson (2011) cautioned against relying exclusively on one-on-one support provided in intensive short-term workshops and argued that to improve students' academic writing skills and self-confidence in their abilities, the support of the language needs of international nurses should be on-going and intensive.

Medicina. For international nursing students, a lack of medical vocabulary knowledge is a major contributor to communication problems in both academic and professional settings (Müller, 2012). To address the issue, the medical vocabulary video-game Medicina was developed to assist nursing students in Australia for whom English is an additional language in learning challenging medical and medication terminology. In the game, a player watches the action on a computer, listens to audio instructions, and chooses among five confusable medication names. The game is based on 50 groups of five similarly looking medical terms and has a continuous flow of background noise to create distraction typical in real-life hospital situations. Based on the findings of the mixed methods study, which included a pre- and post-test assessment and a qualitative survey of 25 international nursing students who participated in the study, increased motivation to learn medical vocabulary, better comprehension of lecture material, and overall improvement of the learning experience in the face-to-face setting were reported (Müller, 2012).

Speak for success. Phase I.   Speak for Success was a two-phase research-based linguistics program designed to improve communication competence of post-hire international nurses in the USA. The first phase focused on linguistic competence and improving communication skills of foreign-born nurses. During this phase, internationally-educated nurses attended a 10-week phonological accent reduction training course in order to improve pronunciation. The course was taught by a certified speech pathologist who specialized in foreign accent reduction. Looking at the total number of errors made by individual participants, the difference in the total number of phonological errors and the percentage of phonological errors made by the study participants between the pre- and post-assessments, Shen et al. (2012) reported a substantial reduction in phonological errors due to the intervention, so the linguistic competence of the international nurses did improve significantly. In addition to the reduction of errors, the linguistic gap between international nurses from non-English and English speaking countries narrowed. While the authors acknowledged that the results of this pilot study were not generalizable due to the small sample size (Shen et al., 2012), the findings were important enough to propose to add this accent modification course to the general curriculum offerings (Carter, Staples, Shen, & Xu, 2013).

Intercultural communication workshop.   The US Commission on Graduates of Foreign Nursing Schools outlined several major challenges faced by IENs regarding language use, which include "(1) intelligibility (phonology and syntactic patterns), (2) vocabulary, (3) conversation, and (4) context-dependent speech (discourse)" (Van Schaik, Lynch, Stoner, & Sikorski, 2014, p. 12). To address these challenges, the Intercultural Communication Workshop, which was a multimedia, Internet-based self-directed educational tool, was developed in order to improve communicative competence of IENs. The program focused on improving oral communication skills by expanding the knowledge of intonation and phonological rules, and overall listener understanding. The program exercises were built on nurse-specific terminology whenever possible and included 86 lessons which allowed users to compare their pronunciation with a native speaker. Using a single-group, pre-post-test design, and a sample of 22 nurses from nine institutions in the United States, Van Schaik et al. found that participants significantly improved on the knowledge test and verbal performance test and benefited from the instruction in the mechanics of speech as well as the cultural information. While a small sample size, lack of a control group, and the short duration of total practice time (eight hours over a three-month period) were recognized as the study limitations, the findings were still significant enough to continue with the implementation of the program and to expand the program offerings by developing several additional support features for users, such as a personalized homepage to track progress, progress reports to encourage daily practice, and social network support.

Programs Addressing the Socio-Cultural Competence

The Centre for Canadian Language Benchmarks described sociocultural competence (also known as sociolinguistic competence) as follows:

> [Sociocultural competence] focuses on considerations of appropriateness in producing and understanding utterances. These include rules of discourse politeness; sensitivity to register, dialect or variety; norms of stylistic appropriateness; sensitivity to 'naturalness;' knowledge of idioms and figurative language; knowledge of culture, customs, and institutions; knowledge of cultural references; and uses of a language through interactional skills to establish and maintain social relationships. (Holmes et al., 2001, p. 3)

Speak for success. Phase II.   The first phase of the program which targeted the linguistic competence was addressed in the section "Programs Addressing Linguistic Competence" above. The second phase of Speak for Success consisted of four workshops targeting the socio-cultural competence of 28 IENs employed by two hospitals in Nevada in the USA. The workshops focused on rapport building, non-verbal cues, therapeutic communication skills, and telephone communication. In a quasi-experimental pilot intervention study, Xu, Shen, Bolstad, Covelli, and Torpey (2010) conducted pre- and post-assessments after the workshops and found no significant improvement in the participants' socio-cultural skills. Xu et al. explained that the participating nurses, whose mean stay in the US was almost 14 years, appeared already adjusted to the American culture which could have explained why no statistically significant differences between the experimental and the control groups were found. Another possible explanation for the statistically nonsignificant results could be lack of interest in the second phase of the program and fatigue from participation in the Phase I activities. Xu et al. acknowledged that the results were not generalizable due to the small sample size and non-random sampling and suggested targeting newly arrived international nurses in future research.

Clinically speaking.   Clinically Speaking was a structured 20-hour language program offered to ESL students at the University of Technology in Sydney, Australia (San Miguel, Rogan, Kilstoff, & Brown, 2006). The goal of the program was to assist students identified during their first clinical placement as in need for additional language support with specially designed language workshops. These workshops offered opportunities for students to develop linguistic and cultural knowledge of clinical placements using simulated clinical situations. For instance, students were taught how to introduce themselves to patients, how to explain clinical procedures to them or ask them for health information, how to make small talk with colleagues at the hospital, and how to switch from using professional terminology with hospital staff to everyday language when communicating with patients. Students reported improved communication skills, better understanding of clinical placements and overall felt better prepared to interact with patients and staff (San Miguel et al., 2006). In a follow-up study on the long-term effects of this program, San Miguel and Rogan (2009) found that the program was indeed beneficial to students as it contributed to their greater confidence in knowing how to communicate with patients and colleagues, and what to expect from clinical placements. Students seemed to apply the language knowledge and strategies they learned in the Clinically Speaking program in their later nursing studies.

While the majority of the programs targeting linguistic and socio-cultural competencies of IENs were described as successful (such as Boughton et al., 2010; Guhde, 2003; Symes et al., 2002), some research demonstrates otherwise (Seibold et al., 2007; Xu et al., 2010). Clearly, more research about the effectiveness of the language support programs targeting different communicative competencies of IENs in different geographical areas is needed.

TEACHING STRATEGIES FOR LANGUAGE DEVELOPMENT

An efficient and satisfactory solution regarding how to address language challenges of nursing students who speak English as an additional language is yet to be found (Starr, 2009). Clearly, language support programs targeting all five types of communicative competence should be developed and implemented, particularly in the context of Canada, since research on language support for Canadian IENs is limited. In addition, it is a challenge to identify a set of strategies which would work effectively for every group of students regardless of their background or language proficiency level. It is important to continue developing strategies to help students succeed in improving their language competency (Abriam-Yago et al., 1999). Abriam-Yago et al. (1999) used the Cummins Model of Language Acquisition, which conceptualizes language proficiency along two continua – the degree of cognitive involvement in communicative activities and contextual support – and suggested the following set of strategies for international nursing students to tackle their language challenges,

(a) investigating previous learning experience, (b) identifying prerequisite knowledge, (c) preparing individual learning objectives related to communication, (d) leveling the playing field, (e) permitting expression of identity and sharing their world, (f) preparing for casual conversation, (g) providing bilingual and bicultural opportunities, (h) managing groupwork, (i) modeling the use of texts and resources, (j) assessing continuously, and (k) evaluating a clinical log. (p. 145)

The following teaching strategies identified by Flinn (2004) may also be implemented in multicultural classrooms to help IENs improve their language proficiency. The strategies ranked from the most to less often used are as follows:

> discussion, active learning, brainstorming, examples, small group tasks, lesson models, teacher working with student(s), questioning, clarifying critical questioning, broad themes, learning activity packets, problem solving, peer tutoring, simulations, reciprocal teaching, reframing, friendship/partnership, guided reciprocal peer questioning, hands-on activities, role modeling, informal learning groups, learning contracts, learning stations, storytelling, writing groups, experiential learning, case studies, cultural events, focus groups, formal learning groups, multimedia, games, dramatic readings, teams, seminars, imaging, and journaling. (Flinn, 2004, p. 11)

Another approach, identified as particularly helpful when working with groups of international nursing students, included delivering lectures with consistent outlines, using visual displays, reviewing content at the beginning and the end of each class session, employing the "round robin" approach when asking content questions, using random group assignment, and developing note-taking guides (Flinn, 2004).

DISCUSSION

IENs should be provided with opportunities to improve their English language competencies and be able to practice all four language skills, listening, speaking, reading and writing, jointly (Hansen & Beaver, 2012). However, the majority of the language programs designed to improve the language ability of IENs targeted only one language skill, for instance speaking with the focus on pronunciation (Carter et al., 2013; Shen et al., 2012; Van Schaik et al., 2014) or writing (Weaver & Jackson, 2011). A more holistic approach to language instruction is needed to facilitate language acquisition and, subsequently, the integration into the workforce and society. In addition, most available research on language support for IENs focused on two of the five competencies as discussed by Pawlikowska-Smith (2002), i.e., linguistic competence (Boughton et al., 2010; Carter et al., 2013; Guhde, 2003; Guttman, 2004; Müller, 2012; Shen et al., 2012; Symes et al., 2002; Van Schaik et al., 2014; Weaver & Jackson, 2011) and socio-cultural competence (San Miguel et al., 2006; Xu et al., 2010). It would be beneficial to develop language programs targeting other competencies, either individually or combined. Geographically, empirical research on language support programs is limited to the US and Australia; therefore, given the uniqueness of the IENs status in Canada, programs specifically addressing the needs of IENs in the Canadian context are highly recommended.

Simplicity of content and lack of appropriate and professionally-relevant context are named when inefficiency of these language support programs is discussed in the literature (Starr, 2009). The overall recommendation found in the literature was to make cognitively-demanding and context-reduced activities in nursing programs more context-embedded (Crawford & Candlin, 2012). Also, instead of providing generic support of grammar and writing instruction to international nursing students on a voluntary basis, the emphasis should be made on helping these students acquire the language specific to the nursing context and offering this support as part of the nursing curriculum (San Miguel et al., 2013). Finally, utilizing appropriate teaching strategies (such as discussed in Flinn, 2004 or Abriam-Yago et al., 1999) is also important in helping the IENs cope with their language challenges and to become fully integrated in Canada, both socially and professionally.

CONCLUSIONS

Changes in the Canadian immigration policies welcomed people with a variety of backgrounds into the country, eventually allowing economic class immigrants to move to Canada. Many of these immigrants are IENs, and even though they have always been considered an asset to the Canadian economic and social development, they face many challenges while adjusting to their new social and professional environment in Canada. One of the main challenges for IENs is their level of English language proficiency, which may be enough to meet the immigration requirements, but not enough for them to be fully integrated into the new society and secure employment.

The need to address language as a major contributor to IENs' success in academic and professional settings is widely recognized in the literature. However, most research available on IENs language support programs and interventions is descriptive in nature and generally reports students' attitudes and perceptions towards available bridging programs and language workshops. Very few empirical studies focusing on particular language interventions and programs have been conducted to assess how language competencies and language skills of the IENs are affected by these programs. More empirical research is needed to investigate the impact of available language support for IENs to facilitate their integration into the Canadian workforce and society.

ACKNOWLEDGEMENT

The authors would like to thank Ray Bennett at York University English Language Institute for his support and valuable comments on the earlier draft of the chapter.

REFERENCES

Abriam-Yago, K., Yoder, M., & Kataoka-Yahiro, M. (1999). The Cummins model: A framework for teaching nursing students for whom English is a second language. *Journal of Transcultural Nursing, 10*(2), 143–149.

Atack, L., Cruz, E. V., Maher, J., & Murphy, S. (2012). Internationally educated nurses' experiences with an integrated bridge program. *Journal of Continuing Education in Nursing, 43*(8), 370–378. doi:10.3928/00220124-20120615-62

Baumann, A., & Blythe, J. (2009). *Integrating internationally educated health care professionals into Ontario workforce*. Hamilton: McMaster University.

Boughton, M., Halliday, L., & Brown, L. (2010). A tailored program of support for Culturally and Linguistically Diverse (CALD) nursing students in a graduate entry Masters of Nursing course: A qualitative evaluation of outcomes. *Nurse Education in Practice, 10*(6), 355–360. doi:10.1016/j.nepr.2010.05.003

Canadian Association of the Schools of Nursing. (2012). *Pan-Canadian framework of guiding principles and essential components for IEN bridging programs*. Ottawa: ON: Author. Retrieved from http://www.casn.ca/2014/12/2010-2012-pan-canadian-framework/

Canadian Association of the Schools of Nursing. (n.d.). *2010–2012 background*. Retrieved from http://www.casn.ca/2014/12/2010-2012-background/

Canadian Institute for Health Information. (n.d.). *Regulated nursing workforce profile, Canada, 2008 and 2012*. Retrieved from https://www.cihi.ca/en/quick-stats

Canadian Nurses Association. (2012a). *2010 workforce profile of registered nurses in Canada*. Ottawa: Author. Retrieved from https://www.cna-aiic.ca/en/download-buy/nursing-statistics

Canadian Nurses Association. (2012b). *2010 workforce profile of nurse practitioners in Canada*. Ottawa: Author. Retrieved from https://www.cna-aiic.ca/en/download-buy/nursing-statistics

Canadian Nurses Association. (2013). Statistics on CRNE writers for calendar year 2012. *CRNE Bulletin, 17*. Retrieved from http://www.cna-aiic.ca/~/media/cna/page%20content/pdf%20en/2013/07/ 25/13/54/crne_bulletin_17_2013.pdf

Carter, K. F., & Xu, Y. (2007). Addressing the hidden dimension in nursing education: Promoting cultural competence. *Nurse Educator, 32*(4), 149–153. doi:10.1097/01.NNE.0000281085.58335.0e

Carter, N., Staples, S., Shen, J., & Xu, Y. (2013). American English pronunciation and the internationally educated nurse. *Nursing Management, 44*(4), 52–55. doi:10.1097/01.NUMA.0000428195.06765.22.

CELBAN Centre. (2015). *Institutional CELBAN*. Retrieved from http://www.celbancentre.ca/institutional-celban.aspx

Centre for Canadian Language Benchmarks. (2012). *Canadian Language Benchmarks: English as a second language for adults*. Ottawa: Author. Retrieved from http://www.language.ca/index.cfm?Voir= sections&Id=17355&M=4038&Repertoire_No=2137991327

Choi, L. L. S. (2005). Literature review: Issues surrounding education of English-as-a-Second Language (ESL) nursing students. *Journal of Transcultural Nursing, 16*(3), 263–268. doi:10.1177/1043659605274966

Coffey, S. (2006). Educating international nurses: Curricular innovation through a bachelor of science in nursing bridging program. *Nurse Educator, 31*(6), 244–248. doi:10.1097/00006223-200611000-00006

College of Nurses of Ontario. (2016). *Nursing registration exams report 2015*. College of Nurses of Ontario: Toronto. Retrieved from http://www.cno.org/en/what-is-cno/nursing-demographics/statistical-reports/

Covell, C. L., Neiterman, E., & Bourgeault, I. L. (2014). Forms of capital as facilitators of internationally educated nurses' integration into the registered nursing workforce in Canada. *Canadian Public Policy/Analyse de politiques, 41*(S1), 150–161.

Crawford, T., & Candlin, S. (2012). A literature review of the language needs of nursing students who have English as a second/other language and the effectiveness of English language support programmes. *Nurse Education in Practice, 13*, 181–185. doi:10.1016/j.nepr.2012.09.008

Cummins, J. (1980). The cross-lingual dimensions of language proficiency: Implications for bilingual education and the optimal age issue. *TESOL Quarterly, 14*(2), 175–187.

Flinn, J. B. (2004). Teaching strategies used with success in the multicultural classroom. *Nurse Educator, 29*(1), 10–12. doi:10.1097/00006223-200401000-00004

Government of Canada. (2012). *Canadian multiculturalism: An inclusive citizenship* [Online]. Retrieved from http://www.cic.gc.ca/english/multiculturalism/citizenship.asp

Government of Canada. (2016). *Notice: Supplementary information 2017 immigration levels plan*. Ottawa: Government of Canada. Retrieved from http://www.cic.gc.ca/english/department/media/notices/2016-10-31.asp

Guhde, J. A. (2003). English-as-a-Second Language (ESL) nursing students: Strategies for building verbal and written language skills. *Journal of Cultural Diversity, 10*(4), 113–117.

Guttman, M. S. (2004). Increasing the linguistic competence of the nurse with limited English proficiency. *The Journal of Continuing Education in Nursing, 35*(6), 264–269. doi:10.3928/0022-0124-20041101-08

Hansen, E., & Beaver, S. (2012). Faculty support for ESL nursing students: Action plan for success. *Nursing Education Perspectives, 33*(4), 246–250. doi:10.5480/1536-5026-33.4.246

Holmes, T., Kingwell, G., Pettis, J., & Pidlaski, M. (2001). *Canadian Language Benchmarks 2000: A guide to implementation*. Ottawa: Centre for Canadian Language Benchmarks.

Malecha, A., Tart, K., & Junious, D. L. (2012). Foreign-born nursing students in the United States: A literature review. *Journal of Professional Nursing, 28*(5), 297–305. doi:10.1016/j.profnurs.2012.03.001

Marsden, S. (2011). Assessing the regulation of temporary foreign workers in Canada. *Osgoode Hall Law Journal, 49*(1), 39–70. Retrieved from http://digitalcommons.osgoode.yorku.ca/ohlj/vol49/iss1/2

Müller, A. (2012). Research-based design of a medical vocabulary videogame. *International Journal of Pedagogies and Learning, 7*(2), 122–134. doi:10.5172/ijpl.2012.7.2.122

Olson, M. A. (2012). English-as-a-Second Language (ESL) nursing student success: A critical review of the literature. *Journal of Cultural Diversity, 19*(1), 26–32.

O'Neill, F. (2011). From language classroom to clinical context: The role of language and culture in communication for nurses using English as a second language: A thematic analysis. *International Journal of Nursing Studies, 48*, 112–1128. doi:10.1016/j.ijnurstu.2011.02.008

Pang, M. (2013). *Temporary foreign workers: Background paper* (Publication No. 2013–2011-E). Ottawa: Library of Parliament.

Pawlikowska-Smith, G. (2002). *Canadian Language Benchmarks 2000: Theoretical framework*. Ottawa: Centre for Canadian Language Benchmarks. Retrieved from http://eric.ed.gov/?id=ED468319

Picot, G., & Sweetman, A. (2012). *Making it in Canada: Immigration outcomes and policies* (IRPP Study, 29). Montreal: Institute for Research on Public Policy. Retrieved from http://irpp.org/research-studies/study-no29/

San Miguel, C., & Rogan, F. (2009). A good beginning: The long-term effects of a clinical communication programme. *Contemporary Nurse, 33*(2), 179–190. doi:10.5172/conu.2009.33.2.179

San Miguel, C., Rogan, F., Kilstoff, K., & Brown, D. (2006). Clinically Speaking: A communication skills programme for students from non-speaking English backgrounds. *Nurse Education in Practice, 6*(5), 268–274.

San Miguel, C., Townsend, L., & Waters, C. (2013). Redesigning nursing tutorial for ESL students: A pilot study. *Contemporary Nurse, 44*(1), 21–31. doi:10.5172/conu.2013.44.1.21

Seibold, C., Rolls, C., & Campbell, M. (2007). Nurses on the move: Evaluation of a program to assist international students undertaking an accelerated bachelor of nursing program. *Contemporary Nurse, 25*(1–2), 63–71. doi:10.5555/conu.2007.25.1-2.63

Shen, J. J., Covelli, M., Xu, Y., Torpey, M., Bolstad, A. L., & Colosimo, R. (2012). Effects of a short-term linguistic class on communication competence of international nurses: Implications for practice, policy, and research. *Nursing Economics, 30*(1), 21–28.

Starr, K. (2009). Nursing education challenges: Students with English as an additional language. *Journal of Nursing Education, 48*(9), 478–487. doi:10.3928/01484834-20090610-01

Symes, L., Tart, K., Travis, L., & Toombs, M. S. (2002). Developing and retaining expert learners: The student success program. *Nurse Educator, 27*(5), 227–231.

Terry, L. M., Carr, G., & Williams, L. (2013). The effect of fluency in English on the continuing professional development of nurses educated overseas. *Journal of Continuing Education in Nursing, 44*(3), 137–144. doi:10.3928/00220124-20130201-97

Tomblin-Murphy, G., Birch, S., Alder, R., MacKenzie, A., Lethbridge, L., Little, L., & Cook, A. (2009). *Tested solutions for eliminating the Canadian registered nurses shortage*. Ottawa: Canadian Nurses Association.

Touchstone Institute. (2015a). *Facts & figures. Issue 1: A historical review*. Toronto: Author.

Touchstone Institute. (2015b). *Facts & figures. Issue 2: A year in review*. Toronto: Author.

Van Dyk, L. (2016). *Canadian immigration acts and legislation*. Halifax, CA: Canadian Museum of Immigration at Pier 21. Retrieved from http://www.pier21.ca/research/immigration-history/canadian-immigration-acts-and-legislation

Van Schaik, E., Lynch, E. M., Stoner, S. A., & Sikorski, L. D. (2014). Can a web-based course improve communicative competence o foreign-born nurses? *Language Learning and Technology, 18*(1), 11–22. Retrieved from http://llt.msu.edu/issues/february2014/action1.pdf

Weaver, R., & Jackson. D. (2011). Evaluating an academic writing program for nursing students who have English as a second language. *Contemporary Nurse, 38*(1–2), 130–138. doi:10.5172/conu.2011.38.1-2.130

Xu, Y. (2010). Transitioning international nurses: An outlined evidence-based program for acute care settings. *Policy, Politics & Nursing Practice, 11*(3), 202–213. doi:10.1177/1527154410384879

Xu, Y., & He, F. (2012). Transition programs for internationally educated nurses: What can the United States learn from the United Kingdom, Australia, and Canada? *Nursing Economics, 30*(4), 215–239.

Xu, Y., Shen, J., Bolstad, A. L., Covelli, M., & Torpey, M. (2010). Evaluation of an intervention on socio-cultural communication skills of international nurses. *Nursing Economics, 28*(6), 386–408.

Zietsma, D. (2010). Immigrants working in regulated occupations. *Statistics Canada Catalogue, No. 75-001-X*, 13–28.

Nadezda Kulikova
University of Victoria
Victoria, Canada

Yuliya Miakisheva
English Language Institute
York University
Toronto, Canada

CUI BIAN AND RÉGIS MALET

5. LANGUAGE(S) OF POWER AND POWER OF LANGUAGE(S) IN INTERNATIONAL STUDENT RECRUITMENT IN FRENCH HEIS IN THE CONTEXT OF INTERNATIONALIZATION

Student mobility has always been one of the popular research issues since the late 1990s when studies on internationalization of higher education became a research hotspot. Many themes have been explored and developed from individual, institutional, national and transnational perspectives. As the most longstanding and principal component of international education activities, student mobility also serves as a consistent driving force for the internationalization of higher education in different national and institutional contexts. This chapter builds upon a particular interest on the roles of language in international student recruitment in France, a non-English speaking country amongst the top destinations for international students. It examines how French HEIs react to the "normalization" of English and maintain the coherence of French language requirements in recruiting and hosting international students. The empirical data used in this chapter come from a doctoral research project done between 2012 and 2015 on international student recruitment strategies in French HEIs in the context of internationalization.

INTRODUCTION

Language acts as a map that describes, demarcates and shapes worldviews, and native language provides individuals with a baseline for viewing the world (Lee, 2006). Language is also the key and the door keeper for accessing a culture. For international students, a key aspect of the mobility experience is achieving the academic and socio-cultural integration in the host institutions and the host society as well, during which the acquisition of sufficient fluency in the host language is primary and decisive. However, the normalization of internationalization and the increasing impact of evaluative logics introduced in the field of higher education have reinforced the role of English in research publications and educational programs. On the one hand, as the Latin of the 21st century (Altbach, 2004), English has emerged as the lingua franca of academia in the context of internationalization and has become almost a necessity in the current world where cross-border collaboration is an effective and efficient way to solve problems. On the other hand, it is undeniable that the power of English language is closely related to the impact of Anglo-American culture and

M.-A. Détourbe (Ed.), Inclusion through Access to Higher Education, 83–99.

ideology. Furthermore, developing English-Taught Programs (ETP) is an effective method for attracting international students and the number of ETPs becomes a barometer for measuring the level of institutional internationalization (EUA, 2013). In this study, we do not want to question the rationality of all this, but rather seek to understand how the French HEIs use the French language in international student recruitment and how they react to the "invasion" of the English language.

To answer these questions, the first section of this chapter will review the international student policy development in France over the last two decades with the aim of clarifying the transformation in posture and identification of priorities that prevail in international student recruitment. The second section will give general information on international student population in French HEIs and draw a global picture of this group of population. The third section will present the empirical analysis of the interview data related to the research questions. The last section will sum up the findings and invite further discussions about language(s) of power and power of language(s) in international student recruitment.

THE TREND OF INTERNATIONAL STUDENT POLICIES IN FRANCE

Many studies on the internationalization of higher education have highlighted its rationales, necessities and modalities. Both conceptually and empirically oriented researches in the field indicate the normalization of the trend worldwide. The stages of internationalization in many countries can be categorized into four groups. For the norm-makers in the trend of internationalization, mostly Anglo-Saxon countries, the involved agents and stakeholders in higher education are in a period of harvesting the "goods" and exploring more efficient ways to improve their performance in international education markets. The norm-makers and takers, mostly European continental countries, are in a phase of confronting the conflicts between the Anglo-American model and their own national contexts and cultures in the process of internationalization and searching for a suitable local version of their own. For the norm-takers with some experience in the internationalization of higher education, particularly newly emerging economic entities such as countries in South Asia, we found a coexistence of the situations happening in the previous two groups; however, the complexities of their specific problems and practices have enriched research in this field. Finally, the new starters, particularly African countries, are still in the phase of learning how to internationalize their higher education systems and are mainly dependent on the guidance and aid of the norm-makers. The stage of internationalization for each country has a direct impact on its policy-making and strategies for international student recruitment.

Another important factor deserving our attention is the higher education governance model. It is considered as a combination of elements of state authority, the market and the academic oligarchy and it also plays an important role in policy development regarding international students. When considering Clark's triangle (1983), three models of governance have been identified: a state-control model, a

Humboldtian model of academic self-rule, and an Anglo-American market-oriented model (Neave, 2003; quoted in Dobbins, Knill, & Vögtle, 2011).

France, which is both norm-maker and norm-taker, has been inevitably influenced by the Anglo-American model of internationalization in the competitive arena of international education and research. Since the late 1990s, a series of reforms have aimed at decentralizing state control over higher education institutions in France. The implementation of new public management theories and the introduction of excellence-oriented evaluation of higher education and research show the influence of the Anglo-American model. At the same time, France was compelled to confront its historical and socio-cultural heritage, including its centralized administrative system, the fact that university education is presented as a public service which is oriented towards national interest, a close relationship with its former colonies, etc. The marketization of higher education developed in major English-speaking countries has emphasized economic interest in recruiting international students. Facing the great economic potential and benefits, the French public HEIs remain committed to a quasi-free tuition policy in international student recruitment. Moreover, the rising of "regionness" (Hettne & Söderbaum, 2000), through the construction of the European Higher Education and Research Area demands a more global approach from France to contribute to regional development.

The first part of our analysis focuses on the policies developed since the late 1990s mainly due to the very active reforms conducted both in France and in Europe. The size of the international student population hosted in France (including metropolitans and overseas) increased tremendously, by 77.4% over the period from 2000 to 2015 (DEPP, 2016). The most important growth took place in the early 2000s, with an increase of 52.3% between 2000 and 2005, which is closely related to the reforms in French higher education.

Loi Réséda (1998): The Beginning of Voluntarist Policies for Welcoming International Students

This reform was initiated and pushed through by Claude Allègre who was then French minister of higher education and the Loi Réséda was adopted on May 11th 1998. Some important measures were implemented, which included softer and more flexible diplomatic policies towards international students such as visa distribution; the creation of EduFrance with the task of promoting French education programs abroad in order to attract more students on the basis of individual mobility, helping French HEIs with their organizations and program offers abroad etc. and responding to international education and pedagogical demand; the creation of EIFFEL scholarship programs to attract the most talented international students, especially from emerging countries like India, China, Mexico, and Brazil.

The reform was expected to respond to both internal and external demands. From an internal perspective, the institutions were worried about the falling demographic of student population because in France, public grants are based on the number of registered students at each institution. Facilitating the international student recruitment process was supposed, to some extent, to solve this issue and maintain their funding level. From an external perspective, the implementation of a more flexible international student policy was intended to promote student mobility, particularly in Europe, and to increase the international attractiveness of French HEIs. Meanwhile, the Sorbonne Declaration was also initiated by Claude Allègre and announced in Paris in May 1998, with participants from Germany, Italy, and the United Kingdom. The joint declaration intended to harmonize the architecture of the European higher education system (Sorbonne Declaration, 1998), marking the beginning of a series of reforms for different national higher education systems in Europe leading to the construction of a European Higher Education Area (EHEA).

Since 2003: A Shift from Quantitative to Qualitative Development

After the implementation of Loi Réséda, many official reports (Cohen, 2001; Dufourg, 1999; Flitti, 2000) were published in the late 1990s and early 2000s regarding the development of international student mobility in France. The Dufourg Report, introduced to the Chamber of Commerce and Industry in Paris (CCIP) in 1999, analyzed the positioning strategies which had been effectively deployed by major developed countries in the international education market and presented a detailed analysis of the strengths and weaknesses of the French model of higher education. In this report, several weaknesses in the way French HEIs hosted international students were pointed out, including the low quality of various hosting services, the lack of visibility of higher education programs in the international education market, the insufficient communication between French HEIs and their counterparts abroad, and the insufficiently developed higher education provision in foreign languages and cultures. Then, the Flitti Report, published in 2000, addressed directly the 'timidity' of French international student policies compared with some major host countries, such as the USA and the UK, where welcoming and hosting international students were prioritized. The lack of HEI strategies for recruiting international students and developing international education, and the need for structured service arrangements were highlighted. Moreover, The Cohen Report in 2001 emphasized the weak influence of French HEIs in Asia and Latin America, where higher education import was highly solicited; however, only a small number of international students from these geographical regions were hosted in France.

The issues raised in these reports in terms of policy-making strategies were brought out together with some propositions for enhancing the visibility and attractiveness of French higher education in the global education market. The policy reform initiatives shifted from focusing on a quantitative increase of international students in the French HEIs to a more quality-oriented focus. More specific and targeted objectives were developed in terms of education programs and recruitment priorities, which included prioritizing master's and doctoral level recruitment, attracting top researchers abroad, developing mobility programs with countries possessing advanced science and technology, promoting French education programs and attracting students from Asia, Latin America and new EU member countries. In order to fulfil these objectives, some strategies were also developed, such as the application of the LMD system (*Licence-Master-Doctorat*/Bachelor-Master-Doctorate) to improve the visibility of French higher education in the recruitment; the generalization of French intensive language courses to facilitate students' academic integration, changing French language acquisition to a major educational objective other than a basic tool of selection for HEIs; developing courses in foreign languages and more specific programs responding to international demand; improving both pastoral and academic support for international students (before and after their arrival). Despite all the good will, these strategies were only partially put into place.

Loi Fioraso (2013) and Afterwards: More Big Steps Forward

After some ups and downs in international student recruitment policy development, the *Loi Fioraso* was implemented in 2013, which was considered as a big step forward. Several major reforms were implemented: multi-annual resident cards for students at postgraduate level and above; one-year temporary resident cards for graduates to work and gain their first professional experiences in France; permanent visa for international doctoral students; a unified service counter for international students' resident card application; green light given to taught programs in a foreign language. The reform continues with the establishment of a new law on March 7th 2016, which became effective from November 1st 2016, in order to maintain the popularity of France as a host country, to reinforce the simplification of administration for international student entry and sojourn, and to attract talented international students as future employees for French economic development. Some new measures have been developed to facilitate international student recruitment and their institutional and professional integration in France. For example, regarding the generalization of the delivery of multi-annual resident cards, all international students can submit their application after one year of study in France and the validity period of the cards varies from two to four years per students' study level. The multi-annual resident card is also renewable. Besides, the creation of the "talent passport" aims at giving talented foreign residents – young graduates, international employees, international researchers, entrepreneurs and innovative economic project initiators – more opportunities to work in France.

When studying the trend of international student policies in French higher education, we noticed some important elements directly related to language issues: generalization of intensive French language courses, the authorization of foreign language taught programs, geographical priority in student recruitment and international collaboration with non-French-speaking countries. Have these policies proven relevant and effective over the years? The changing makeup of the international student population will give a direct answer to this question.

INTERNATIONAL STUDENT POPULATION IN FRENCH HEIS

According to the definition given by the UNESCO Institute for Statistics (UNESCO, 2009), international students are those who leave their country or territory of origin with the objective of studying in another country or territory of which they are not permanent residents. Considering the regionalization of higher education in the EU, the intra-European mobility and immigration legislation, international students are generally defined as "students who are not permanent or usual residents of their country of study or alternatively as students who obtained their prior education in a different country, including another EU country" (OECD, 2016, p. 332).

In 2013, over four million students were enrolled in tertiary education outside their country of citizenship (OECD, 2016, p. 352). The United States, the United Kingdom, Australia, Canada, France, Germany, and Japan host over 50% of all international students around the world. In 2014, around 1.3 million international students were recruited for Master's and Doctoral or equivalent programs in OECD countries (OECD, 2016, p. 332). Among the OECD countries, the United States received 26% of these groups of international students, followed by the United Kingdom (15%), France (11%), Germany (10%) and Australia (8%). Students from Asia are the largest group of international students. In particular, students from China represent 22% of the overall students registered at the master's and doctoral or equivalent programs.

In 2015, HEIs in France hosted 309,642 international students, an increase of 3.3% from 2014. As indicated in Table 1, the number of international students in French HEIs has considerably increased across all fields of study and multiplied by 1.92 since 1990–1991. The most noticeable increase took place between 2000 and 2005. Meanwhile, the international student population has been stable in French HEIs, at 12% in the last ten years, with 11.6% in 2005–2006 and 12.1% in 2015–2016. In 2015, 72.8% of international students studied in universities, representing 14.1% of the total student population and the percentage differed at different levels of studies: 10.7% at undergraduate level, 17.2% at postgraduate level and 41.1% at doctoral level.

Regarding students' countries of origin, in the year 2015–2016, nearly one international student out of two in French HEIs came from Africa: 24% from Maghreb, 20% from the rest of the Africa; 23% from Europe among which 19% were from the EU member countries; 22% were from Asia or Oceania and 9% from America. In 2015, the top sending countries to France in descending orders were Morocco (36,768), China (28,043), Algeria (22,660), Tunisia (12,077), Italy (11,188), Germany (8,532), Senegal (8,975), and Cameroon (6,963). Among the top three groups of students, their preferred institutions showed some nuances. For students from Morocco, 69% chose universities (including University Diplomas in Technology (DUT) and engineering education programs), 11% engineering schools and 8% business schools. For students from China, 59% chose universities, 9% engineering schools and 17% business schools. For students from Algeria, 88% chose universities, 1% engineering schools, and 2% business schools.

Table 1. Share of international student population in French higher education institutions from 1990 to 2016

Types of institutions	1990– 1991	2000– 2001	2005– 2006	2010– 2011	2015– 2016	2015– 2016 (%)
Universities	131,901	137,559	209,523	218,364	225,366	14.1
Engineering Education Schools (university programs not included)	2,259	4,272	8,678	1,3081	14,964	12.7
Business Schools	2,519	6,273	11,047	17,164	21,524	15.8
Schools of Arts, Architecture and Journalism	5,328	5303	8,459	8,103	8,505	11.5
STS (Scientific and Technology Section) and similar education	5,969	8,280	8,134	5,831	9,346	3.7
CPGE (preparatory class for *grandes écoles*)	1,310	2,166	2,961	3,176	3,345	3.9
Other	11,862	10,704	16,908	19,226	26,592	5.2
Total	161,148	174,557	265,710	284,945	309,642	12.1
Student percentage %	9.4	8.1	11.6	12.3	12.1	12.1

Source: (DEPP, 2016)

Regarding the choice of fields of study, during the year 2015–2016, 12.9% of the total number of international students studied Law, 21.5% Economics and Business Administration, 14.4% Arts and Social Sciences, 17.4% Sciences, Physical Education and Health, 7.6% Medicine, Odontology and Pharmacy, 5.6% DUT programs. Meanwhile, as indicated in Table 2, the statistics also showed an interconnection between students' continent of origin and their choices of study.

The official statistics from which the data above was extracted provide detailed information about aspects of the international student population in French HEIs, including students' nationalities, fields of study, institutional choices, etc., which are expected to impact language issues in international student recruitment. The statistics show the effectiveness of the international student recruitment policies, and more particularly an important increase of the student population from non-French speaking countries, especially those from geographical priorities, which is consistent with the generalization of French intensive courses and the authorization of foreign language taught programs.

The following empirical analysis is part of the research findings from a doctoral thesis. Four HEIs were selected as research sites, two universities and two *grandes écoles* which specialize respectively in social sciences, sciences and technologies.

*Table 2. International students' continents of origin and
choices of study in the year 2015–2016*

Continent of origin / Fields of study	EU (%)	Africa (%)	Asia (%)	America (%)	International students (%)
Law	25.8	48.3	12.1	8.6	12.9
Economics and Business Administration	11.4	56.2	22.2	5.6	21.5
Arts and Social Sciences	28.3	30.2	20.8	14.2	14.4
Sciences, Physical Education and Health	12.6	57.8	20.2	6.3	17.4
Medicine, Odontology and Pharmacy	25.9	52.7	14.2	3.7	7.6
DUT (University Technology Diploma) programs					5.6

Source: (DEPP, 2016)

The choice was based on the different fields of study and types of institutions. A qualitative approach was used for data collection, incorporating interviews and documentation analysis. A total of 38 interviews were conducted with administrative employees in international relation services, faculty/researchers, and international students registered in master's programs at these institutions. The following analysis focuses on the roles of French and English in international student recruitment. In this study, international student recruitment is considered as a process that includes institutional promotion, selection and admission, as well as student integration.

LANGUAGE(S) IN INSTITUTIONAL PROMOTION

According to the Eurobarometer special report 386 (European Commission, 2012), French was classified as the second most spoken foreign language just behind English, and it was the third most useful foreign language in Europe behind English and German. At global level, almost 67% of French speakers came from different parts of Africa and 2% from Asia (OIF, 2010). With the prospect of demographic growth in Africa between 2025 and 2050, the number of French speakers and learners is well expected to increase. At national level, the Toubon law implemented in 1994 made it compulsory to use the French language in all official government publications, government-funded schools, advertisements, workplaces, commercial contracts, and in some other contexts. In other words, the law defended the French language officially and supported its use in all public fields. As a top host country, with very rich language cultures, it is not easy for

France or French intellectuals to dampen down their self-esteem, which appears clearly in institutional promotion.

Institutional websites are the first portal of information for international students and the language used on the websites reflects indirectly the institutional attitude towards foreign languages. Around 58% of the universities provided an English version of their websites (Bian, 2016). Very few had a complete version in English, especially for educational programs. Among the four institutions in this study, SSGEA, a social sciences *grande école*, and SSUB, a social sciences university, had one English page related to the history of the institution; STGEC, a science and technology *grande école*, had a very well-developed English version of its website while STUD, a science and technology university, had no other language version of its website beside French. The underlying message seemed to be that most institutions assumed that students should have acquired a sufficient level of French before they were recruited. Some respondents from the international office and faculties were aware that having no English website for their institution was an obstacle somehow. However, they explained that their major difficulty resulted from lack of funds and human resources.

LANGUAGES IN STUDENT SELECTION AND ADMISSION

As mentioned in the evaluation report of the situation of international students' registration and study experience in French universities conducted in 2005 by the General Inspection of National Education and Research Administration (Szymankiewicz, Boutet-Waiss, Luc, Roignot, & Simon, 2005), international student recruitment at different study levels has its own characteristics. For the recruitment at undergraduate level, the first two years, serious selection criteria were based on students' linguistic and academic competences and only around one third of applicants could be retained. The recruitment at this level was the most administratively structured and selective one. The French language test comprised two parts that evaluated students' skills in listening, reading, grammar and writing. The regulation of exams, jury membership, and design of tests have been under the authority of the International Center for Pedagogical Studies (*Centre international d'études pédagogiques*) since 2004. The exam results are categorized into six levels in ascending order as A1/A2/B1/B2/C1/C2 or 1, 2, 3, 4, 5, 6, and language requirements can differ from one institution and field of study to the other. However, a minimum level (B1 or B2) is required so that students can at least understand subject contents, take notes and write exams. As the report indicated, students from non-French-speaking countries, particularly from Asia, often found themselves in the most difficult situations. Compared to the sophisticated selection process at undergraduate level, the master's and doctoral levels seem more straightforward, and some postgraduate programs are financially dependent on the recruitment of international students. Doctoral student recruitment is mostly based on students' motivation, researchers' individual decisions and research needs.

In this study, 19 international students at master's level from the four institutions were interviewed, five from SSGEA, five from SSUB, five from STGEC and four from STUD. Based on the types of programs, these participants were categorized as Erasmus (including Mundus) students, institutional exchange students and free movers. Based on language of instruction, three of them followed English-taught programs in Economy and Management and one attended the Erasmus Mundus program. As for the free movers recruited in French-taught programs, they had to provide evidence of a certain level of French language when they applied – B2 or C1 depending on the field of study. The students from the latter group who applied for the first time to French universities could complete the application forms online through CEF (*Centre d'études en France*) in their home countries, and send it together with a French B2 or C1 language certificate. As for the free movers in English-taught programs, a sufficient level of English was required and some knowledge of the French language was also recommended but not mandatory. As for traditional Erasmus students, as per respondents, they needed to pass a French language test before their application for mobility. Due to a lack of applicants but a great number of vacancies, French language requirements were symbolic or a matter of diplomacy in the selection. Students' mobility lasted between one semester and one academic year. The main goals were to obtain some credits and an intercultural experience. In the interviews, some researchers mentioned that although Erasmus programs went very well in the European network, they were comparatively less satisfied with the quality of students, in particular students' unpreparedness for the French language. Students recruited through institutional programs (double or joint-degree programs between institutions) were selected in their home institutions by professors from home and/or host institutions and the selections were mainly based on their academic records, motivations, interview performance, in which a sufficient French level was required but not essential.

In the four institutions, we observed that the fees for English-taught programs were far higher than for the similar French-taught programs. The French MENESR (Ministry of National Education, Higher Education and Research) set the registration fees for national degree programs (medicine, odontology and pharmaceutical studies excluded) in 2016–2017 to 184€ for undergraduate degrees, 256€ for master's level and 391€ for doctoral level degrees; 610€ for education in engineering schools. In other words, as international students pay the same registration fees as local students, the cost of a national master's degree only amounts to 256€/year in the French higher education system. In the interviews, three students from the English-taught program in Economy and Management at SSUB mentioned that their program also existed in French, with only standard national fees, but their own tuition fees amounted to 2,600€ for the first year of study and 4,200€ for the second year. The program officer explained the price gap as a mean of offsetting the invitational cost of visiting international professors. As for this group of students, they considered the price to be acceptable compared to English-speaking countries and the program taught in English saved their time and energy in learning the French language. Two other programs in the STUD were also taught in English: one is the ALGANT master's program (mathematics), open to international students from Europe and the rest of the world and the tuition fees were 8,000€/year for non-European students and 4,000€ for European students and excellency scholarship holders; the other one is the MER program (marine studies) and the tuition fees were 8,000€ for non-European students and 4,000€ for European students. There were similar courses taught in English and French in the two programs but the fees were totally different. The program officers defended the rationality of the set price and explained that the fees were well spent for the best interests of students. Furthermore, according to the respondents, French language courses were provided for students on Erasmus programs, institutional exchange programs and English-taught programs and they also expressed their interest in French language learning.

LANGUAGES IN STUDENTS' INSTITUTIONAL INTEGRATION

Students' institutional integration is a two-dimensional process, which depends on both host institutions and international students. International students' linguistic acquisition level is the decisive element guiding the whole process. The way institutions position students (students' role), and students position themselves (students' motivation, intention, and competences) in the host institution directly impacts this process.

Language learning, as a highly contextualized learning process, needs to be analyzed and de-constructed for better understanding. According to poststructuralists, language is not "a set of idealized forms independent of their speakers or their speaking, but rather situated utterances in which speakers, in dialogue with others, struggle to create meanings" (Norton & Toohey, 2011, p. 416). In other words, language learning is dependent both on the context and on the changing power relationship between learners/speakers and their interlocutors. Some researchers argue that language learning is a joint engagement with others in activities with the help of cultural tools, which indicates that the process is not a one-man show, and the result of learning depends on both learners' previous and actual acquisition of cultural capital. These views explain why speakers' position affects their speaking privilege, and linguistic and cultural capital has a direct impact on learners'/speakers' participation in activities. As Bourdieu elaborated, linguistic discourse is "a symbolic asset which can receive different values depending on the market on which it is offered" (quoted in Norton & Toohey, 2011, p. 416). When language is not just a set of utterances but a kind of social capital, its social and economic functions can turn into a generator for learning. Moreover, linguistic and cultural affinity could accelerate or slow down language learning and the integration process in the host countries.

In this study, three out of 19 participants were from French-speaking countries, Senegal and Morocco. All of them had an excellent French level and two of them had been educated in French schools since childhood. According to their own experience, although they had no problem with the French language, they still mentioned some difficulties in their institutional integration process. Among them, the student from STUD failed his first year of study due to inadequate academic competency and lack of financial support, which is quite a common phenomenon, as previous studies of international students' experience in France highlighted. The other two girls from Morocco were recruited to STGEC via very competitive entrance selection and both had good academic records. They considered themselves well integrated in the host institution. Nevertheless, when they were questioned about their interactions with French students in the classroom, they showed preference to be with students from the same cultural backgrounds as theirs. Unlike these three interviewees, the other respondents had difficulties because of insufficient linguistic and academic skills. They all mentioned limited contact with local students due to lack of personal motivation and the campus atmosphere, among which language became the first and most important barrier for getting involved. When they were questioned about their performance in class, most of the students majoring in social sciences expressed their feeling of awkwardness. Some of them had expected to contribute to the class as speakers for their culture and country in order to share their views with local peers. However, for this group of students, their goodwill sometimes could not overcome the linguistic challenge. Some of them just wanted their presence in class as a "silent" symbol of cultural diversity. Therefore, by avoiding eye contact or lowering their heads, they reached a mutual understanding with their professors. In the interviews, we also asked students about their professional plans and categorized them into three groups based on their responses. The first group was composed of "traditionalists," mostly intent on getting a degree, and they often chose to go back to their home country after studying abroad. Factors such as strong attachment to families, patriotism, and lack of the linguistic competence needed to find a job in France, mainly explained their choices. Students in this group also conveyed their concern about their inadaptability to the cultural and linguistic environment in France. The second group was composed of "strategists" who showed a strategic vision of their future careers and considered their mobility experience as a process of human capital accumulation. They often chose to live their first professional experience abroad for several years before finally going back to their home countries. The added-value they gained during this experience could enrich their profiles. The third group consisted of "internationalists," whether this was voluntary or not. They chose to study abroad for different reasons and for some, unstable political and bad economic situations in their home countries forced them to find another country to start their careers. We noticed that the different groups of students showed different attitudes towards language learning, which resulted in various levels of language acquisition and choices in language instruction.

If we now turn to HEIs' roles in the integration of international students, it is essential to note that in France, equality, hospitality and autonomy have been established as three basic premises since the admission process was put under the responsibility of universities in 1981 (Chandler, 1989). Firstly, equality conveys the idea that international students benefit from equal rights to their local peers'. This indifferent attitude to difference becomes a double-faced coin in the international student recruitment process. On the one hand, the equal tuition fees and equal access to social welfare and medical care have always been attractive for international students and were once top incentives for French HEIs. However, the equality in international student policy has been criticized by some researchers and policy-makers over the last two decades: they state that this generous policy could turn into a financial burden and put the already difficult national economic situation into an even worse situation. On the other hand, it also means same requirements in students' admission and attainment which, as previously noted, could pose problems for students from non-French speaking countries.

Secondly, the policy of hospitality includes two aspects: the international students are selectively welcomed based on their French language level and academic skills; meanwhile, once the international students get accepted in French HEIs, the HEIs are responsible for offering them better academic and pastoral support services. In the interviews with international office staff, we were informed that the offices were created quite recently in these institutions and composed of 3 to 10 employees. In general, the international relations office is led by two directors: an administrative director for the daily management of international relationships, and a general director for the strategic development. The size of the institution is usually directly related to the number of staff in the international relations service and in this study, only three people were working in such services, one at SSGEA and two at STGEC. The IR service acts as the hub of policy implementation and support provision both internally and externally. It is endowed with different missions: research collaboration at European and international levels, student, academic and administration staff mobility, and other forms of internationalization programs, like the export of teaching programs, offshore campuses, etc. Its missions were perceived as not being properly carried out in the different institutions due to various reasons, such as a lack of human resources, an over-centralized hierarchy in administration, the institution's visions and priorities, etc.

Connecting the student interviewees' responses with the international office staff's answers to the question of service provision from the host institutions led us to make two general observations: the ones who pay more are better served; the ones who were recruited in more structured programs get better services. Students' accommodation was considered as the biggest difficulty, according to student respondents. International students can apply for a room via the CROUS (*Centre régional des oeuvres universitaires et scolaires*) website once they get their admission from French HEIs. However, some untold rules were implied in the interviews. The group of students from Erasmus programs, institutional exchange programs and programs that charged extra tuition fees, were prioritized and they also got pedagogical help with their course choices and other related administrative issues. Even though some staff expressed their awareness of the presence of the large group of free movers in their institutions, this group of international students were still only partially taken care of in the four institutions, if at all, and in the eyes of some researcher interviewees, they were considered in the same way as local students.

Finally, the policy of autonomy mainly refers to the university's pedagogical autonomy and to the fact that universities need to take responsibility for their recruitment decisions, which is closely related to the roles of international students entrusted by host institutions. The international student policy-making is a process in which the national demand and strategic priorities need to be considered in terms of diplomacy, economic development, educational needs and immigration policies. In this study, the international student population was equated with infinite resources for the institutions, its researchers and the local students. Combining student interviewees' profiles in this research and institutions' strategies for developing international student recruitment, we observed that French HEIs intended to form more ambassadors for non-traditional partners, particularly former French colonies, and to expand the soft power of French education to other parts of the world.

The intention explains a transformation of institutional attitude from passively receiving international students to more active recruitment strategies. Institutional needs were valued more in developing student recruitment strategy. To attract and recruit talented students remains the common interest of the four institutions in this research. The researcher respondents in the interviews showed their great passion towards students who had excellent academic backgrounds and were interested in research and for them, the French or English language was not a definitive issue for selection. The development of English-taught programs and program exported abroad at SSUB and STUD, the engineering training programs for Brazilian and Chinese students at STGEC, the integrated and double-degree programs development at SSGEA, all implicitly demonstrated the institutions' interest in the economic benefits hidden behind the programs and the institutions managed to make good use of their advantages respectively.

In a word, as noted by an international student in an interview, no matter what language was used in the education program, he felt that studying in France, in a French-speaking society, whether he liked it or not, was an opportunity to be immersed in French culture. The English language is only a facilitator for students from non-French speaking countries to get a pathway or shortcut to achieving their study objectives, and for institutions to expand their influence internationally and gain economic or other kinds of benefits based on internal needs.

CONCLUSION

This chapter intended mainly to answer the question of the roles of two languages, French and English, in the international student recruitment in the context of internationalization of French HEIs. The interview data and the related institutional documents used in this analysis derived from a research in international student mobility development. Due to the limited number of interviews and the choice of institutions, the findings related to language issues in the international student recruitment are not exhaustive because this study did not account for all possible situations. However, the analysis covered the major phases in the whole recruitment process, from information diffusion and communication, selection and admission to students' integration into the institution's life. Based on the data from the field investigation, we found that French still acts as the major filter for the selection of international students and holds the key to students' academic success and professional development in France. For most international students, the mastery of French language is critical to a successful study experience and academic career. However, English, as the most popular and widely used language worldwide, functions as an added-value to French HEIs in pulling in more international students, and attracting some unique talents. It can also be seen as a cash-cow and as a factor that pushes local students out, especially in collaborative or exchange programs with English-speaking countries. In general, the two languages exercise their power in different arenas. In research, the popularity of global rankings leads nations and institutions to play the game of competition voluntarily or involuntarily, and apply an external referencing system and evaluative logic into their institutional functioning system. For some fields of research, such as economics and management, sciences and technology, English is a "must" language for academic publication, a necessary tool for international communication. However, we must consider the particularity of some fields in the social sciences and humanities, historically constructed and highly contextualized in France where only the French language can accurately and authentically express the knowledge. In teaching, English is welcomed in French HEIs but only for a small number of programs, in special study fields, for students at certain levels. The use of English language in teaching and the development of English-taught programs are encouraged but not mandatory, which could be good for both the internationalization of the academic profession and students' future employment.

To develop further understanding of language issues in international student recruitment, we need to expand our vision to factors such as the competition and cooperation among different nations, the changing brain drain patterns, the changing relationships between nations and HEIs in the internationalization of higher education and economic globalization. In the era of knowledge economy where technology and innovation become the generator of economic productivity and marker of national strength, talents are the vital resources for competing nations (Pan, 2011) as they seek higher platforms to enrich their standings on the global market. The talent flow is a complex phenomenon greatly influenced by global political, economic and cultural relationships between nations (McMahon, 1992). The world-system theory implies an interactive network composed of different social entities structured as core, periphery and semi-periphery based on the power hierarchy of the entities. This global structure is not stable because of the instability of absolute power and in this network, countries in the periphery could possibly enter the semi-periphery, however, they may never be able to gain access directly to the center (Chase-Dunn &

Grimes, 1995). Therefore, France, as one of the core countries in the center, will continue to attract international students from other spheres, and students from other core countries as well. As noted by Chandler, a nation's international student policy reflects its "philosophical biases and the consistent or contradictory themes contained in its culture" (Chandler, 1989, p. 15). France keeps a strong commitment to education as a public good and its higher education is closely coordinated with the state, serving the higher interest of the nation. Unlike the other top host English-speaking countries where international students are often considered as a kind of commercial goods, France follows and will most likely continue to adopt a distinctive approach to international student recruitment. Indeed, the increasing importance of the English language as the prevailing lingua franca in business and academia around the world threatens the French cosmopolitan culture and the pride of French intellectuals. However, it could only be a threat but not a replacement. The conflicts between the use of these two languages in international student recruitment reflect the competition between France and other major English-speaking countries. Furthermore, the complementary role of English could benefit French HEIs in the internationalization of higher education. In sum, the gist of the matter is not simply language but rather power.

REFERENCES

Altbach, P. (2004). Globalization and the university: Myths and realities in an unequal world. In National Education Association (Ed.), *The NEA 2005 almanac of higher education*. Washington, DC: National Education Association.

Bian, C. (2016). International students in French universities and grandes écoles: A comparative study. Springer Singapore & Higher education press.

Clark, B. C. (1983). *The higher education system: Academic organization in cross-national perspective*. Berkeley, CA: University of California Press.

Chandler, A. (1989). Obligation or opportunity: Foreign student policy in six major receiving countries IIE Research Report No. 18. New York, NY: Institute for International Educatuon.

Chase-Dunn, C., & Grimes, P. (1995). World-system analysis. *Annual Review of Sociology, 21*, 387–417.

Cohen, E. (2001). *Un plan d'action pour améliorer l'accueil des étudiants étrangers en France: Diagnostic et propositions*. Paris: Ministère de l'éducation nationale.

DEPP. (2016). *Repères et références statistiques*. Paris: Ministère de l'Éducation nationale, de l'Enseignement supérieur et de la Recherche.

Dobbins, M., Knill, C., & Vögtle, E. M. (2011). An analytical framework for the cross-country comparison of higher education governance. *Higher Education, 62*, 668–683.

Dufourg, B. (1999). *Compétitivité éducative internationale de la France*. Paris: Chambre de Commerce et d'Industrie de Paris.

EUA (2013). *European higher education: European policies, institutional strategies and EUA support*. Brussel: Author.

European Commission. (Ed.). (2012). *Europeans and their languages. Special eurobarometer 386*, conducted by TNS opinion & social. Retrieved from http://ec.europa.eu/commfrontoffice/publicopinion/archives/ebs/ebs_386_en.pdf

Flitti, E. (2000). *L'accueil des étudiants étrangers dans les universités françaises*. Paris: Rapport.

Hettne, B., & Söderbaum, F. (2000). Theorising the rise of regioness. *New Political Economy, 5*(3), 457–473.

La loi du 7 mars. (2016). *Relative au droit des étrangers en France*. Retrieved from https://www.legifrance.gouv.fr/affichTexte.do?cidTexte=JORFTEXT000032164264& categorieLien=id

Lee, R. (2006). *Globalization, language and culture*. New York, NY: Chelsa House.

McMahon, M. (1992). Higher education in a world market: A historical look at the global context of international study. *Higher Education, 20*, 465–482.

Neave, G. (2003). The Bologna declaration: Some of the historic dilemma posed by the reconstruction of the community in Europe's system of higher education. *Educational Policy. 17*(1), 141–164.

Norton, B., & Toohey, K. (2011). Identity, language learning and social change. *Language Teaching, 44*(4), 412–446.

OECD. (2016). *Education at glance 2016: OECD indicators*. Paris: OECD Publishing.

Organisation Internationale de la Francophonie. (2010). *La langue française dans le monde*. Paris: Nathan.

Pan, S.-Y. (2011). Education abroad, human capital development and national competitiveness. *Frontiers of Education in China, 6*(1), 106–138.

Sorbonne Declaration. (1998). *Sorbonne joint declaration: Joint declaration on harmonization of the architecture of the European higher education system*. Paris: The Sorbonne. Retrieved from http://www.ehea.info/cid100203/sorbonne-declaration-1998.html

Szymankiewicz, C., Boutet-Waiss, F., Luc, J.-C., Roignot, M., & Simon, T. (2005). *Les conditions d'inscription et d'accueil des étudiants étrangers dans les universités*. Paris: Ministère de l'Éducation nationale, de l'Enseignement supérieur et de la Recherche.

UNESCO. (2009). *Global education digest 2009: Comparing education statistics across the world*. Montreal: UNESCO Institute for Statistics.

Cui Bian
Research Institute for International and Comparative Education
Shanghai Normal University
Shangai, China

Régis Malet
LACES EA7437, ESPE d'Aquitaine
Université de Bordeaux
Bordeaux, France

PART 3

THE BROADER ISSUE OF INCLUSION THROUGH ACCESS TO HIGHER EDUCATION

JULIA CARNINE

6. INTERNATIONAL STUDENTS' SOCIAL INCLUSION AND LONG-TERM BENEFITS

The Case of Chinese Students in France

INTRODUCTION

Chinese students have greater access to higher education (HE) than ever before, yet domestic education opportunities do not meet the ever-growing demand (Soo, 2015). This situation causes many Chinese university students to study abroad and today they represent the world's largest international mobile student group (UNESCO, 2016). Whereas their short term study abroad sojourns are widely reported (Carnine, 2016; Liu, 2013; Vignes, 2013; White, 2011; Zhang, 2010), this chapter asks to what degree Chinese graduates' longer term settlement intentions are based on social inclusion and contribute to long term benefits towards the host country.

Studies have shown that greater inclusion social networks can impact settlement decisions (Boyd, 1989; Fawcett, 1989; Gurak & Caces, 1992; Hosnedlová, 2017). Granovetter's (1985) holistic social network analysis (SNA) approach relies on his theory of social "embeddedness" where an individual's choices are a result of decisions filtered through interactions with others in her or his social network. In such social dynamics, relationships may impose pressures as well as open up opportunities. Further research shows that among other processes of local adaptation, specific "embedded" relationships, not necessarily family ties, developed by migrants in their host country can influence their intentions to stay (Hosnedlová, 2017). We know that mobile students have some relationships that enrich their social networks, providing key types of adaptive and linguistic resources and thus aiding in socializing individual students during their sojourn abroad (Carnine, forthcoming).

Using a longitudinal view of Chinese mobile students' (N = 45) personal social networks during and after their sojourn, this chapter studies relative degrees of Chinese student inclusion in France with special focus on how they manage social integration and attachment to their host country. How does this group manage local social integration and long term attachment to their host country? Examining integration via institutionally-based and social network analyses, it aims to answer the following research questions: are Chinese students integrated to some degree into local structures of French HE? What are the processes (formal or informal) of integration via HE institutions? Further, mobile students have long contributed to diasporic knowledge economies upheld by HE academic mobility (Drucker & Smith, 1967;

M.-A. Détourbe (Ed.), Inclusion through Access to Higher Education, 103–121.

Yang & Welch, 2010) and the long-term benefits that are associated with them. This research shows how HE integration in France may or may not foster and/or favor more long-term benefits for this particular knowledge diaspora. An outcome from this study points to influential relationships with French language instructors. It also recommends certain inclusion practices that may enhance long term benefits to these transnational knowledge sharing networks. Lastly, it shows the impact of favourable economic factors in China on returnees, and points to French policies that may foster beneficial support bolstering these transnational networks.

CHINESE MOBILE STUDENTS IN A GLOBAL CONTEXT

Global academic mobility is changing the landscape of HE giving rise to networks of vital transnational human capital while also impacting institutions and socio-cultural practices. Increased academic mobility is a shaping force of the future of HE in new ways beyond the traditional "brain drain" from less developed to more developed nations (Agrawal, Kapur, McHale, & Oettl, 2011; Zweig, 2006). Within this group the Chinese mobile student population represents a majority. Further, contemporary Chinese mobile students do not reproduce migratory patterns of earlier waves of immigration that often relied on extended family and social relations in the host country (Carnine, 2016), instead they make new types of social networks. Given the enduring trend of Chinese mobile students in our increasingly inter-dependent global economy, it behooves us to better understand the social dynamics of this significantly sized Chinese knowledge diaspora (Welch & Zhang, 2008), matriculating in great numbers in international HE institutions.

There is a strong trend for Chinese study abroad: in 2016, UNESCO's Statistical Institute cited 712,157 Chinese students studying worldwide. According to the Chinese Ministry of Education (2015), the number of students studying abroad increased by 17.7% between 2011 and 2012, with around 399,600 Chinese students going abroad to begin further study. North America and Europe HE institutions are the top destinations for most Chinese. In China, prestigious foreign degrees imply rigorous language training as well as conferring social status more important than ever in today's increasingly competitive market (Tan, 2013).

In Table 1, the large gap between the number one European destination, the UK and France suggests that English language study and highly ranked UK universities are prioritized by this group. Similarly, the UK Higher Education Statistics Agency reported that 67,325 Chinese students were registered on degree courses in UK universities (HESA, 2015). Yet growing numbers of Chinese students in other Western European countries, unmatched in number by other national groups, speaks to an important change in student population. Non-Anglophone countries like France and Germany have also seen substantial increases. Over the five-year period (2008–2013) Campus France data show double the number of matriculated students from China (Campus France, 2015) In 2013, French president François Hollande signed several new French and Chinese university partnerships with the aim of increasing student mobility between the two countries to 80,000 and 10,000 respectively by 2020 (Marshall, 2013).

Table 1. UNESCO's statistical institute numbers of Chinese students in Western European HE 2016

Country	Number of students
United Kingdom	86, 204
France	25, 388
Germany	19, 441
Italy	9778

The growing number of such students greatly increases culture and knowledge exchange with China and aids these top destination host countries in creating new sorts of "knowledge economies." Several decades ago Drucker and Smith (1967) introduced this globalization-driven concept centered on the production and circulation of ideas, knowledge and information over previous forms of labor intensive economies. We can now observe that this is also a borderless economy nourished by trends in academic mobility. Yang and Welch (2010) introduce the phenomenon of "brain circulation" where semi-permanent study abroad favors the development of diasporic knowledge communities fueled by study abroad and largely maintained by modern communications technology. Of these, the Chinese is the fastest growing, making them key to development both within and without Chinese borders. Diasporic knowledge economies are upheld by academic mobility and imply specific immigration patterns. It would stand to reason that there would be knowledge economies benefitting from this fluid group of graduates.

Specific host country policies can also impact trends of student migration and decisions to remain in the host country at the conclusion to their studies (Yang & Welch, 2010). Han et al. (2015) highlight how beyond global competition among research institutions, the complex, restrictive nature of US immigration policies threatens American HE's spot as the world's premier HE destination. In France's case, upon election in 2012, newly elected president François Hollande repealed the controversial 2011 Guéant memorandum that imposed stiff visa restrictions on foreign students and graduates. Such a move is considered a way to attract and retain international French degree holders. Thus, on an institutional level, France may be working to retain this foreign-born talent. In addition, there may be other ways French HE is creating conditions for different types of inclusion (legal, social, and professional) for this consequential degree seeking group. This chapter asks if France is cultivating and circulating knowledge exchange within these Sino-French transnational social networks and if so, how?

Quantifying academic mobility for outgoing Chinese students to host countries is one-dimensional, and longitudinal; mobile research is helpful to complete the picture. After all, successful employment abroad was generally considered the best marker for return on investment in international education for elite Chinese. However, that tradition is changing, contrary to previous trends, there is a greater number of mobile Chinese graduates returning to China to seek employment. A 2011 Chinese study cites that rapid paced domestic economic growth combined with difficulties in securing jobs abroad contributes to this massive homecoming among recent graduates (EIC, 2011). Of special interest to the discussion regarding social network contributions to future immigration intentions, the study highlights the fact that Chinese graduates' low language ability, lack of adaptation skills and poor social skills also contribute to the choice to return home. Therefore, there are more than simply economic factors influencing the future decisions of these students. This chapter explores the degree and type of social networks as well as the institutional practices that affect Chinese students' future plans and migratory patterns. Specifically, do they seek employment in their host country? If so, to what end? If not, why not? Are there different ways in which their learning abroad represents a new type of transnational human capital in their specific knowledge diasporas?

RESEARCH RATIONALE

Studying specific pathways of Chinese mobile students demonstrates issues of international accessibility and inclusion of external groups into HE. Schnapper (2007) suggests that integration needs to be understood and measured on at least four distinct levels:

- institutionally in terms of the structures that serve as intermediaries (HE institutions, host country immigration policies, etc.),
- socially in terms of local relationship development,
- culturally, when looking at shifts in values and beliefs,
- identity-based that depends on one's subjective views of belonging.

Institutionally speaking, research suggests that although Chinese student populations in France are growing, HE's role is often relegated to simply administrative tasks of course registration and issues related to student legal status (Hui, 2010; Vignes, 2013). French HE considers all students, regardless of nationality, as fully operational independent individuals and there are few services directed at them. What is intended as a complement to their maturity as young adults often leaves Chinese students resorting to co-national resource sharing. Compared to the service oriented US model of international student integration efforts, France's version is limited. Subsequently the norm is a high level of socio-cultural segregation for Chinese students in France (Carnine, 2014).

Beyond institutional factors, a growing body of research on Chinese mobile students seeks to understand mostly exclusive co-national Chinese groupings.

Several studies conducted in the US and the UK point to this phenomenon of Chinese students sticking together (see Barry, 2003; Carnine, 2014; Chen, 2006; Gaeris, 2012; Harrison & Peacock, 2009; Zhang, 2010). Chinese cultural norms, influencing certain types of social practices, are seen as obstacles as well as underlying definitions and patterns of what is considered to be "friendship" in different cultures. Additionally, linguistic factors are also cited (Hussmann, 2011; Spencer-Oatey & Xiong, 2006; Turner, 2006; Vignes, 2013) contributing communication difficulties and thus further distancing Chinese students from their hosts. To remedy this segregation, some argue that institutional level intervention is necessary, that institutions of HE need to be active in the inclusion process, providing opportunity for greater accessibility and inclusion (Vande Berg et al., 2009). As suggested previously, establishing more local social contacts may create greater potential to physically stay in and/or virtually stay in contact with persons in the host country thusly enhancing diasporic knowledge exchange.

Lastly, a more balanced analysis should also take into account Chinese student agency in terms of their own social inclusion, which Schnapper considers as an "identity based" type of integration. Which forms of intercultural language practice does this new generation of increasingly technologically connected Chinese students devise (Li & Zhu, 2013)? In what ways are student motivations modified from simply degree seeking to active intercultural practice (Carnine, 2016)?

METHOD AND DATA

Both quantitative Social Network Analysis (SNA) as well as qualitative interviews in the form of autobiographical narratives were used to gather this data. The mixed-method, longitudinal study began in 2010, with follow up in 2015 in Paris and Toulouse, France. Colleagues within French universities provided access to more than 100 Chinese students and 45 responded. Beyond their common nationality, this Chinese cohort constituted a relatively homogenous group ranging from middle-to upper-class urban dwelling university students, between 18 and 26 years' old, yet, their fields of study were wide ranging (e.g., finance, fashion, math, French, and political science). Additionally, their average sojourn in France was three years' long. These participants filled out individual questionnaires detailing their personal social networks. SNA elicits personal, social networks based on one or more "name generator" question(s) detailing their relationships (Bidart & Charbonneau, 2012). In this study the prompt was "Who are the most important persons to you during your stay abroad?" after which they were asked to further characterize the relationship by type (family, schoolmate, school resource person, professional contact, etc.). In particular, questions that connect the type of relationship with the type of resource provided helped us understand to what degree institutionalized HE structures are actively aiding this student group in their integration processes.

In the interest of comparison between different types of institutional practices of social inclusion, the Chinese cohort will also be compared here to both French and US study abroad students, additional participants in the extended field work of the Phase 1 2010 study (N = 180).[1] These "egos," were all given the same written questionnaire, translated into their native language that then yielded a total of 1,571 relationships or "alters." All three national student sub-groups were also invited to participate in face-to-face semi-structured interviews, although only one in four did so. In all, 45 interviews (15 per national group) were transcribed and coded using Nvivo software. This phase of the research ended in 2011.

In its second phase, from Toulouse in 2015, additional, in-depth qualitative interviews were done via Skype and email with two Chinese students who had recently left France to return to China for work. Here, a biographical narrative approach popular among applied linguists when approaching academic sojourners in complex socio-cultural interactions, was employed (Barkhuizen, Benson, & Chik, 2013; Lantolf & Pavlenko, 2001; Norton & Toohey, 2001). Although all 15 Chinese participants from Phase 1 were asked to participate in this second phase, only two students volunteered. It is important to note that their willingness to engage in this continued research makes them interesting cases, not that their social networks are representative of the overall cohort. The Chinese students in France cohort (N = 45) had relatively small personal networks made up almost exclusively of parents and a few school friends. Financial help and emotional support are the principal resources provided by these networks. In contrast the two participants described here were both highly successful in their studies, had bigger and broader networks while also experiencing more than average institutionalized help in French language class. Nonetheless, when understood with these limitations, they offer rich, salient examples of how institutionalized processes of student integration in HE, immigration legislation as well as socially based inclusion may or may not contribute to potential long-term mutual benefits for the greater Sino-French knowledge diaspora circulating via these mobile students.

INSTITUTIONAL INTERVENTION LEADS TO GREATER NUMBER OF DIVERSE SOCIAL TIES

When comparing the different student cohorts (N = 180) in Phase 1, the role of institutional intervention in creating social inclusion was revealed. Settings with little to no structured international social integration in terms of language focus or multi-national integrated lodging, favored co-national social networks. The opposite was also true, the more intentional social integration in program design, the more international relationships appeared in diverse networks, averaging around 50%, even allowing for a majority (61.2%) of international relationships. These results suggest that interventionist programs favor more integrated social networks and counteract co-national segregation. A host country dimension emerged also, the rate of co-national social relations rose to its highest (73.8%) for the French subgroup in China and 73.2% for Chinese students in France. The Chinese student cohort in France maintained a majority of non-familial relationships with their co-national peer group reinforced by co-national housing. Different from the American model, where international student programs provide support personnel, enhance transnational socializing and international housing, French students in China and Chinese students in France tended to look to their immediate co-national peers while overseas.

Further, when examined closely, it was clear that certain socially inclusive institutional frameworks correlate with certain resource providing roles. Social networks of the Chinese in France cohort showing a co-national dominance rarely included institutionally based persons (those mentioned were almost exclusively French language instructors). In contrast, students in the American HE model had social networks with higher rates of different types of HE support persons. The Chinese studying in the US described social networks that helped with schoolwork, language, and cultural adaptation. In these cases, several support persons from the HE institution appeared in social networks, be they international program staff, residential staff or language instructors. In this Phase 1, major points arose regarding social integration of international students; institutional frameworks could offer structures for integration as well as pathways to resource persons aiding students' integration processes.

In order to better understand how Chinese students are integrated, if at all, into local structures of French HE and how this may have impacted their settlement plans over a longer time frame, Phase 2 began in 2015. Two Chinese students agreed to participate in extended interviews regarding their personal social network composition. Quantitative name generator questionnaires as well as qualitative biographical interviews resulted in the following social network maps. These maps show two distinct time frames, the personal network they described as "important persons" during their stay in France, and then the personal network they now participate in since their return to China. In each case the 'ego' is represented in either France (during their sojourn) or China (upon return) and their relations span outward via different shapes corresponding to the different nationalities (those in France, French etc.), and the type and number of relations (school resource person, professional, school friend, family). Their interviews were analyzed in terms of their biographical narrative describing the relationships, the specific dynamics that lead to their creation and what types of aid and support was offered by each relationship.

NETWORKS DOMINATED BY CO-NATIONAL TIES

Of these two participants, Li's network size during her sojourn is the most representative in terms of type and size of the Chinese in France cohort (N = 45) studied in 2010–2011, as is her overall approach to her time in France. Li lived with other Chinese classmates and socialized almost exclusively with that group. "Tan and I met before we left for France when we were organizing our visas and we became roommates. We cooked together and shopped together, we had many classes together too." They also shared a similar vision of this time away from all the social pressures of being at home in China, it was a liberating chance to travel and explore.

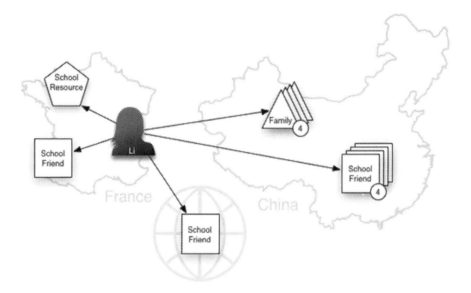

Figure 1. Li's personal network during her stay in France

"We were young and wanted to see so many places with great history. We took buses and trains and airplanes all over Europe! Soon enough we would have to get back to 'real life' and find a job and get married…that was a time to be more free." Despite the lack of social interaction with her European peers, Li held a high regard for European culture and considered herself lucky to see many important sights. For Li, Tan and her family and friends back in China with whom she kept in almost daily contact, were the extent of her network; only rarely did she break that pattern with an exceptional French or international friend. Although she admits that she did not make many attempts to use her French language, she was fortunate in her studies: "My French was never that good, but I had a great language teacher that was so kind and patient. She took us out for activities and really made us feel welcome. Once I had a letter from the bank that I didn't understand, and my teacher was the only person I knew to help me re-read it. I was embarrassed to ask for help, but we [*Li and her roommate* Ed.] were really helpless."

Regarding longer term stay in France, Li knew that she was interested in continuing work in academic related research as her career. While still completing her Masters in France she learned how difficult it would be to secure employment domestically. "My classmates were talking about how the French government was cutting back and that there was a real lack of funding for research positions, even support positions in the future." Indeed, France and China have almost exactly opposite economic prospects in terms of funding research positions. The Chinese government is investing domestically just at a time when France tends to be reducing HE funding. Further, during Li's stay the restrictive Guéant memorandum was acted. In the broader context of the immigration issue, Li's situation is one where her degree of "embeddedness" in relationships with other doubtful Chinese students exacerbated her fear. Like her peers she thought that regardless of her motivation and hard work she would have no legal recourse to stay in France. "We all thought about how it would affect us, even those who had French or international boyfriends and girlfriends and didn't really want to go back to China...we knew we had little choice." In Li's case she was ultimately pleased to go back to China: "even though it was kind of fun at first [*to be in France* Ed.], I was tired of always being different and not feeling comfortable. I wasn't very happy to have to go to work, but I was happy to finally be going home."

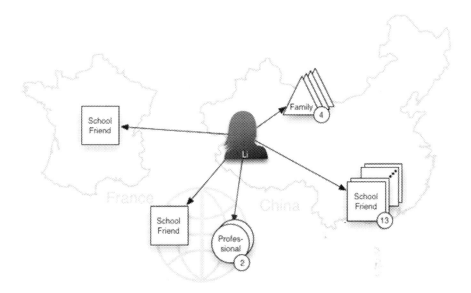

Figure 2. Li's personal network upon her return to China

Upon her return to China Li expanded her already large group of Chinese school related friends and included two international professional relationships that stemmed from her current job. She maintained one French classmate friendship; she specifies that they hope to meet up to travel in Asia someday, but there are no specific plans. Now Li has a much bigger social circle in China than she did in France, yet in terms of its composition it is still largely homogenous consisting of Chinese peers.

After spending four years in France, Li now works in academic administration and her French language does not serve her on a daily basis. However, there is an international dimension that she attributes to skills learnt while abroad. "Before, I never would have made an effort to get to know my Korean colleague, but I was also a foreigner and I know how hard it can be to be on the outside [*from a different country* Ed.]. I try to be friendly and ask questions about how she is doing in China. Her Mandarin is much better than my French ever was, so it is easy to chat."

The fact of Li's French-earned diploma was helpful in acquiring her current employment, but she also admits that her family and close-friend social connections or "*guanxi*" were even more influential (Gold, Guthrie, & Wank, 2002). "Luckily my father knows many people; job hunting is very competitive in China … I am too young to have any real experience." She adds that the Chinese friends she made in France all have returned to China and they make a helpful bunch of connections for her future: "I know that the next step for my parents is that I get married and have a child, so maybe I will meet my future husband through them [*the Chinese friends from abroad* Ed.]…I think Chinese men who have studied abroad make a great pool of talent from which to choose a husband."

Li refers to the time spent sojourning in France as a time of discovery and personal growth. The relationships made in French HE were limited to a French language teacher who she truly benefitted and learned from. Other international relationships did exist, both with a French national and an international person, but they were still limited as Li was mostly dependent on her Chinese roommate and her pre-existing social network located in China for the time of her stay. In terms of knowledge-based outcomes from this time, she cites the value of her degree and her enhanced intercultural curiosity, reaching out more easily to international persons. However, overall, not using her French language or specific training gained in country, there is nothing particularly "French" about the ways she refers to her time abroad.

TRANSNATIONAL CONTACTS THAT OUTLAST TIME AND DISTANCE

Jiang's network size while in France is not representative of the average network size of the Chinese in France cohort (N = 45) studied in 2010–2011. The cohort had an average of seven relations that were largely concentrated between Chinese family and friends. Therefore, Jiang has proportionately more local and international social ties, almost double that of his Chinese peers for the time abroad. Unseen in most other Chinese student networks, Jiang cited three important relationships with school resource persons. Two of them were French instructors with whom he maintained strong ties as they were very helpful and encouraging, explaining cultural differences and introducing specific parts of French culture that he would never have learnt otherwise. Consistent with Li's portrayal, French language learning via key teacher relationships can be a very important resource. The third HE resource person was an adjunct teacher that he only briefly had in class, but this instructor was very interested in China. Jiang made his acquaintance and then kept contact sometimes getting together, sharing their common interest in China and as it happens, French wine. In this case, the integration pattern via this school related tie depends more on shared individual preferences over given institutional roles.

As is evidenced by the greater number of relations, Jiang considers himself very "out-going" and somewhat iconoclast. Studying abroad in France was a dream for

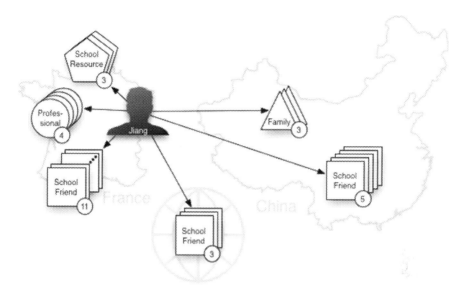

Figure 3. Jiang's personal network during his stay in France

him, although his parents wanted him to study in the world of finance. In the end, they compromised and Jiang worked towards a degree in business. When he reached his Masters' degree, it required an internship in France. He explains his difficulties:

> In my first years there, I spent so much time investing in making French friends… more than other Chinese students I had gotten to know upon arrival. After my first year, besides my girlfriend, all my friends were non-Chinese, French or international. Yet, two years later when it was time to secure an internship, I started to seriously doubt my choice to be so open internationally. While my Chinese acquaintances simply used their Chinese student network to find a spot to work… and it went very quickly for them, I could tell that they were not willing to help me. It was like I had betrayed them, that by making all foreign [*non-Chinese*, Ed.] friends somehow I considered myself better than them. So I was on my own… using all the international and local connections I had, but I still just barely got the position [*as an intern,* Ed.] in time to count for the coursework. In the end, my internship was really beneficial, it granted me a way into my current profession. But I was really too stressed out by all that I had to go through just to get it. That with the fact that my student visa was not necessarily going to be renewed convinced me that I wouldn't have any real chance to work in France… and so I set my sights on returning to China, but working with French companies and products.

Interestingly, given his openness, Jiang seemed to be an ideal candidate to remain working in France, yet his lack of resources in finding an internship coupled with potential visa problems dissuaded him.

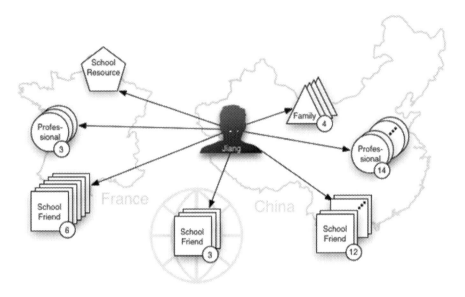

Figure 4. Jiang's personal network upon his return to China

Looking at his social network shift during and after the sojourn we see that after a total of eight years, (five years of study in France and three years working in China), Jiang still maintains contact with many persons that he met in France. Despite the distance and time, there is enough common desire to maintain the relationship.

When approaching the Chinese job market, Jiang was able to capitalize on certain country-specific skills. He continues to use his French professionally and regularly uses his multilingual and multicultural capacities. "Today in the wine industry in China I have worked in Beijing and Shanghai, both very international cities where I meet all kinds of different people. My time in France really prepared me for this kind of work." Even though he has more Chinese friends than when he was in France, and he explains that all of these are new friends, "Chinese friends who studied abroad like myself, though not necessarily in France. These friends can see how life is different outside of China and that is a big part of why we get along." Jiang explains that he was often surrounded by pressures to conform while growing up in China, the idea of "filial piety" or always obeying your parents despite your own opinions. Now he refers to a way of seeing the world that he finds altered among this group of friends who have also traveled and lived abroad.

However, he can also point to clear differences between the sense of what it means to simply be a graduate, or to be a graduate of a more well-known school. "Some friends wear their famous school name a lot, their clothes, their bags, they love to show that they were a part of that place. Wearing your school name is something we rarely saw in France. I am not sure if I would want that, but it seems to make good business!"

DISCUSSION

In Phase 1 of the study, the social networks of Chinese students in France proved to have a majority of same nationality ties with a marked absence of French HE support persons. Formally, in their coursework, both Li and Jiang benefitted from incredibly helpful and open French instructors, but no other support staff were mentioned. Informally, Li and Jiang had very different approaches to conducting their social lives. Li's co-national network heavily centered on her relationships based in China, follows the tendency seen in the Phase 1 study of the Chinese in France cohort group (N = 45). This trend is supported by research of other Chinese student communities abroad where cultural factors (such as collective versus individually based social interaction) are used to explain the failure of some Chinese students overseas to befriend host nationals (Barry, 2003; Chen, 2006; Liu, 2013; Spencer-Oatey & Xiong, 2006; Turner, 2006). Yet, it is important to remember that co-national socializing is a widely reported phenomenon and is not exclusive to Chinese nationals (Carnine, 2015; McManus, Mitchell, & Tracy-Ventura, 2014). Moreover, Jiang socialized in a way entirely different to Li despite their similar context; he chose to informally and independently build transnational relations that later brought him many new communication and intercultural skills.

In both cases, Li and Jiang ended up leaving France and returned to China to pursue professional opportunities, but not necessarily for the same reasons. Although they both cited the impact of the Guéant memorandum of 2011 that was perceived as a general rejection of international students, there were divergences in their settlement plans. Displayed by her Chinese dominant social network and her personal growth opportunity narrative via the sojourn, Li showed less specific interest in France, but more so in the sojourn abroad itself and subsequent joining of the ranks of overseas student returnees in China. Jiang, however, was motivated to apply himself in a specific market and gain knowledge and skills that would have served him, as well as his future employers, in either country. A gregarious individual, Jiang also performed the rare task of creating a polyvalent relationship – a formal French teacher/Chinese student relationship – was transformed into a less formal friendship through which intercultural learning was shared (Bidart, Degrenne, & Grossetti, 2011). Further, his network map after the sojourn shows that he maintains different types of social connections in both countries that provide for continual personal and professional links. This is a case where the Sino-French knowledge diaspora has clearly gained largely due to Jiang's openness in creating new conduits socially and professionally.

Nowhere beyond the French language classroom were HE institutionalized frameworks active in creating social inclusion for these two students. As stated above, international relations officers at French university traditionally fulfill an administrative role, guaranteeing student status and course registration, but not one that aids toward socio-cultural integration. Yet, there are signs of convergence toward a broader internationalized service-oriented model. In Paris and other university cities and within the elite *Grandes Ecoles* as well as universities, there are greater efforts for recruitment and retention of international students (Bian, 2014). Among the new offerings, international and domestic students are now asked to participate in HE sponsored student integration activities that create a sense of collective student identity and to actively meet others.

Such long term institutional relationships can be further pursued in terms of creating institutional image or branding (Brown & Mazzarol, 2009), nurturing a continued student relationship to the institution via its alumni, which has also been touted as an important job seeking tool for graduates. Jiang's remark about his Chinese returnee friends literally "buying" into the sense of belonging to their schools speaks to this sense of continued identification with one's alma mater, especially when it concerns a well-reputed institution. It further points to the different traditions regarding school affinity and attachment between French and British or US HE. Such a student identity affiliated with one's school has a history in France, but considerably less strong and visible as is the UK or US school identity tradition.

Indeed, mobile Chinese students in this diasporic knowledge network are savvy consumers. Different host countries attract different profiles as they represent different financial investments in terms of tuition, but also in terms of status and social networking. Reinforcing the importance of social networks, Li explains that "most Chinese students would prefer a US or UK degree," not simply for the generally preferred English language training, but for the fact that further job opportunities tend to occur among graduates of certain top schools in countries with strong economies. The symbolic importance of a foreign degree coupled with her father's connections ultimately made Li's time in France a good investment professionally. However, one could argue based on her description that her sojourn offered her an equally important time for personal development, a finding echoed by Papatsiba (2003) when studying Erasmus students. Alternately, for Jiang, France is a place to develop niche market talent such as in aeronautics or luxury goods, "there are few jobs, but good jobs because there are not always good candidates" but, he adds, "everyone knows that on the job market, English is the language that matters." Further, Chinese are keen on global university rankings as a gauge of a "good school." It is important to note that on this type of HE ratings scale, domestic Chinese universities are currently outperforming their French counterparts. Nonetheless, Jiang's academic to professional trajectory is a good example of how specific training in France leads to such a coveted and rare work opportunity. He benefitted from his French academic background as he is working directly with French products destined for the Chinese market. His hard-won internship working in the French wine industry, his intercultural and language skills made him a perfect candidate.

Together with many recent stimulating and attracting policies put forth by the Communist central government, economic factors impact settlement intentions creating favorable conditions for students to return (Biao, 2003; Zweig, 2006). Li and Jiang are members of the newer "returnee" generation in China, sometimes referred to as "sea turtles" (*hai gui*) in Chinese (Hao & Welch, 2012). Whereas some top tier students are lured abroad by what is seen as world class research facilities, combined with opportunities to work alongside leading researchers with access to significant research grants, China's booming economy greatly mitigates such an intention.

CONCLUSION

Drawn home by greater job opportunities and a growing economy in China, hindered by short-lived restrictive visa policies, and socially segregated while abroad, what if anything makes France an attractive destination for settling down? Certainly continued adjustments in France could create opportunities for more permanent or semi-permanent settlement. On an institutional level, social inclusion efforts could structurally reverse some of this segregation creating more support towards integration of international students. These data suggest that upgrading and promoting French language study is a fundamental welcoming portal. Also, based on the comparisons with less segregated US models, advocating inclusive housing, along with specific integrative socio-cultural programming in France could all positively affect both home and host students. However, if Li and Jiang are any example, we could reasonably argue that fewer Chinese students may emigrate to France than previously. In cases like Jiang's, he offers specific skills circulating in a knowledge diaspora that benefit a transnational zone including home and host countries. To achieve this, he made a deliberate attempt to seek out transnational relationships, partially, but not solely, as instrumental players in his network that could enhance and increase his intercultural learning. HE institutions can likewise foster resource-heavy social networks for international students whether they be in France or in China during and after their academic sojourns.

Several government-funded legal provisions and institutional efforts are underway that should offer more solid Sino-French HE cooperation, although they do not specifically address social inclusion. Investing in knowledge diasporas also means permitting multi-directional academic flows. The projects mentioned here reverse previous trends of one-way Chinese mobility to France, rather they encourage circulation back and forth. Although the Guéant memorandum was cited as a deterrent for Li and Jiang, a different 2011 measure was passed allowing all Chinese Masters and Doctoral alumni to obtain a "circulation visa" for unlimited numbers of 90-day stays for up to five years. Additionally, in early 2016, a law passed by the French National Assembly introduced a multi-year residence permit for all foreign students in France. In terms of HE collaboration, the new satellite campus of Aix-Marseille University in Wuhan follows other French institutions already implanted in China such as Centrale Pékin and Paris Tech Shanghai-Jiaotong. Further internationalization programs seek to increase Sino-French student mobility, yet they also involve multi-level teacher exchanges, creation of joint courses and collaborative research. Highly specialized knowledge diasporas receive important support as well; CNRS Institut de Physique du Globe de Paris will collaborate on international research which includes China as well as renewing multi-party research pacts such as CNRS, Inserm and Institut Pasteur with Shanghai-Jiaotong Ruijin hospital (Campus France, 2015). However, this research funding addresses a selective scientific group: what about more general efforts to maintain mutually beneficial Sinophile and Francophile graduate networks?

Campus France, France's government sponsored HE mobility administration, has launched "France Alumni" and specifically for Chinese alumni "Club France." The latter is an alumni group based in China which aids in socio-professional networking. According to their website, its members are largely young (90% are under 40 years' old), masters-level professionals residing in large urban areas (Beijing, Shanghai, etc.). Their common purpose is professional insertion into the Chinese workforce in ways that favor Sino-French cooperation in a variety of professional sectors. For example, Shanghai's 2015 job fair was composed of 40 different French companies and in that same year, their website posted over 200 job offers. Not unlike the social networks established by Li and Jiang upon their return to China that tended to seek company with other returnees, this formal online group creates connections via a virtual knowledge diaspora among graduates sharing specific types of knowledge and skill sets. Instead of appealing to specific school alumni, Club France is seeking to maintain graduates' identification with French HE overall in order to benefit both French and Chinese job markets. Among the institutional social inclusion initiatives explored in this chapter, Club France may represent the most applicable and thus the most beneficial to today's highly mobile and specially trained Chinese graduates from French HE. This shift shows the reality of how international graduates make contributions to permeable knowledge diasporas across national borders and markets. Yet this observation remains exploratory, based on small study samples and individual biographies. Further research on a larger scale and with a longitudinal scope is needed to understand the exact impact of such an institutionally sponsored group among social networks and relative to job searching.

NOTE

[1] These students studied abroad in France, the United States or China thus somewhat limiting the range of host country variables (Carnine, 2014).

REFERENCES

Agrawal, A., Kapur, D., McHale, J., & Oettl, A. (2011). Brain drain or brain bank? The impact of skilled emigration on poor country innovation. *Journal of Urban Economics, 69*(1), 43–55.

Barkhuizen, G., Benson, P., & Chik, A. (2013). *Narrative inquiry in language teaching and learning research*. London: Routledge.

Barry, D. T. (2003). Cultural and demographic correlates of self-reported guardedness among East Asian immigrants in the US. *International Journal of Psychology. 38*(3), 150–159. doi:10.1080/00207590244000287

Bian, C. (2014). *A local comparative study of inbound student mobility and internationalization in grandes écoles and universities* (Unpublished Doctoral dissertation). University of Bordeaux, Bordeaux.

Biao, X. (2003). Emigration from China: A sending country perspective. *International Migration, 41*(3), 21–48.

Bidart, C., & Charbonneau, J. (2012). How to generate personal networks: Issues and tools for a sociological perspective. *Field Methods. 23*(3), 266–286. Retrieved from https://halshs.archives-ouvertes.fr/halshs-00512180

Bidart, C., Degrenne, A., & Grossetti, M. (2011). *La vie en reseau: Dynamiques des relations sociales* [A networked life: Dynamics of social relations]. Paris: Presses Universitaires de France.

Boyd, M. (1989). Family and personal networks in international migration: Recent developments and new agendas. *International Migration Review, 23*(3), 638–669.

Brown, R. M., & Mazzarol, T. W. (2009). The importance of institutional image to student satisfaction and loyalty within higher education. *Higher Education, 58*(1), 81–95. doi:10.1007/s10734-008-9183-8

Campus France. (2015). *Alumni dossier*. Retrieved from http://www.campusfrance.org/fr/dossier/france-alumni

Carnine, J. (2014). *French "mobilité estudiantine internationale," American "study abroad" and Chinese 留学 Liu xue: A comparative look at cross-border study via social networks and national identities* (Unpublished Doctoral dissertation). University of Toulouse, Toulouse.

Carnine, J. (2015). The impact on national identity of transnational relationships during international student mobility. *Journal of International Mobility, 3*(1), 11–30.

Carnine, J. (2016). The social networks of Chinese students studying in France (中国留学生在法国的社会关系). *Journal of Chinese Overseas, 12*(1), 68–95.

Carnine, J. (forthcoming). Among oysters and chameleons: Chinese and French students' social networks and social integration during overseas academic sojourns. Special Asian edition, *Study Abroad Research in Second Language Acquisition and International Education.*

Chen, Y. W. (2006). Intercultural friendship from the perspective of East Asian international students. *China Media Research, 2*(3), 43–58.

Chinese Ministry of Education. (2015). *Educational statistics*. Retrieved from http://en.moe.gov.cn/Resources/Statistics/edu_stat_2015/2015_en01/

Club France Events. (2015). Retrieved from http://www.clubfrancechine.org

Drucker, P. F., & Smith, J. M. (1967). *The effective executive*. London: Heinemann.

EIC. (2011). *Key China education statistics for international educators*. Retrieved from http://partners.eic.org.cn/images/PDF/eicstatreport2.pdf

Fawcett, J. T. (1989). Networks, linkages, and migration systems. *International Migration Review, 23*(3), 671–680.

Gaeris, E. (2012). Intercultural friendship: Effects of home and host region. *Journal of International and Intercultural Communication, 5*(4), 309–328.

Gold, T., Guthrie, D., & Wank, D. (Eds.). (2002). *Social connections in China: Institutions, culture and the changing nature of guanxi*. Cambridge: Cambridge University Press.

Granovetter, M. (1985). Economic action and social structure: The problem of embeddedness. *American Journal of Sociology, 91*(3), 481–510.

Gurak, D. T., & Caces, F. (1992). Migration networks and the shaping of migration systems. In M. M. Kritz, L. Lin, & H. Zlotnik (Eds.), *International migration systems: A global approach* (pp. 150–176). Oxford: Clarendon Press.

Han, X., Stocking, G., Gebbie, M. A., & Appelbaum, R. P. (2015). Will they stay or will they go? International graduate students and their decisions to stay or leave the US upon graduation. *PLoS ONE, 10*(3), e0118183.

Hao, J., & Welch, A. (2012). A tale of sea turtles: Job-seeking experiences of hai gui (High-skilled returnees). *China Higher Education Policy, 25*(243). doi:10.1057/hep.2012.4

Harrison, N., & Peacock, N. (2009). Cultural distance, mindfulness and passive xenophobia: Using Integrated threat theory to explore home higher education students' perspectives on 'internationalisation at home.' *British Educational Research Journal, 36*(6), 877–902.

Higher Education Statistics Agency (HESA). (2015). *Students in higher education.* Retrieved from https://www.hesa.ac.uk/stats

Hosnedlová, R. (2017). Embedded settlement intentions: The case of Ukrainians in Madrid. *Social Networks, 49*, 48–66.

Hui, M. Y. (2010, January). Parcours chinois dans l'université Française [Pathways of Chinese students in French universities]. *Le Français dans le Monde.*

Hussmann, A. (2011). *Interim report: Students' learning experience in a multi-cultural environment* (Unpublished doctoral dissertation). Teesside University, Middlesbrough.

Lantolf, J., & Pavlenko, A. (2001). Second language activity theory: Understanding second language learners as people. In M. Breen (Ed.), *Thought and actions in second language learning: Research on learner contributions* (pp. 141–158). London: Longman.

Li, W., & Zhu, H. (2013). Translanguaging identities and ideologies: Creating transnational space through flexible multilingual practices amongst Chinese university students in the UK. *Applied Linguistics, 26*(1), 42–56.

Liu, C. (2013). From language learners to language users: A study of Chinese students in the UK. *International Journal of Applied Linguistics, 23*(2), 123–143.

Marshall, J. (2014, May 04). Pacts with China to boost cooperation and mobility. *University World News.* Retrieved from http://www.universityworldnews.com/article.php?story=20130502125304518

McManus, K., Mitchell, R., & Tracy-Ventura, N. (2014). Understanding insertion and integration in a study abroad context: The case of English-speaking sojourners in France. *Revue Française de Linguistique Appliquée, 19*(2), 97–116.

Norton, B., & Toohey, K. (2001). Changing perspectives on good language learners. *TESOL Quarterly, 35*(2), 307–322.

OECD. (2015). *Education data.* Paris: OECD. Retrieved from https://data.oecd.org/fr/chine-republique-populaire-de.htm#profile-education

Papatsiba, V. (2003). *Des étudiants européens: Erasmus et l'aventure de l'alterité* [European students and the adventure with 'otherness']. Berne: Peter Lang.

Schnapper, D. (2007). *Qu'est-ce que l'intégration?* [What is integration?] Paris: Gallimard.

Soo, K. T. (2015). Recent trends in graduate unemployment and higher education in China. *Contemporary Chinese Political Economy and Strategic Relations: An International Journal, 1*(3), 637–661. Retrieved from http://envoy.dickinson.edu:2048/login?url=http://envoy.dickinson.edu:2151/docview/1790497634?accountid=10506

Spencer-Oatey, H., & Xiong, Z. (2006). Chinese students' psychological and sociocultural adjustments to Britain: An empirical study. *Language, Culture and Curriculum, 19*(1), 37–53.

Tan, G. Y. (2013). Higher education reforms in China: For better or for worse. *International Education, 43*(1), 101–118.

Times Higher Education. (2015). *World university rankings. Times Higher Education.* Retrieved from https://www.timeshighereducation.com/student/where-to-study/study-in-china

Turner, Y. (2006). Chinese students in a UK business school: Hearing the student voice in reflective teaching and learning practice. *Higher Education Quarterly, 60*(1), 27–51.

UNESCO. (2016). *Global flow of tertiary level students.* Paris: UNESCO. Retrieved from http://www.uis.unesco.org/Education/Pages/international-student-flow-viz.aspx

Vande Berg, M., Connor-Linton, J., & Paige, R. M. (2009). The Georgetown consortium project: Interventions for student learning abroad. *Frontiers: The Interdisciplinary Journal of Study Abroad, 18*, 1–75.

Vignes, L. (2013). Témoignages d'étudiants chinois à l'université en France: De la culture d'enseignement apprentissage aux stratégies personnelles [Chinese students in France focus groups: From the culture of teaching to personal strategies]. *Synergies Chine, 8*, 125–135.

Welch, A., & Zhang, Z. (2008). Communication networks among the Chinese knowledge diaspora: A new invisible college? In R. Boden, R. Deem, D. Epstein, & F. Rizvi (Eds.), *Geographies of knowledge, geometries of power: Higher education in the 21st century. World yearbook of education 2008* (pp. 338–354). London: Routledge.

White, A. (2011, February 1). Chinese students' international study: Factors feeding the decision process. *World Education News and Reviews*. Retrieved from http://wenr.wes.org/2011/02/wenr-januaryfebruary-feature

World Bank. (2014). *Gross enrollment ratio, tertiary, both sexes*. Washington, DC: World Bank. Retrieved from http://data.worldbank.org/indicator/SE.TER.ENRR

Yang, R., & Welch, A. R. (2010). Globalisation, transnational academic mobility and the Chinese knowledge diaspora: An Australian case study. *Discourse: Studies in the Cultural Politics of Education, 31*(5), 593–607.

Zhang, Q. (2010). Asian Americans beyond the model minority stereotype: The nerdy and the left out. *Journal of International and Intercultural Communication, 3*(1), 20–37.

Zweig, D. (2006). Competing for talent: China's strategies to reverse the brain drain. *International Labour Review, 145*(1–2), 65–90.

Julia Carnine
Dickinson College/LISST-CERS
University of Toulouse
France

HIMABINDU TIMIRI

7. ON THE MARGINS OF INCLUSION

Higher Education Challenges Faced by Immigrant
Techworker Spouses in the United States

INTRODUCTION

For immigrant women, access to post-migration higher education involves negotiating a matrix of market regulations and familial gender norms, besides race and class intersections where they are located (Alfred, 2003, 2005). Both migration and higher educational trajectories are a function of immigration policy and labor market choices made by immigrant women and their families as they seek to fulfill their aspirations (Raghuram, 2004). In the absence of policy that is attentive to the complexity of their condition, they may be led to pursue higher educational goals as neoliberal subjects in the market of education – calculating and measuring their market value as academic capitalist subjects (Slaughter & Rhoades, 2004). For women who migrate through family reunification in particular, their higher educational pathways would have to be approved and funded by their families, who may also take a return-on-investment approach to the educational aspirations of these women.

In the United States (US), one category of middle-class immigrant women in particular, faces a range of challenges in fulfilling their post-migration higher educational goals. Located at the juncture of immigration regulation and access to higher education, their condition underscores the need for policy to consider the diverse contexts that frame immigrant women's lives. This chapter examines the case of so-called "dependent" immigrant women. They are the spouses of immigrant techworkers residing in the US on the H-1B visa. The H-1B program facilitates high-skilled guest workers to migrate to the US in order to perform specialized jobs in the American knowledge economy.[1] As "high-skilled[2]" immigrants, H-1B workers perform jobs requiring at least a bachelor's degree and specialized skills, primarily in information technology (IT) related fields, besides science and engineering (United States Citizenship and Immigration Services [USCIS], 2015). The H-1B program also offers these guest workers and their families a long-term pathway to American citizenship.

Since it began in 1990, the H-1B visa program has remained contentious for favoring foreign workers and low-cost international labor (Chakravartty, 2005). It is alternately described as a "magnet for global talent" or a "high-skilled body

M.-A. Détourbe (Ed.), Inclusion through Access to Higher Education, 123–139.

shop" (Chakravartty, 2006, p. 28). Nevertheless, it has expanded considerably with the lobbying support of high-tech corporate interests that seek the competitive advantage of globally-sourced human capital (Banerjee, 2006). But these interests rarely extend to the families of these techworkers, the H-4 visa holders. The spouses and children of H-1B techworkers migrate through the sub-category of the H-4 visa, also officially known as the "dependent[3]" visa category. This chapter focuses specifically on "dependent" immigrant women, spouses of these techworkers, and their access to higher education. Despite pre-migration higher education as well as skills comparable to those of their partners, "dependent" immigrant women are not allowed to work after migration. Instead, current immigration policy allows them to volunteer or pursue higher education on arrival. This chapter contends that this seemingly inclusive clause in immigration policy is countered by other micro and macro socio-economic factors, which effectively make it difficult for "dependent" immigrant women to access post-migration higher education.

Based on the current demographics of this immigrant population, the majority of H-4 "dependents" are women from India[4] (Kelkar, 2012). H-4 women cannot seek employment, are not given social security numbers, and in effect, cannot function as independent legal subjects after migration (Balgamwalla, 2014). Advocacy by South Asian activists in the US, including some H-4 women, has ensured tentative policy remedies over the last decade (Lodhia, 2010). In response to such activism, the state has advanced policy reform. First, it addressed the condition of women in this population who were victims of domestic violence. The Violence Against Women Act (VAWA) of 1993 ensured that victims of domestic violence, including those who were on the H-4 visa, could independently apply for a permanent resident status, rather than rely on their abusers for the process (Kelkar, 2012). More recently in November 2014, through the Presidential Executive Action on immigration, a limited number of "dependent" immigrants were allowed to apply for work permits (USCIS, 2014). Still, the vast majority of "dependent" immigrant women are excluded from these reforms as well, including all 30,000 or so newly arriving "dependent" immigrants each year. They can expect to wait six years to a decade or more to qualify for work permits; for this process, again, they are dependent on the lead migrant, their techworker partner.

At the outset, it would appear as if current H-4 immigration policy has an inclusive higher education clause – it explicitly permits the pursuit of higher education for this category of immigrant women. But it is important to note here that "dependent" immigrant women typically possess higher education from India, and often, a few years of work experience (Balgamwalla, 2014; Chang, 2013). Nevertheless, as "dependents" and immigrants, they are only permitted the pursuit of higher education, as they wait five years to a decade or more for their green cards to be processed, after which they can seek employment of their own. This chapter argues that immigration and higher education policies combine with familial gender norms to set these women on tangential pathways, away from accomplishing their higher educational goals. Indeed, it is not a single factor such as the state, the global market or the institution of family/marriage that contributes to their condition. Instead, a web of factors creates and maintains the "dependent" condition of these immigrant women. Through three case studies of "dependent" immigrant women who sought to access and pursue post-migration higher education, this chapter details the roadblocks that lead to migratory "dead ends" (Cuban, 2010) for them. In the process, these middle-class immigrant women scale down or even abandon their educational aspirations. The chapter argues that higher education and immigration policy ought to work in tandem and be more attentive to the situation of "dependent" immigrant women, so as to pave the way for their progressive inclusion as future citizens. Before exploring individual cases, the following section details gender and migration research that addresses women's post-migration labor market participation and higher educational aspirations.

GENDERED MIGRATION AND HIGHER EDUCATIONAL PATHWAYS

Migration scholars have described the phenomenon of "de-skilling" that is specific to the population of high-skilled immigrant women (Iredale, 2005; Mojab, 1999; Salaff, 2000; Suto, 2009). De-skilling research suggests that notions of being "educated" shift for immigrant women after migration, governed as they are by their intersectional location in the labor market and as immigrants in their new country. In a de-skilling study on Chinese immigrant women in Canada, Guida Man (2004) upholds from such an intersectional perspective that in migratory decisions, immigration processes as well as patriarchy within the family lead to men's education being more valued than women's education. Thus, immigrant women are more likely to become "dependents" rather than lead migrants in family migration. Man suggests that for high-skilled immigrant women, gendered and racialized institutional processes tend to compound such gender inequalities. She found that Canadian professional regulatory bodies, such as those for teachers and doctors, made it difficult for Chinese immigrant women to transfer their pre-migration education and training. Also, requirements for local work experience and language skills ensured that immigrant women were kept out of jobs at their former skill level. Hence, a combination of institutional factors and household responsibilities as caregivers led to immigrant women working far below their previous skill levels: they were effectively de-skilled. Similarly, family-based migration decisions dictate that women from India migrate to the US as "dependents" of their techworker spouses, the lead migrants in the majority of the H-1B/H-4 population. Further, since H-4 women are legally prohibited from seeking employment, they can be seen as effectively de-skilled even before they enter the labor market.

From a slightly different approach, Meares (2010) has argued that processes of downward occupational mobility among highly skilled immigrant women cannot simply be understood through the labor market. They require an examination of the "iterative relationship between the public sphere of paid work and the private sphere of the home" (p. 475). Among skilled South African immigrant women living in

New Zealand, Meares demonstrated the overlap of family and career decisions. For these immigrant women, choosing further education after migration was a function of whether they found work to match their prior qualifications in the first place. Likewise, Raghuram (2004) too explicitly connects education to the migratory decisions of the families of Indian immigrant women. Much like Meares, Raghuram captures the deep imbrication of family and work decision processes for middle-class Indian immigrants. In the case of immigrant women from India who were medical doctors in the United Kingdom, Raghuram found that despite their former medical training, institutional factors determine whether these educated women become the lead migrant or the "dependent" trailing spouse. For instance, family-based patriarchy and the general demand in the global labor market for their educational specialization, medicine, would often dictate who became the lead immigrant in the family.

Immigrant women face additional challenges through credentialing systems that do not recognize their former education (Cuban, 2010; Man, 2004; McDowell, 2008; Shan, 2009). Even among those women who are motivated to seek higher educational pathways after migration and are able to access higher education, a range of sociocultural factors complicate their learning. Alfred (2003) explores these factors in her study of the higher educational experiences of immigrant Caribbean professional women in the US. Alfred uses a sociocultural perspective and the notion of discourse communities of learning. Instead of individual-based learning, she argues the need to closely examine the sociocultural context where immigrant women's learning takes place, that is the relational and discourse communities aspects of their higher educational experiences. Caribbean immigrant women in the study spoke of being disadvantaged by language and race. Besides, their own pre-migration notions of education as being teacher-centered made it difficult for them initially to adapt to the US model of learning. Later, however, their perspective provided them much-needed structure to their learning.

As discussed, much of the scholarship on immigrant women and post-migration work and higher education decisions captures the overlap of labor market needs, immigration policy, familial patriarchy and the specific context of women's migration. Indeed, it is not advisable to generalize the condition of all "immigrant women" in order to suggest policy reform. Their intersectional location amidst class, ethnicity and race-based considerations significantly alters the experiences of women after migration (Alfred, 2005; Man, 2004). A context-specific reading of the experiences of immigrant women, their labor market participation and higher educational choices, would offer practicable insights, rather than a generalized frame that risks glossing over differences of race, class, ethnicity, and gender among immigrants (Brah, 1993).

Following the model of such gender and migration scholarship that accounts for the intersectional location of skilled immigrant women, this chapter examines the issue of "dependent" immigrant women and their access to higher education. The condition of "dependent" Indian immigrant women is similar to yet different from much of the research on middle-class and skilled immigrant women. They are located at the intersections of familial and market-based gender, race and class axes (Balgamwalla, 2014; Banerjee, 2006). Yet, they are also subject to a specific policy clause that allows them to study but not seek employment. Therefore, it can be said that in their case, de-skilling research portends the uneven road ahead for them, if and when they meet the criteria for work permits in the US. Indeed, it would appear that obtaining some form of post-migration higher education could potentially hedge their risk of being de-skilled in the future. So, on the one hand, "dependent" immigrant women are formally channelled by immigration policy towards higher education. On the other hand, as detailed in the three cases below, their higher educational pathways are roadblocked at various stages through market, migration and marriage factors that must be recognized in devising policies to better address their condition.

AN ETHNOGRAPHY AND THREE CASES

This chapter draws on data from an ethnographic study of the immigrant techworker community in the metropolitan area of Atlanta. The city of Atlanta is an upcoming immigration hub in the Southern United States where the Indian immigrant community has doubled over the last decade (United States Census Bureau, 2014). Fieldwork and interviews began in June 2015 and spread over a year and a half. A focal group of five "dependent" immigrant women from India were interviewed multiple times over the duration of the study, besides interviews with six other participants, their techworker partners and a community activist. The study included numerous visits to the homes of focal participants, as also to Indian community spaces and events in Atlanta. Interviews were conducted in English and Tamil with some code-switching in Hindi during the English interviews. English is not the first language for the majority of Indians, including the researcher and the participants in this study. But it is widely taught in urban schools in India and used for Indian urban and middle-class social interactions, as also among its middle-class diaspora.

Among focal participants in the study, three young women in their twenties, Maya, Nisha, and Lila,[5] stated that before migration they had goals to pursue higher education in the US. Maya had aspired to do research in her field of biotech engineering and imagined herself completing a doctoral program to accomplish her goal. Nisha had engaged in a long-term search for a master's program in the US ever since she had graduated from an engineering program in India. Lila too expressed a long-held desire to complete a US-based master's program. But unlike Maya and Nisha, Lila had to first obtain a bachelor's degree that would complement her vocational training diploma in India. Maya and Nisha posed typical cases of the general population of "dependent" immigrant women who, not unlike their techworker partners, tend to possess a bachelor's degree or higher qualification (Chang, 2013; Kelkar, 2012). As an outlier to this general trend, Lila's case underscored factors that could derail even rudimentary higher educational plans for "dependent" immigrant women. Below, each case is considered in detail, before a discussion of their implications for policy and research on immigrant women and higher education.

EDUCATIONAL PATHWAYS AND ROADBLOCKS

In the specific case of "dependent" immigrant women, challenges to accessing higher education are twofold. First, the high costs of post-secondary education mean that the women have to assume student loans or rely on family resources to realize their educational aspirations both in India and in the US. Next, among the skilled professionals of middle-class India and its diaspora, such as those in the field of IT, the pursuit of education is largely weighted towards marketable skills that would guarantee future high-demand employment (Lukose, 2009). Therefore, after migration, the steep costs of higher education in the US mean that the women cannot justify educational expenses to their families, other than as a guaranteed pathway to jobs that would be similar to those currently held by their techworker partners.

Current immigration policy explicitly allows "dependent" immigrant women to pursue higher education on arrival. In fact, they are eligible for in-state tuition rates, provided they are residents of their state. In-state rates reduce tuition costs to half of those paid by out-of-state and international students. However, if "dependent" immigrant women are new to the country or the state where they reside, and attempt to pursue higher education, they will be charged out-of-state tuition rates. It typically takes about a year to establish residency in most US states. Again, unlike all other students in the US, including international students, "dependent" immigrants are not eligible for assistantships or work-study of any kind. Therefore, in order to study, most H-4 visa holders prefer switching to a F-1 or international student visa, which gives them eligibility for funding their education through assistantships and a limited number of on-campus work opportunities. Also, the F-1 or student visa has yet another advantage, unavailable to H-4 visa holders: after obtaining the degree, F-1 visa holders can work for a year or two through a program called the OPT (Optional Practical Training). While these pathways to higher education and employment are available to all "dependent" immigrant women and many do avail them, the roadblocks that prevent them from advancing on these pathways are just as numerous.

AN UNCERTAIN EDUCATION

Since the majority of their work is project-based, techworker immigrants and their families tend to lead insecure lives. Typically, projects last an arbitrary period – anywhere from three or eight months up to three years, after which the project may be extended and their visas renewed. Project timelines depend on corporate clients, who have the power to terminate a project at any time, stating dissatisfaction with the progress of work. For the techworker and his family, this translates to a tenuous position, where from the moment they relocate to the US, they are uncertain about how long they will remain in the country, or in a particular town or city. The H-1B worker may find himself without a job in less than a month and face a return to India with his family.

Work and visa-based uncertainty affects the educational pathways of "dependent" immigrant women as well. Of all the participants in the study, Maya had most ardently expressed how the need to "do something" had consumed her since she had moved to the US a year ago. Maya had a master's degree in biotechnology from India and had graduated at the top of her class at an engineering institute in her home state of Tamil Nadu. So, when Maya migrated to the US with her techworker husband, Krishna, she had been determined to find employment based on her master's degree in biotechnology despite her restrictive visa situation. At the same time, she hesitated about her next step. She was not sure if they would have to relocate the following year, if Krishna's project were to end abruptly. Still, Maya discovered that a large public university was located not too far from their residence. So she decided to apply for a PhD program there in order to realize her long-held dream of doing research in her field.

> When we are caught in a situation we don't know what to do. Only when we come out of it we realize oh we can do this. I've tried to put my current situation aside, come out of it mentally and tried to think sometimes. Then I think I should have done a master's here. I did a master's in India but that's ok for India. My husband says it's best to get used to this system first and learn some things. Only then can you adapt to it. But my position is that I don't have a job now and I'm just sitting at home and it's very difficult. When I think by coming out of it then I think I should also better qualify myself if I want to survive here. I should do the GRE. I don't know where that might lead. But I know it's the first step. So I've made up my mind to do it now and I'm preparing for it. (Maya, July, 2015)

Maya describes here the decision-making process that led her to decide to pursue a doctoral program. She understood the need to adapt progressively to the US system, and higher education was a means to this end. Over the course of this study, Maya wrote both the international entrance tests required to pursue higher education in the US, namely the Graduate Record Exam (GRE) and the Test of English as a Foreign Language (TOEFL). Yet, right through the process of test-preparation and test-taking, Maya was unsure if she would have to move before completing the application process. Her husband, Krishna, was supportive of her decision to apply for a doctoral program. However, within eight months of their arrival, there was talk at Krishna's work about the project ending ahead of schedule. His colleagues were being let go or moved to the head office in Connecticut, a state in the Northeast. In the midst of this uncertainty, Maya wrote her tests and submitted her application to the PhD program. But, a little over a year after they had first arrived in the US, as teammates dispersed and found other opportunities, Krishna too found another project, this time in California. Before she left, Maya was cautiously optimistic about her chances to pursue further education. She had searched for and located a university not too far from their new town in California. She planned to reapply for a doctoral program at the new location.

In Maya's case, her educational goals and pathway were interrupted by the temporary, flexible nature of the neoliberal tech labor market. She had initially considered seeking employment based on her master's in biotechnology. When she could not find a research position, she had considered doing a doctoral degree instead, since it appeared to be the right path to a research position in the US. Thus, Maya hoped to create an educational pathway towards a research position. Notwithstanding the support of her husband for her educational aspirations, the uncertainty of the tech labor market meant that she could not complete the admission process and had to relocate to California.

In a sense, study participants anticipated such uncertainty. On numerous occasions during the study, Maya took stock of her uncertain situation. She would often express a passion for doing research in her field and spoke of wanting to teach. She felt too that her master's degree and training should qualify her for work in the US. Her urgency to seek employment came from a need to contribute to her family in India, who she felt could use her financial assistance. But she also understood the need for immigration policy to maintain what she termed a "lock" on H-4 visa holders by disallowing employment for them:

> It's good they've kept a lock on employment for us, but that lock should be such that if you do a six-month course then you are eligible for employment. In six months you have to learn the standards in the US. If they set it that way, we can think ok in six months we can learn and sharpen ourselves. For a PhD there are so many steps. GRE is a must. Besides, I don't have money. I have to find funding since up till now I've used my parents' money and studied everything. Krishna will give me money for studies. But I can't keep asking everyone for money to study. I've come to a position in life where I must earn and give others. All that is difficult. Else they could arrange funding and give those of us who are willing to study. We will also put in our hard work. I am ready to work that's how we are. As such it is too much to expect that they allow me to work right away. They need us to gain some experience and they need to give preference to Americans. All this I understand. But if they open some of the other gates that will be good. (Maya, September, 2015)

Here, Maya tries to balance her own career and educational aspirations with the need for policy to maintain a tight control on "dependent" immigrants, what she terms a "lock." She extends her metaphor of the "lock" to the availability of funding for higher education. Funding would open a "gate" towards releasing the "lock," she says. The lack of funding contributes to keeping the "lock" in place. In a way, Maya also addresses the issue of de-skilling of immigrant women like herself whose master's degree did not lead to employment after migration. She suggests a potential pathway to help "standardize" immigrant women's skills through a short-term course that would bring them up to par with the local labor market. Also, the question of funding her education gave rise to guilt about her inability to repay those who had supported her education thus far. She implies that scholarships for "dependent" immigrant women willing to pursue an education like herself, would counter some of the roadblocks faced by them in their current situation. In the absence of these policy remedies, Maya finds that her dependence on her family is compounded as she seeks to advance her educational and career aspirations.

Like Maya, many "dependent" immigrant women struggle with the uncertainty of their partner's typically short-term projects and the resulting uncertainty of residence in the US. Moreover, they deal with the uncertainty of funding for their educational goals, even if they secure the support of their partners. With prior market-worthy skills and qualifications, they find it difficult to justify pursuing further expensive higher education after migration. While some manage to secure support at home and funding at school by converting to an F-1 student visa, many simply move from state to state unable to give roots to their educational aspirations.

NEOLIBERAL CONCEPTIONS OF HIGHER EDUCATION

Ever since she had graduated with an engineering degree, Nisha, an IT engineer from Bengaluru, India, had been motivated to pursue higher education in the US. Despite an outstanding educational loan for her engineering studies, Nisha had considered pursuing a master's degree in the US. She believed that it would enhance her long-term earning potential. But Nisha's parents had been reluctant to send her unaccompanied to study in the US. They had decided instead to arrange her marriage with a US-based engineer, Akash. Nisha had reasoned that her marriage could pave the way to the higher education that she had sought. So she had been firm in expressing her educational goals to her future husband:

> I saw nothing bad in it. I said see if he has no issues with me studying there, then I don't see any problem. I told my parents if you feel good that I am married and not staying alone, I'm fine with it. When Akash and I met, I told him everything clearly. I told him see I want to do a master's and after doing a master's, I don't want father to repay the study loan himself. So until I can repay the entire loan, at least till then I want to stay in the US. I just told him that it will take me about four to five years for sure. (Nisha, July, 2015)

Before she met Akash, Nisha had taken the GRE and TOEFL tests in India, the same tests that Maya had taken as well after moving to the US. However, Nisha had not scored well on one of these tests. So her educational consulting firm in Bengaluru had suggested that she pay for additional coaching classes in order to assure her admission to a master's program in the US. Again like Maya, Nisha had been reluctant to spend more of her father's money on her education, since the family was yet to repay the study loan for her bachelor's in engineering. So, she decided to apply for master's programs in the US with her poor test scores and was unable to secure admission. Subsequently, Nisha turned to employment and was recruited at a top IT firm in Bengaluru:

> By then my plan to do a master's had gone down on my list. This was because I had started working. But even when I began working, I still thought that after a year maybe I will go to the US. I will think of writing TOEFL again and do a master's. But once I started working I realized something. What you study in theory you don't really come across that a lot in your work. So instead of a master's if you have two years of experience, that adds more value rather than you saying I did a master's. I realized that. Then I thought why should I study. Instead let me work for that period and gain experience. That's why studies went down on my list. I just didn't have master's at all on my list. But somewhere I thought if my company allows me after a few years, I will do an MBA part-time while working and move to the manager level. But it was not a priority on my list. It was not that I was not interested in studies anymore. I *was* [her emphasis] but not in a master's. More in something that could help me with promotions at work. (Nisha, July, 2015)

Nisha describes here a shift in her thinking about higher education. When she began working in IT, she realized that on-the-job training and experience mattered more in the field of IT than theoretical knowledge and an additional degree. Soon after her graduation with an engineering degree, she had seen the value of obtaining a master's degree in the US. But, after a difficult attempt at applying for admissions and being reluctant to ask her family to support her aspirations, she leaned towards a more neoliberal conception of education. Nisha now preferred a return-on-investment approach and valued a part-time MBA program, sponsored by her employer, rather than a self-funded master of science (MS) program. Hence, when she did migrate to the US after her marriage with Akash, Nisha preferred to apply for an H-1B visa of her own, rather than pursue a MS program. It was only when she could not get her own H-1B and a tech job like her husband's, that she re-considered her educational goals:

> When I started looking for options here, there was studies. Studies were the easiest thing you could do while waiting to apply for the H-1B. So then I looked at a few universities nearby. Georgia Tech, Georgia State, Herzing University. I used to call them up and chat. From all these I liked Southern University. So I went to their college and spoke to them. I will be an in-state student, now that I am a resident of Atlanta. So tuition fee is also much lower. I went in person and spoke to them. I was interested in their MS in Data Analytics. So I went to that department. There was an Indian professor there. He guided me through everything, this is how the course works and so on. I said I would prefer a one-year course which they had. So they walked me through the course. I was happy. Finally they told me the price. It was too high like forty-one thousand

dollars a year! My plan was that if it was less than twenty thousand, I would go for it. I would get one year of OPT and then I was sure I could repay the loan 'coz I was sure I could earn twenty thousand by then. If I did nothing and put all my salary on the loan, I could repay it. (Nisha, July, 2015)

Nisha clearly still embraced neoliberal notions of obtaining higher education. For instance, she spoke interchangeably about public and private universities. Also, the deciding factor for her had been how much a degree would cost her from a return-on-investment perspective. Nisha's experience of seeking access to higher education in the US only fortified her neoliberal notions about education. She was told that she could do a one-year program as she desired, but that it would cost her to obtain the tailor-made degree that she had sought. Nisha figured that the OPT (the year of post-graduation work allowed for all international students) would offer her a way to repay an educational loan of about twenty thousand dollars. This was also her estimate of her annual earning potential after a MS. In this manner, investment, skills and returns are all tallied in this assessment of higher education. Later in the study, when Nisha finally decided to update her skills, she chose a short-term Oracle certification course that would add immediate value to her IT skills and raise her earning potential.

The very nature of IT work compounds the difficulty of the task that "dependent" immigrant women face in justifying the costs of formal higher education. Immigrant techworkers are required to have a bachelor's degree and specialized IT skills. Most techworkers develop these skills over years of experience and may or may not hold a master's degree. For "dependent" immigrant women who are IT workers themselves, like in Nisha's case, the pressure to justify assuming high costs of education are not so much external as internalized. Despite her long-term goal to complete a master's degree, Nisha struggled to rationalize shouldering yet another educational loan to fulfill her aspirations. Instead, she adopted a market-based logic that devalued formal higher education and knowledge, opting instead for the immediate returns of a short-term skills-based course. Nisha's sense of urgency to complete a one-year master's program and then to repay the loan came from her own conception of education as skills-based. But it was also the result of a need from her family in India that the couple be available to return to India at any time to take care of Akash's widowed mother. In the third case below, such family-based concerns compound the difficulty of accessing higher education as a "dependent" immigrant woman.

FAMILIAL GENDER NORMS AND EDUCATIONAL ASPIRATIONS

More than graduate education, undergraduate studies pose a bigger challenge for immigrant women. Lila had a post-secondary vocational degree in electronics engineering, also known as a polytech diploma, which in general is not seen as the equivalent of a bachelor's degree. Lila's case was atypical because the majority of immigrant techworker spouses tend to have qualifications that match those held by their partners, since many of them meet through an arranged marriage and belong to the middle class in India. In Lila's words, she had always had the "aim" and "desire" of pursuing a MS degree in the US. But without a bachelor's degree from India, she could not fulfill her aspiration. Also, her vocational degree from India did not meet job and work-based visa requirements in the US. Lila did not have a bachelor's degree as the circumstances of her middle-class family in India had been difficult – her widowed mother had raised her sister and herself doing tailoring work, her late father had been a bus conductor, and they received no support from the extended family. These familial conditions meant that Lila's marriage had been arranged early on to a US-based engineer, Siva, though she had aspired to pursue further studies:

> My case is that I don't have a degree. I only have a polytech diploma from India. Before I could do higher studies, my marriage was arranged. Since I didn't have a father, my mother got me married early. Within two months of the wedding, we moved to the US. Here I've visited so many colleges, more than fifty both in Virginia and in Atlanta. But everyone says it would cost something like eighteen thousand dollars a year to do MS. Now I just have a non-bachelor's degree which means I cannot do MS right away. I'm unable to do anything further. Things have stopped for me. But my husband wants to stay here. If I go back to India for a bachelor's degree, I have to sacrifice three years of our marriage. My husband says there's no need for such a situation. (Lila, October, 2015)

Throughout the study, like Maya and Nisha, Lila too expressed deep concern about placing further financial burden on her widowed mother. She could not afford to spend on tuition for an undergraduate degree in the US. Like Nisha, she had enquired at colleges in Virginia, where the couple had lived before, and in Atlanta. But she had discovered that the pathway from a foreign vocational degree to a bachelor's in the US was long and expensive. It required expensive accreditation of her Indian vocational diploma in electronics engineering. Thereafter, the US degree would still cost her thousands of dollars each year for four years.

As she mentioned in the previous excerpt, Lila spoke at times of returning to India and completing a bachelor's degree there, so that she could return to the US later for a master's program. But her family, including her mother, discouraged her from living apart from her husband, Siva. Instead of paving and supporting her educational trajectory, marriage and migration appeared to have impeded her path to a master's degree. Yet, like Nisha, Lila too framed her marriage as a step towards fulfilling her educational aspirations:

> Even now I still can't believe though I'm here that my life is fulfilled. Since 10th standard in India I only wanted to study in the US. I would ask people and they'd say you could go do a M.S. This inspired me to get the top rank in school so I could go to the US. Though I've come here through marriage, I'm simply following my ambition and cannot really focus on my family life. I feel

that only if I go to college here and take exams for the first semester, that's when I will feel like I am in the US. That's what I'm looking for now. The first day I landed here in Virginia, it was 7PM. My husband said there's a college behind our house. We went there together and took a picture. So everything in this country has been about going to college, college, college. It's fixed in my mind. It's as if I've come here only for studies. My cousins in India say just be thankful about where you are right now. We don't get that opportunity. But I'm unable to sense the opportunity that I have now. Only if I study and get a degree, I will be content here. (Lila, April, 2016)

Here, Lila links the promise of being a new immigrant to her dream of pursuing higher education. She is unable to acknowledge her newly gained privilege without access to higher education. Everything about her migration spoke of "college, college, college" to her. It is clear that it was not a deficit of motivation that prevented Lila from pursuing higher education. There was also ample evidence of her level of perseverance. In the two years since she had migrated to the US, Lila had constantly explored different avenues to further her educational goals. After a bachelor's degree in the US proved unaffordable, she had looked into the possibility of a distance program, a bachelor's in computer applications (B.C.A.) from a university in her home state of Tamil Nadu in India. She had asked her mother and sister to help her collect sealed transcripts from her former polytech institute there. But it proved impossible to file an application with Lila being located in the US. The university in India had insisted that the student be physically present at the time of admission. Again, Lila explored other pathways towards a bachelor's degree in the US. She learned about community colleges and the fact that she could transfer credits from some of these colleges to a bachelor's program. She enquired at one of these colleges near her apartment in Atlanta. She was told that she would have to take standardization tests, get her polytech diploma accredited and then apply for admission. Even then, it would take her a total of four years to complete undergraduate studies, and only partially lower her costs. Once again, her dream of accessing higher education reached a dead end.

As mentioned in the other two cases, the nature of IT work itself makes it difficult for "dependent" immigrant women to justify the costs of higher education. As seen in Nisha's case, most techworkers develop their skills over years of experience on a range of IT projects and may or may not hold a master's degree. So it is difficult for the lead migrants, the techworker partners of "dependent" immigrant women to readily understand the long-term utility of their wives pursuing a master's or doctoral degree. At times, Siva was supportive of Lila's aspirations, saying he would find work wherever her studies took her. But he also discouraged her from pursuing a four-year engineering program in India, saying she would be out of touch with studies after marriage. Instead, Siva had suggested that his wife should consider doing a distance program in India for a bachelor's in computer applications or a B.C.A. Siva's rationale had been that since he was familiar with the field of IT, it would be easy for him to guide Lila towards a job. In fact, it is quite common for "dependent" immigrant women to abandon their pre-migration training in favor of IT-related work once they migrate to the US. Frequently, the husband is known to teach software skills to his wife so that she would qualify for her own H-1B tech job. Lila, however, fell short of the requirements for a H-1B visa and job, since she did not have a bachelor's degree. So it made sense to Siva that she complete a distance bachelor's program from India in an IT-related field:

> My aim is of course to study engineering but my husband says that after marriage I may not be in touch with studies to do a tough program like engineering. So computers and B.C.A. is the best way for me, he says. He's in software testing and suggests that I go the same way and do software testing. There is a software training institute close to our apartment here in our suburb. (Lila, October, 2015)

In this short excerpt, Lila scaled down her ambition from pursuing a competitive engineering program to a short-term course in software in her neighborhood. Her motivation to complete a master's program is nowhere in the picture that she paints here. Lila's educational goals had to pass through the filters of family approval, financial feasibility and a neoliberal rationale for the market. All these filters distilled her motivation from pursuing a formal higher educational degree to settling for a short-term training course that she could access from her apartment.

Lila's case represents the gamut of roadblocks that derail the educational aspirations of "dependent" immigrant women. Unlike Nisha's neoliberal conception of higher education, Lila described her goals in the realm of feeling, as "desire" and lifelong aspiration. Yet, in the end, she too was obliged to correct her perspective to fit a neoliberal stance – do a short-term training course so that she could obtain skills for immediate productivity.

CONCLUSION

Notwithstanding the marginally inclusive higher education policy for "dependent" immigrant women, diverse familial and market factors condition the access of educational pathways for these immigrant women. As seen in the three cases in this chapter, those who sought to pursue higher education had to simultaneously negotiate familial norms around marriage and gender, as well as justify the high costs of education through a neoliberal conception of education.

Maya's case illustrated the first overarching challenge encountered by many of these women as they seek to pursue post-migration higher education – the uncertainty of project-based IT work and the ensuing uncertainty of visa renewals and family relocation. Despite support from her partner, Maya could not complete her application process to a doctoral program and had to relocate to a different state when her husband's project abruptly ended. Nisha, on the other hand, had embraced ideas of education as a monetary investment, based on her experience as a techworker in India. Therefore, she sought ways to repay the educational loan that she might assume through an expensive master's program in the US. But Nisha's calculations of her earning potential after the master's degree fell short of the actual cost of completing the degree. Consequently, she was led to abandon her higher educational goals. Though Lila did not begin her journey through a return-on-cost mindset, she too had to concede to pursuing a short-term course over her dream of completing a master's program. In her case, familial norms around gender and marriage dictated the turns that her educational pathway took, often overriding her own aspirations.

Current policy for "dependent" immigrants appears to be inclusive in allowing them to pursue higher education in the US. However, as this chapter revealed, this is only a marginal form of inclusion that provides for little else in terms of funding or pathways to realize higher educational aspirations. Such marginal inclusion deters immigrant women who are otherwise marginalized as well through their legally "dependent" status. It is in this regard that higher educational policies could specifically address diverse categories of immigrant women in conjunction with immigration policy. Such policy change would be attentive to the development of vital human resources represented by these middle-class immigrant women, who typically channel their energies into homemaking and motherhood in the absence of higher educational pathways.

In view of the constantly growing need for greater numbers of foreign techworkers to help secure IT and global competitiveness, immigration policy makes greater room to accommodate expanding numbers of techworker immigrants. Yet, a primordial factor in the migration of these techworkers is left out of policy reform – the quality of life that their families experience once they migrate to the US. Immigration and higher education provisions for their families matter immensely to keeping this skilled labor force in the US. As suggested by Maya in this study, higher education policy could work in tandem with immigration policy and provide for limited sources of funding for "dependent" immigrant women who are motivated to access higher education. Again, when H-4 visa women convert to a student visa, they are subject to the additional challenges of stamping and visa approvals, which could be waived in their specific case. Such nominal provisions would also partly overcome family-based gender discrimination faced by "dependent" immigrant women. These policy changes would incentivize and encourage them to pursue higher education, since the women would now have a pathway to access the labor market other than by assuming large family-funded educational loans.

NOTES

[1] "Knowledge economy" here refers to the non-manufacturing sectors of the global economy, where knowledge/education replaces material production as the key economic driver (Walby et al., 2007). Guest workers, the majority from diverse Asian countries, perform specialized jobs predominantly in the American information technology sector (USCIS, 2015).

[2] Feminist scholars problematize the notion of work being low or high-skilled since it inherently devalues unpaid labor such as domestic work and care work (hooks, 1984/2000; Piper, 2008). Still,

the terminology is widely used for immigration categories. In migration literature, these terms concurrently reference different social classes of immigrants.

3   The term "dependent" is in quotes throughout the chapter to problematize its usage, particularly in its gendered connotation when applied to immigrant women (Fraser & Gordon, 1994).

4   There is no official demographic breakdown of the population of "dependent" immigrants. But Indian men make up more than half of the annual inflow of 85,000 H-1B workers (USCIS, 2015). So a conservative annual estimate of 30,000 to 45,000 is generally applied for "dependent" immigrant women from India (Kelkar, 2012).

5   Pseudonyms are used throughout for participants.

REFERENCES

Alfred, M. V. (2003). Sociocultural contexts and learning: Anglophone Caribbean immigrant women in US postsecondary education. *Adult Education Quarterly, 53*(4), 242–260.

Alfred, M. V. (2005). Overlooked in academe: What do we know about immigrant students in adult and higher education? *New Horizons in Adult Education and Human Resource Development, 19*(1), 4–14.

Balgamwalla, S. (2014). Bride and prejudice: How US immigration law discriminates against spousal visa holders. *Berkeley Journal of Gender, Law and Justice, 29*(1), 25–71.

Banerjee, P. (2006). Indian information technology workers in the United States: The H-1B visa, flexible production, and the racialization of labor. *Critical Sociology, 32*(2–3), 425–445.

Brah, A. (1993). 'Race' and 'culture' in the gendering of labour markets: South Asian young muslim women and the labour market. *Journal of Ethnic and Migration Studies, 19*(3), 441–458.

Chakravartty, P. (2005). Weak winners of globalization: Indian H-1B workers in the American information economy. *AAPI Nexus: Asian Americans and Pacific Islanders Policy, Practice and Community, 3*(2), 59–84.

Chakravartty, P. (2006). Symbolic analysts or indentured servants? Indian high-tech migrants in America's information economy. *Knowledge, Technology and Policy, 19*(3), 27–43.

Chang, S. (2013). Dreams of my father, prison for my mother: The H-4 nonimmigrant visa dilemma and the need for an 'immigration-status spousal support'. *UCLA Asian Pacific American Law Journal, 19*(1), 1–29.

Cuban, S. (2010). It is hard to stay in England: Itineraries, routes, and dead ends. An (im)mobility study of nurses who became carers. *Compare, 40*(2), 185–198.

Fraser, N., & Gordon, L. (1994). A genealogy of dependency: Tracing a keyword of the US welfare state. *Signs, 19*(2), 309–336.

hooks, b. (2000 [1984]). *Feminist theory: From margin to center.* Cambridge, MA: South End Press.

Iredale, R. (2005). Gender, immigration policies and accreditation: Valuing the skills of professional women migrants. *Geoforum, 36*(2), 155–166.

Kelkar, M. (2012). South Asian immigration in the United States: A gendered perspective. *Harvard Journal of Asian American Policy Review, 22,* 55–60.

Lodhia, S. (2010). Constructing an imperfect citizen-subject: Globalization, national 'security', and violence against South Asian women. *WSQ: Women's Studies Quarterly, 38*(1–2), 161–177.

Lukose, R. A. (2009). *Liberalization's children: Gender, youth, and consumer citizenship in globalizing India.* Durham, NC: Duke University Press.

Man, G. (2004). Gender, work and migration: Deskilling Chinese immigrant women in Canada. *Women's Studies International Forum, 27*(2), 135–148.

McDowell, L. (2008). Thinking through work: Complex inequalities, constructions of difference and trans-national migrants. *Progress in Human Geography, 32*(4), 491–507.

Meares, C. (2010). A fine balance: Women, work and skilled migration. *Women's Studies International Forum, 33*(5), 473–481.

Mojab, S. (1999). De-skilling immigrant women. *Canadian Woman Studies, 19*(3), 123–128.

Piper, N. (2008). Feminisation of migration and the social dimensions of development: The Asian case. *Third World Quarterly, 29*(7), 1287–1303.

Raghuram, P. (2004). The difference that skills make: Gender, family migration strategies and regulated labour markets. *Journal of Ethnic and Migration Studies, 30*(2), 303–321.

Salaff, J. W. (2000). Women's work in international migration. In E. Chow (Ed.), *Transforming gender and development in East Asia* (pp. 217–238). London: Routledge.

Shan, H. (2009). Shaping the re-training and re-education experiences of immigrant women: The credential and certificate regime in Canada. *International Journal of Lifelong Education, 28*(3), 353–369.

Slaughter, S., & Rhoades, G. (2004). *Academic capitalism and the new economy: Markets, state, and higher education.* Baltimore, MD: *Johns Hopkins* University Press.

Suto, M. (2009). Compromised careers: The occupational transition of immigration and resettlement. *Work: A Journal of Prevention, Assessment and Rehabilitation, 32*(4), 417–429.

US Census Bureau. (2014). *State and country quick facts: Atlanta (city), Georgia.* Retrieved from http://quickfacts.census.gov/qfd/states/13/1304000.html

USCIS. (2014). *Employment authorization for certain H–4 dependent spouses.* Retrieved from http://www.regulations.gov/USCIS

USCIS. (2015). *Characteristics of H-1B specialty occupation workers: Fiscal year 2014 annual report to congress.* Retrieved from https://www.uscis.gov/sites/default/files/USCIS/Resources/Studies/H-1B

Walby, S., Gottfried, H., Gottschall, K., & Osawa, M. (2007). *Gendering the knowledge economy: Comparative perspectives.* Basingstoke: Palgrave Macmillan.

Himabindu Timiri
College of Education and Human Development
University of Minnesota
Minnesota, USA

MICHELLE HENAULT MORRONE

8. INCREASING ACCESS TO HIGHER EDUCATION FOR "NEWCOMER" PUPILS IN JAPAN

INTRODUCTION

Equal access to education is an aspiration any democratic nation has for its citizens. Postwar Japanese education has been praised for its meritocracy and boasts a nearly 98 percent high school graduation rate, one of the highest in the world, with more than 50 percent of these pupils continuing on to higher education. But pupils who are not citizens, even though they may be permanent residents, are not included in these statistics, making their academic success or failure difficult to determine. This chapter examines the educational situation faced by non-national pupils in Japan and discusses their prospects for higher education within the Japanese meritocracy. Because Japan is a *gakureki-shakai* or school-credentialed hierarchical society, higher education success correlates very closely with future economic and social success. Those who are not endorsed by the *gakureki* system face an uncertain road in such a lockstep culture. Growing numbers of non-national pupils entering the educational system without proper school guidance or parental support risk being left on the fringes of society with limited possibilities for future careers and greatly circumscribed life-choices. Although at this writing, the non-national population is under two percent of the national total, its presence adds to the challenges faced by Japan's post-bubble society, a society in which many of its own citizens are at increasing risk of becoming marginalized as a result of ongoing economic and demographic changes (White, 2002).

NON-NATIONALS IN JAPAN

In 2014, according to the Justice Ministry, there were approximately 2.23 million long-term and permanent foreign residents in Japan (2.086 million not including those with permanent residency). Although these numbers fell somewhat after the financial downturn in 2008 and the Fukushima earthquake of 2011, they are expected to rise further as the Japanese government allows the entry of more foreign workers, many to help with the care of its rapidly ageing society. The greatest number of foreigners in Japan is Chinese, followed by Koreans, Filipinos, Brazilians, and Vietnamese ("Statistics on resident aliens," 2014). All those entering have varied reasons for coming to Japan as well as diverse educational and cultural backgrounds; yet they share one characteristic in the eyes of their Japanese hosts: their non-Japanese-ness,

M.-A. Détourbe (Ed.), Inclusion through Access to Higher Education, 141–157.
© *2018 Sense Publishers. All rights reserved.*

which is reflected in the terms by which Japanese society refers to them. Members of the first and oldest group of immigrants are termed, "*zainichi-Nihonjin*," or "in-Japan Japanese." This refers to the descendants of the Koreans taken into Japan after Japan's annexation of Korea at the beginning of the 20th century. Traditionally isolated from mainstream Japanese society, Koreans in this category were the first foreigners to secure legislation granting citizenship (with the stipulation that they take Japanese surnames). The peculiar name for them in Japanese suggests their "not quite" status, however, since "in-Japan" accentuates their essential foreignness.

This chapter deals mainly with a second group of non-nationals. These are referred to as "newcomers," most of whom came from South America and Asia when the Japanese Immigration Control and Refugee Recognition Act was revised in 1990 to allow certain low-skilled workers entry into Japan. In particular, the law allowed Japanese-descended Brazilians and Peruvians, up to the third generation removed from their Japanese roots, to come and work in Japan, the government believing that people of Japanese extraction would be more easily acculturated. More recent "newcomers," the result of a further revision to the law in 2009, include many groups from Asia and Southeast Asia, including Vietnamese, Chinese, Malaysians, Indonesians, Filipinos, Indian, and Nepalese (Immigration Control and Refugee Recognition Act, 2009).

In addition to these two groups of newcomer foreigners, there is a third category of long-term foreign residents. This group has no official name but might be referred to as "partial/non-Japanese residents." The Japanese government does not recognize these persons as "newcomers" because they did not enter Japan under the special newcomer long-term visa. Members of this group came to Japan originally as students, researchers, teachers, or highly skilled workers with international companies, or they were born in Japan and have one non-Japanese parent. Those who came on temporary visas continue to be seen as visitors no matter how long they actually stay in Japan. Their children often grow up speaking Japanese and living to varying degrees in Japanese society but in most cases they do not have Japanese citizenship. Being born in Japan does not confer citizenship rights, though having at least one Japanese parent does. Although the children of mixed unions may have citizenship, they remain only partial citizens in a sense. They have legal status as Japanese but in the eyes of many Japanese they can never have the same social status. This is because the Japanese tend to regard Japanese identity more in terms of blood than passports. For these reasons, I have referred to the members of this varied group as "partial/non-Japanese" since even when they are technically Japanese, their position in Japanese society and in the Japanese school system is always somewhat provisional.

The "foreign" pupils from the three categories hail from different backgrounds and have different reasons for being in Japan. Some have a Japanese parent and therefore citizenship, some have two Asian parents and share some cultural affinities with the Japanese, some have Japanese-descended parents from South America, and some have western parents and a privileged though segregated status. They come from all household income levels. Despite their differences, all of them to varying degrees share a marginal position within the educational system because they are not fully Japanese. While some of the Brazilian and Peruvian newcomers are in fact fully Japanese in the sense that their ancestors maintained their Japanese bloodlines even in South America, it is not enough to "look" Japanese. One must also speak Japanese natively and share with one's fellow Japanese thousands of identical experiences, experiences which do not include having parents who immigrated from South America. Since even partial/non-Japanese residents with Japanese citizenship are generally not accepted as Japanese in everyday life, those who have even less claim to Japanese-ness can expect even less acceptance and less equal treatment. This has important implications for newcomer pupils, who tend not to receive the same degree of help and encouragement as their Japanese counterparts.

JAPANESE LAW REGARDING SCHOOL ATTENDANCE

The Japanese Ministry of Education, under the authority of the Japanese Constitution and the Japanese Education Laws, oversees education policy, the creation of a credential system for teachers and the accreditation of schools and curricula. It also creates the general policies that manage Japan's school curriculum, making changes via educational reforms as required. According to Article 26 of the Japanese Constitution of 1947, "All citizens shall have the right to receive an equal education correspondent to their ability, as provided for by law. All citizens shall be obliged to have boys and girls under their protection receive ordinary education as provided for by law. Such compulsory education shall be free" (Constitution of Japan, 1947). The Fundamental Law of Education, which was enacted in the same year as the constitution, provided the legal basis for the right to education set out in Article 26, "clarifying the aim of education" in the "spirit of the constitution" (Fundamental Law of Education, 1947). It replaced the Imperial Rescript on Education that some felt had contributed to the rise of Japanese militarism. The new law was designed to address the changed circumstances in the aftermath of WWII and to establish the "foundation for a new Japan."

By the twenty-first century, circumstances had changed enough to warrant a major updating of the Fundamental Law. In 2006, an extensively amended version of the law was passed. The updated law shifted the aim of education from the full development of the "personality" to the full development of the "individual character," and further expanded educational opportunities, even providing for the education of the disabled. However, it continues to specify that these rights are those of citizens, implying non-citizens are exempt from the provisions of the law. For example, Article 4, on Equal Opportunity in Education, states: "Citizens shall all be given equal opportunities to receive education according to their abilities, and shall not be subject to discrimination in education on account of race, creed, sex, social status, economic position, or family origin." Article 5 continues: "Citizens have an obligation to educate their children to cultivate the foundations for an independent life within society." Although these provisions sound very progressive and inclusive, in practice they can be interpreted to mean that non-citizens are not entitled to equal educational opportunities and that non-citizen parents and guardians have no legal obligation to educate their children. Under this interpretation of the law, educators are under no great pressure to address cases of non-attendance by non-nationals, and in fact such statistics are generally not counted with the "citizen" statistics listed for national attendance and graduation rates (Motooka, Totsuka, & Yamashita, 2014). Additionally, school officials may feel they have no right to insist a non-citizen child attend school or any incentive to encourage his/her parents to seek additional academic support as they would in the case of a Japanese national who refused to attend (Watanabe, 2010).

As a signatory to the International Covenant on Economic, Social and Cultural Rights and the Convention on the Rights of the Child, Japan is in fact legally obligated to provide compulsory education to non-national children (Umeda, 2015). However, social norms in Japan usually take precedence over strict legalities, and it is not generally considered normal for non-national children to be in a Japanese school (Goodman, 2003). Local school officials in Japan are probably only dimly aware of the legal right of non-national children to attend public schools and may tend to view them as guests whose attendance is anything but compulsory. Under these circumstances, it is not hard to see why Japanese school officials may take a markedly relaxed attitude toward the non-attendance of non-nationals, particularly when those officials are busy addressing the more pressing issue of non-attendance by Japanese pupils.

Over the past few decades, there has been a significant rise in the non-attendance of Japanese nationals. This is mainly attributable to two causes: (1) *futoko* or school refusal, when a child does not attend school, usually due to bullying or an aversion to the intense social stresses of Japanese school, or more rarely, (2) homeschooling, in which the child or parent chooses an alternative pedagogy over the Japanese system. In 1992, in response to an increasing number of *futoko* pupils refusing to attend school, the government amended the fundamental law as follows: "As any child is likely to turn to avoiding school at any time, children need not be forced to return to school" ("Legality of homeschooling in Japan," n.d.). This rather strangely phrased directive probably only increased school non-attendance. Parents of homeschoolers argued that the law could be understood to mean that the parent is responsible for school attendance only if the child is willing to attend and that the child has no obligation at all to attend (Kugai, n.d.).

Despite this seeming support for school non-attendance, those who refuse to attend school, for whatever reason, face ostracism in a conformist society where such behavior marks one as deviant and "The nail that sticks out is pounded down" continues to be the quintessential Japanese saying. The sheer appearance of attendance, or appearance of the intention, is so valued that usually every effort will be made to keep a Japanese child on the school rolls even when the child rarely, if ever, attends. If the school principal or head teacher can show that an effort has been made to urge the parent and child to ensure alternative education, the child's registration may still serve as an official indication of attendance, and this assures the child's graduation from that school, while at the same time maintaining the school's high attendance and graduation rates. This proof of attendance and graduation eliminates the need to take a difficult high school equivalency test and makes it possible for the child to continue on to higher education. However, schools do not usually go to such heroic lengths to ensure the graduation of non-nationals, no doubt in part because their numbers do not contribute to their school's success rate. Thus, for non-nationals, attendance problems are far more likely to result in a failure to advance through the system.

CLIMBING THE EDUCATIONAL LADDER IN JAPAN

Local ward offices in Japan have the responsibility to see to it that all residents, non-nationals included, receive information about school registration, health checks, and other relevant information. The neighbourhood, too, has long played a role in informing its residences of neighbourhood activities and duties, and even school-related matters (Bestor, 1990). The information is not always as transparent to the non-national parent as it would be to a Japanese citizen who is better acquainted with the language and the workings of the system. These efforts, however, do tend to ensure that all neighborhood children are able to enroll in the local elementary school where they can begin working their way up the educational ladder.

Elementary schools are relatively stress-free in Japan, and tend to focus on the socialization skills that are an essential part of learning to function in Japanese society. Once in middle school, however, testing and tracking take over, with pupil rankings published after each test in order to maintain the pressure to achieve at all costs. For the ambitious, school will often be seen as not providing sufficient preparation for the tests, and these children will spend their evenings and weekends studying in cram schools. High school in Japan is not part of compulsory education. Therefore, high schools often have very competitive admissions standards. The results of the tests a pupil takes in middle school determine the high school that pupil will enter. That high school in turn will in large part, with the aid of many more tests, determine the pupil's college choices, which will then determine the company that person will one day work for, more or less fixing that person's social and economic status for a lifetime. Stepping off this track for almost any reason is considered an indication that something is seriously amiss and is to be avoided at all costs. The rigidity of this system means that what happens in middle school can determine your entire life course. Non-national pupils whose parents have not come up in this system are at a distinct disadvantage in their attempts to navigate these complexities.

FOUR CASE STUDIES

The following case studies illustrate the situations faced by four non-national families within this system. They are intended to offer a cross section of the types of non-national newcomers most prevalent in Japanese schools today and to provide

145

an overview of the various factors that impede newcomers from progressing on to higher education. Four main subjects were interviewed along with their families. The subjects' nationalities are meant to be representative of the main newcomer groups in Japan. Two of the subject families are Japanese-Brazilian, the largest single contingent among the newcomer groups. One family is Japanese-Peruvian, another large group of older newcomers. Finally, one family is Vietnamese, one of the Southeast Asian countries that has provided many of the newest newcomers. Interview subjects were found through an NPO that assists foreigners in the Aichi and Shizuoka area, through inquiries at local universities, and through church programs for newcomers. I conducted most of the interviews in Japanese. The translations presented here are my own. In cases where the main subjects or their parents could speak English, the interview was conducted in English. The interviews took place between January 2015 and August 2016 over the course of multiple visits in each case in order to discuss various issues with the principle interviewee both alone and *en famille*. Interviewees hailed from Aichi Prefecture and Shizuoka Prefecture, areas with high concentrations of newcomer families. Names have been changed to conceal the identities of the interviewees.

Case 1: Julio and His Family, Japanese-Brazilian

Julio, aged 31 at the time of the interviews, works at temporary contract jobs and has no steady income. He was five years' old when he entered Japan. He still lives with his parents. His younger sister, now 21, is enrolled in a private secretarial college and hopes to find a job in a company. The interview was conducted in Japanese.

Julio's parents came to Japan in 1990 to work in a factory under the revised visa law. Both parents are Japanese-descent Brazilians but speak and write no Japanese. The grandparents spoke some Japanese but Julio's parents were raised only speaking Portuguese, although they recognized some Japanese words when they were children. Their son, Julio was five years' old when they arrived in Japan. He recalls his first experience at Japanese school when he was six. He said he could not understand what everyone was saying and remembers crying a lot. Once he said something in Portuguese and everyone laughed and jeered at him, saying, "What language is THAT? Where do you come from? That's not English so you must be from a poor country." Julio learned quickly not to use Portuguese. Even if he looked Japanese, he realized he could never be accepted if he spoke a different language. He explained that from that moment, he knew he absolutely must learn Japanese or he would never fit in. As his mother explained, "In Brazil we could be Brazilians even if we are of Japanese background. Here we can only be Brazilians, low-class Brazilians."

Julio's parents had a high school education and did not worry much about their children's education in Japan as they felt they might return at the end of their contract period. They were told to enroll their children in Brazilian school so they would not lose the language but it got to be too expensive on the family's low income. Julio transferred to a Japanese school, but not until the 5th grade of elementary school.

He thought about continuing on to high school, which is not compulsory, but this was difficult with his inadequate Japanese. He explained that "The complexities of the preparation process and cost of university seemed too much." Since he had little hope of attending university, he decided not to go to high school. As his mother elaborated: "We figured that if he cannot get into a public school or university with his test grades then there was no point in paying such a high cost for education. Plus, there is a lot of learning how to interview for that and he was not confident that he could do it."

Julio added that at least he was glad he had decided to learn enough Japanese to communicate. He explained:

Some of the kids who went to the Portuguese language school never learned Japanese properly, even after taking those stupid Japanese remedial courses. They were a joke. You just hung around and did nothing till you decided to drop out. Anyway, a private school is expensive so that is another reason to drop out. It's easy to drop out because nobody makes you stay. Problem is that if they drop out, they can do nothing because no Japanese company will hire them, and the factory jobs are harder to get now. I kind of wish I had known more about the academic high school and university route because I know kids who were not so smart who went that way and it gave them the credentials you need to do really well here.

For her younger daughter, however, Julio's mother said she had picked up "the way" and saved up money so her daughter could attend a private Japanese high school. She said she had no idea about the quality of the school, but she just followed the advice of the other experienced parents who befriended her. She further justified this decision by saying that her son could work at the factory right away but the daughter needed some finishing if she wanted to have a decent life here and be "respectable."

Julio's mother explained that she thought her children would have a better future if they could stay in Japan, especially since they had learned Japanese. She also felt that perhaps if her daughter received some higher education, the Japanese would see her differently and be more accepting of her. The mother was very proud that her daughter was attending a local private college to learn language and computer skills but was worried whether they could continue to afford it. Private colleges, which are generally easier to enter than public universities, cost approximately 1.5 million yen ($15,000 US) a year, about three times more than the tuition at a national or prefectural university. Brazilian and Peruvian *Nikkeijin* (people of Japanese extraction) are often regarded as third-world immigrants, with a low place in the Japanese social hierarchy (Oda, 2012). Their status as *dekasegi*, which refers to their ancestors having left Japan to seek work elsewhere, carries an implicit suggestion that they are disloyal. Naturally, Julio's mother hopes her children can somehow rise above their origins.

Julio's case shows the difficulties faced by newcomers who were not born in Japan and who learn Japanese as a second language in households where the native language continues to be spoken. Because of the complexities of the Japanese written language in particular, such newcomers may never be able to achieve the level of Japanese necessary to progress on to higher education. This issue is further compounded by the seemingly temporary nature of the initial period of stay. Julio's Japanese might be much better if his parents had known they were going to stay in Japan permanently and had accordingly enrolled him in Japanese schools from the beginning. Julio's case also illustrates the way the expense of higher education in Japan, where even high school is not free, can dissuade newcomers of limited income. It is also clear that Julio's school career suffered from his parents' lack of familiarity with the Japanese system and their own limited educational attainments. Interestingly, as their experience with the Japanese system increased, the parents were able to overcome these handicaps and provide their younger daughter with a better education than Julio received. It is also interesting to note that the mother's motivation for making the sacrifices necessary to send her daughter on to higher education was largely based on her desire for increased respectability. In this we see that the Japanese tendency to look down on newcomers and view them as immigrants from a "poor country" can actually motivate newcomers to use Japan's higher education system to rise above these obstacles in pursuit of acceptance and respect.

Case 2: Maria and Her Family, Japanese-Brazilian

Maria is a 20-year-old student at an education university. She was five years' old when she arrived in Japan. At the time of the interview, she had already received some teacher training experience and was looking forward to becoming a teacher. She works part-time to pay for her school expenses. The interview was conducted in Japanese.

Maria's family is of Japanese-Brazilian descent. Her father went to Japan to work in a factory full time on a special visa. An economic downturn cost her father his full-time position, so her mother started working at a Brazilian restaurant. Neither parent is college educated but they did finish their compulsory education in Brazil. When Maria was six, she entered the local Japanese school but felt that because of her lack of Japanese it was very difficult to make friends. She tried to play with the girls as she would do in her own country, but they laughed at her when she tried to speak Japanese. They often said things like, "Why do you speak so funny?" and "Why are you here? Are you going back to your country soon?" Maria wanted to learn Japanese but said: "There was no program in place to help officially. Finally, a teacher took it upon herself to help me to learn Japanese." She added:

> I really could not understand her instructions and now I realize that the teacher had no formal training in teaching Japanese as a second language, so mostly her teaching was by way of gentle encouragement. Still, she was kind and supportive. I eventually caught on and could kind of keep up in school in

Japanese, although my friends still, even now, consider me a foreigner. Still, I was so lucky. Not everyone had such a teacher. So most of those without any kind of teacher support eventually just dropped out. I lost track of them but I know they are not doing anything. Not studying or working.

Maria explained that her mother spoke neither Japanese nor English, making it very difficult for her to get information about how to apply to schools once the compulsory stage was over. As she said, "I basically had to do it myself. I found out about going to cram school when my studies were kind of behind, and I found out information about high school, and then from there about how to enter university."

Maria was able to enter a private teaching college and works part-time every day in order to afford the high tuition. She finds her university studies too easy, and feels that perhaps she should have tried to enter a more competitive national or prefectural university. In her case, even now, she must translate official documents for her parents. Every weekend she travels two hours by train back to her hometown to take care of her parents and help her brother with his studies. She does this to guide her little brother through the education system:

> No one else can do it. I know what he must do but my parents still do not have a clue and cannot understand the system. Plus, he does not listen to them because he thinks they don't know anything. They are foreigners after all. My brother is a bit embarrassed of them. My brother is better at Japanese at a younger age because he was born here. But he does not know Portuguese very well and cares little about Brazil, which is kind of sad for me. He wants to be Japanese. So I help him with school because there is no one else to do it and he will have to stay here in Japan. Brazil offers nothing for us.

Maria's story shows how important it is for newcomers to receive the help and support of someone within Japan's education system. The fact that her teacher was not actually trained to teach Japanese as a second language was less significant for Maria's progress than the fact that the teacher was "kind and supportive" and willing to try to help her struggling pupil. On the other hand, Maria's case also illustrates the randomness of a system that offers few opportunities for formal "official" support. In Maria's own word, she was "lucky" to have a teacher volunteer to help her. But the clear implication is that the system is not set up to ensure that all its newcomer pupils are so fortunate. As with Julio, Maria had to get by with little parental support. Maria, however, started Japanese school at the age of six and her stronger Japanese skills made it possible for her to better navigate the system, eventually helping her to get all the way to a four-year private college, though even she seems to feel she might have gone further in the system with better advice. This seems to have motivated her to make sure that her younger brother gets the kind of advice, support and information that she had to struggle so hard to get for herself. As a veteran of the system, she can now serve the function that a Japanese parent would in a non-immigrant household. Her feeling that "no one else can do it" makes it clear there is still no effective state-supported system for addressing the special educational needs of newcomer pupils.

Case 3: Teresa and Her Family, Japanese-Peruvian

Teresa at the time of the interview was 22 years' old. She was just about to graduate from a private university and begin a job as a preschool teacher at an international preschool. Teresa arrived in Japan from Peru when she was six and her brothers were eight and twelve. Because of her advanced English skills, the interview was conducted in English. The interviewer also spoke to her mother and brothers in English.

After arriving in Japan about twenty years ago, Teresa's parents quickly developed ties with other Peruvian families in their neighborhood and attended their local church, which further expanded their social circle. The parents, like others in their neighborhood, had no higher education credentials themselves. Teresa, who is now 22 and in university, is the youngest of her parents' children, and in her opinion, the "most Japanese." Teresa was only about six years' old when she and her family left Peru for Japan. Her father came to Japan to work in a factory but became ill soon afterward. Sadly he passed away when she was still in elementary school. To support her three children, her mother made lunch boxes at a factory that supplied convenience stores. The older brother did not attend school at all once he reached Japan. The younger brother left school after finishing his compulsory education at 16. The older brother, now in his late twenties, works in a factory for a while, then quits his job and travels, then starts the cycle again. The other brother also works part time at various factory jobs.

With no higher education credentials, they have little chance of obtaining full-time positions. Teresa worries that, "They are free and happy now, but maybe this situation won't be so good when they reach their thirties. They are in a weak position but so long as they can find factory jobs, they will be okay but…" The brothers have joined the ranks of workers called, *freeta* or free time workers, workers without solid ties to full-time jobs, a category not limited to non-nationals but one in which non-nationals often find themselves. In Japan, *freeta* workers are in a very precarious position, with no job protection, little hope of advancement and no prospect for achieving the regular "salaryman" life that most Japanese aspire to. Most men in such positions find it difficult to attract marriage partners. The recent increase in the number of unmarried men is directly related to increases in the number of *freeta* workers. Not only are such men considered unattractive marriage partners, but the men themselves are often reluctant to enter into a marriage unless they can support a family comfortably (Yamada, 2005, 2008).

Teresa explains that her mother was not really aware of the importance of education when her boys were young. The boys were middle school age when their father became ill. After his death, they had little incentive or funds to consider high school, even if they had known how to apply. But by the time Teresa was middle school age, her mother began to see things differently:

> My mother wanted me to have a job that could be a career, not like hers. She just works making *obento* [lunch boxes] for convenience stores and must start work at 3:30 am. She does not really know enough Japanese to survive doing anything else, but for me, with my Japanese ability, she wants more. I suppose I was more ambitious than my brothers because the factory option was not there for me and after my father died my mother realized how important it was for a woman to have a career. But after middle school and the end of compulsory education, I realized my mother had no clue as to how to help me go to school or even to get a job. I was so worried and no teacher at school said anything to me. But I found out how to enter a high school because I just followed what my friends did since everyone else was applying to high school. My mother worried about how to pay for it but I told her I would help out with part-time work. So I applied to a school that called itself an international high school because my friends said as a non-Japanese maybe I would be able to get in. I had no idea how to judge which school was good but I just knew I needed to get in somewhere. I thought I could do well in English, which perhaps because I speak Spanish I am better at than most Japanese. And I was able to enter a school that did not focus on Japanese skills so much and where I could do more English. Japanese is too hard to be really good at and it was too late for me at the time. Anyway, I am determined, I will graduate and find a job as a preschool teacher and make my mother proud.

Teresa and her brothers show the widest range of educational outcomes among the interviewed families. One brother has virtually no formal education at all, the other brother has only completed his compulsory education, and the sister, Teresa, is about to receive a bachelor's degree. As in the case of Julio's sister, Teresa benefited from being the youngest child. Teresa's mother also gradually realized the importance of higher education for her children's future and encouraged her daughter to pursue it. Like Maria, Teresa found that she had to achieve her ambitions almost entirely through her own efforts since her mother did not have the Japanese language skills or familiarity with the system to help her and there was no older sibling to show the way. Also like Maria, Teresa feels that her inadequate Japanese language skills and limited knowledge of available options have kept her from going as far as she might have. As in all these cases, no official help with newcomer issues was offered to Teresa by the system itself.

Case 4: Catherine and Her Family, Vietnamese

Catherine was born in Japan but holds only Vietnamese citizenship. She was 13 years' old at the time of the interview. The interview was conducted in Japanese, although the mother often added comments in English. The parents speak fluent English and expressed hope that their children would soon be fluent as well.

Both Catherine's parents came to Japan to work as caretakers at a nursing home. The family keeps a very tight connection with the Vietnamese church community and attends church services in Japanese. Catherine is in middle school and her brother is in elementary school. She explained her situation in school:

> Well, school is fun and I have lots of friends. But I was born here and know the language so I never had any trouble. Now the trouble is that I find it more and more difficult to talk Vietnamese, especially to family when I visit Vietnam. And I don't get the culture there anyway. Here my parents insist that we speak Japanese. My mother says that is the only way to get ahead here. So I am enrolled in science courses and cram schools. So is my brother. Mom says that we must study harder than a Japanese person in order to get ahead. I know it was hard for her but she worked hard to pass the nursing test in Japanese. I am proud of her and I understand what she means. We are only Vietnamese and so we are not considered as smart or special as *real* foreigners who are American or something.

When asked about other foreign friends, she said:

> I have a half American/Japanese friend who never seems to have to study very hard. Her parents will send her to a girls' high school, which is much easier to get into than the public school my parents are planning for me. It is also more expensive. My parents are always worried about money, so we cannot do that. Anyway, my friend says she wants to go to an American university someday because Japanese universities are so bad, but I wonder if she can. I don't think her English is very good, actually, as she never studies it and does not speak to her father much, but maybe she can learn it. Anyway, I heard that an American university is easier to get into than a Japanese university. As they say, "American university is easy to get into and hard to graduate from," which is the opposite of here. My parents think that the university system here is very good and reasonable and so I have no choice but to try to get into the national system and then get a good job. So science studies is the only route acceptable for my parents.

When asked if she had teachers in school that encouraged her or her brother, she replied, "not especially. My parents looked into everything and found out how to get through the system. They just did what normal Japanese parents do, right?"

The fact that Catherine feels her parents are no different from "Japanese" parents when it comes to manoeuvering through the system shows the degree to which she and her family believe they have acculturated to the Japanese educational environment. One strong indication of this is that the children have come to believe their efforts will serve to advance them through the system with the same chances of success as those available to their Japanese counterparts. They see the system as essentially fair. The important thing is that you must do things the "right way," which is to say the Japanese way. They have completely subscribed to what they explained as the "mainstream ideology" of Japanese life, one that views the family and work in very traditional ways. Their views adhere very closely to the familial corporate model idealized in a traditional Confucian value system. Young Japanese, however, are increasingly open to different worldviews and different values with regard to work and lifestyle (Ronald & Alexy, 2015). Ironically, as this Vietnamese family follows a model of familial and social success that adheres closely to the postwar Japanese orthodoxy of Japan Inc., an increasing number of their Japanese contemporaries are moving away from that model in search of more individualized definitions of success and fulfillment (White, 2002; White, 2015).

Catherine was the youngest of my interview subjects and her case showed some striking differences with the cases presented by the South American immigrants. For one thing, her parents had higher levels of education when they entered Japan. They were effectively "professionals" even if their actual work as immigrant laborers was somewhat menial. Because they did not work in factories but directly with Japanese people, their spoken Japanese skills improved very rapidly. Moreover, having to pass an official nursing exam in Japanese has given Catherine's parents writing and reading skills far beyond those of the Brazilian and Peruvian parents I interviewed. Equipped with these language skills and a strong educational background, they have been much better able to guide their children through the Japanese education system. The fact that Catherine was born in Japan and that Japanese is in effect her first language is also a significant difference compared with my Brazilian and Peruvian subjects who arrived in Japan when they were elementary school age.

In addition to these differences, it should also be mentioned that Catherine's Vietnamese family may have had a cultural advantage over the South American families. Vietnam shares with Japan, China, and Korea a strong tradition of Confucian values, particularly with respect to education, hard work, and filial piety. It may be that these shared values have made it easier for Catherine's family to adjust to life in Japan. There would be considerable irony in this since Brazilians and Peruvians of Japanese extraction were admitted to Japan in large part because it was assumed their Japanese "blood" would make them better suited to Japanese life than foreigners who lacked a racial connection (Oda, 2012, p. 137).

All of the families in this study have experienced difficulties with the Japanese education system as a result of their newcomer status. All of them have had to struggle with language issues, financial constraints, insufficient information, and a general lack of familiarity with the system on which their children's futures depend. Catherine's family has perhaps surmounted many of these difficulties with less trouble than the other families, but all of them share their essential foreignness in a country that prizes homogeneity and is confounded by difference. The system was simply not set up to accommodate outsiders and these outsider families have all had to deal with that ineluctable fact, as was made clear by the one overriding similarity in all these cases: none of my interview subjects mentioned receiving any significant help with newcomer issues from the Japanese system itself. Maria received the assistance of a kind and dedicated teacher but that was more on a voluntary than official basis. Otherwise all these newcomers have been obliged to navigate the system on their own with varying degrees of success or failure.

THE JAPANESE GOVERNMENT RESPONSE TO NEWCOMER PUPILS

In an attempt to address some of the educational challenges faced by newcomers, the government has set up new policies and guidelines, focusing almost exclusively on the Brazilian community, as it is the largest group of the South American newcomers and a community that has had more than its share of educational and social difficulties in Japan. Initially volunteer programs were set up using local international associations, NPOs, NGOs, and student volunteers. Pilot programs were set up to assist with Japanese language teaching. Some university professors sent their students and graduate students to visit Brazilian schools to tutor the pupils in Japanese. Portuguese speakers who were translating in the court system were recruited to help out in local schools. It was not until 2010, however, long past the point when it had become clear that the bulk of the newcomers would stay on in Japan, that the government created an actual education policy for foreign children, especially with regard to language assimilation. The policy ("Policy points," 2010) states:

> Education systems, as well as enriching the quality of Japanese language education for those children whose first language is not Japanese, should be considered in order to make elementary and junior high schools more accessible. Also, we should promote the authorization by local authorities of private national schools.

This policy to make schools more inclusive came twenty years after the bulk of the newcomers had arrived. Prior to this, Brazilian parents were encouraged to send their children to Brazilian private schools since this would minimize their contact with the Japanese population and better prepare them for life back in Brazil. For a long time, the government failed to realize that an economic downturn might make it difficult for Brazilian parents to continue paying for such private schools without necessarily making them want to leave Japan. Since the original stated policy of the Japanese government was that Brazilian workers were all to leave Japan within a fairly short period of time, the Education Ministry felt justified in thinking that few Brazilian children would stay long enough to need any education beyond the compulsory limit.

The new policy shift in responsibility from local volunteers to schools was also advanced by a resource website for teachers called CLARINET (Children Living Abroad and Returnees) to keep newcomers better informed, and also to assist Japanese nationals returning after living or studying abroad. The education ministry also announced that it would do more to improve: (1) the system of Teaching

Japanese as a Second Language by promoting the development of second-language training programs in university education departments; (2) the support system for foreign resident parents adjusting to Japanese life; and (3) the support system for foreign resident pupils in order to help them progress through the school system ("On Japanese language," n.d.).

As a result of this policy, the government started some well-intentioned programs in the hopes of fostering bilingualism and better cultural understanding. One of these was the Overseas Dispatch Program: it involved sending about ten in-service teachers from Japan to Brazil for a year and eight months, where they were to learn more about the Brazilian educational environment, study Portuguese, teach Japanese, and foster cultural exchange. Another program, under the auspices of the Rainbow Bridge Policy, was aimed at newcomer pupils who had dropped out of school. This six-month program supplied limited support and classes for the pupils if their parents were unemployed.

Other than official government-sponsored programs like these, the government has done very little to address the problems faced by newcomer pupils. Meanwhile Japanese academia has been reluctant to incorporate Japanese as a Second Language (JSL) in university training programs, so there remains a great shortage of teachers to help newcomer pupils overcome their language difficulties. Recently, however, an increasing number of universities have been creating JSL programs that promise to eventually supply the badly needed teachers.

As Watanabe (2010) has shown, the most effective efforts to deal with the difficulties faced by newcomers have not come from the Japanese government but from local volunteers, university teachers and students, the Brazilian government, and private companies that offer funding for volunteer initiatives.

CONCLUSION: ENSURING EQUAL EDUCATION FOR ALL

After nearly thirty years of the newcomer phenomenon, it is clear that newcomer children without adequate Japanese language skills are ill equipped to ascend the educational ladder to the level of higher education, and are thus at a huge disadvantage in their future lives in Japan. Despite this, even more newcomers may come to Japan and stay. The need for health workers to care for Japan's rapidly aging population has led to a surge in immigration from Southeast Asian countries (Soble, 2017). Most likely the Japanese government is hoping that these workers will only stay for a few years. But if the past is any guide, large numbers of them will end up staying in Japan permanently. Their children will grow up there and face many of the same issues discussed in this chapter. To ensure that every child in Japan has access to the country's vaunted meritocracy, the education system will need to be far more solicitous of its newcomers than it has been to date. An outline of the key steps required in any serious effort to ensure the right of "all people" to an "equal education" has already been made clear by the work of volunteers. As the number of newcomer children increases, however, the responsibility for this effort will inevitably need to shift to the government and be incorporated in clearly defined policies and official budgets.

Admitting that the system must work for everyone is the necessary first step in this process. This has particular importance for a country that will have to depend increasingly on foreign-born newcomers and their children. Japan's demographic future is bleak. According to Japanese government estimates, by 2050 nearly 40 percent of the country's population will be over 65, while less than 10 percent is projected to be under the age of 15 (Statistics Japan, n.d.). Japan has little choice but to offset declining numbers of young people with foreign labor. Wealth disparities in Asia continue to make Japan an attractive place for immigrants willing to accept second-class status in order to escape poverty in their home countries. As time goes on, however, Japan may need to become more accommodating to foreign workers and their families—on the one hand to attract them and on the other to reduce the risk of creating a large permanent underclass of non-citizens. Increasing access to higher education for newcomer pupils is one way for Japan to do both.

REFERENCES

Bestor, T. (1990). *Neighborhood Tokyo.* Stanford, CA: Stanford University Press.
Constitution of Japan (The). (1947). *Prime Minister of Japan and his cabinet.* Retrieved August 14, 2015, from http://japan.kantei.go.jp/constitution_and_government_of_japan/constitution_e.html
Fundamental Law on Education. (1947). *Ministry of education, culture, sports, science and technology.* Retrieved from http://www.mext.go.jp/b_menu/kihon/about/06121913/002.pdf (An English translation is available from *The Asia Pacific Journal: Japan Focus* at http://apjjf.org/data/ed.law.file.pdf)
Goodman, C. F. (2003). *The rule of law in Japan: A comparative analysis.* The Hague: Kluwer Law International.
Gottlieb, N. (Ed.). (2012). *Language and citizenship in Japan.* New York, NY: Routledge.
Immigration Control and Refugee Recognition Act. (2009). *Immigration Bureau of Japan.* Retrieved from http://www.japaneselawtranslation.go.jp/law/detail/?id=2647&vm=&re=
Kugai, T. (n.d.). *Frequently asked questions about homeschooling in Japan.* Retrieved from http://www.asahi-net.or.jp/~ja8i-brtl/faq.html
Legality of homeschooling in Japan. (n.d.). *Education in Japan community blog.* Retrieved from https://educationinjapan.wordpress.com/homeschooling-afterschooling/legality-of-homeschooling-in-japan/
Motooka, S., Totsuka, E., & Yamashita, Y. (2014, 07 July–25 July). Discrimination against foreign children in Japan: The right to education of foreign children and the Japanese education laws. *Research Institute of International Human Rights Law Policies (RIIHRLP), Alternate report delivered to the International Covenant on Civil and Political Rights, session 111.*
Nakamura, A. (2008, January 3). Flexible and diverse, international schools thrive. *The Japan Times.* Retrieved from http://www.japantimes.co.jp/news/2008/01/03/national/flexible-and-diverse-international-schools-thrive/#.WNU5ixIrLow
Oda, E. (2012). Cultural citizenship and the hierarchy of foreign languages: Japanese Brazilians' views on the status of English and Portuguese in Japan. In N. Gottlieb (Ed.), *Language and citizenship in Japan* (pp. 137–155). New York, NY: Routledge.
Okada, A. (2012). *Education policy and equal opportunity in Japan.* New York, NY: Berghan Books.

On Japanese Language and Adjustment Guidance for Foreign Pupils. (n.d.). *Ministry of education, culture, sports, science and technology.* Retrieved from http://www.mext.go.jp/b_menu/shingi/chousa/shotou/042/houkoku/08070301/005.htm

Policy Points from a MEXT Policy Panel on the Education of the Children of Permanent Resident Foreigners. (2010, May 19). *Ministry of education, culture, sports, science and technology-Japan.* Retrieved from http://www.mext.go.jp/b_menu/shingi/chousa/kokusai/008/toushin/1294066.htm

Ronald, R., & Alexy, A. (2015). Continuity and change in Japanese homes and families. In R. Ronald & A. Alexy (Eds.), *Home and family in Japan: Continuity and transformation* (pp. 1–24). New York, NY: Routledge.

Soble, J. (2017, February 10). Japan limited immigration: Now it's short of workers. *New York Times.* Retrieved from https://www.nytimes.com/2017/02/10/business/japan-immigrants-workers-trump.html

Statistics Japan. (n.d.). *Ministry of internal affairs and communications bureau of statistics.* Retrieved from http://www.stat.go.jp/english/

Statistics on Resident Aliens. (2014, October 21). *Ministry of internal affairs and communications.* Retrieved from http://www.e-stat.go.jp/SG1/estat/List.do?lid=000001127507

Umeda, S. (2015, June 6). *The education of non-native language speaking children: England, European Union, France, Israel, and Japan* (pp. 17–19). Washington, DC: The Law Library of Congress, Global Legal Research Center.

UNESCO. (2011, June). *World data on education, 7th edition Japan.* Paris: UNESCO. Retrieved from http://www.ibe.unesco.org/fileadmin/user_upload/Publications/WDE/2010/pdf-versions/Japan.pdf

Watanabe, T. (2010). Education for Brazilian pupils and students in Japan: Towards a multicultural symbiotic society. *Procedia Social and Behavioral Sciences, 7,* 164–170. Retrieved from https://doi.org/10.1016/j.sbspro.2010.10.024

Weiner, M. (Ed.). (2009). *Japan's minorities: The illusion of homogeneity.* New York, NY: Routledge.

White, B. (2015). Reassembling familial intimacy: Civil, fringe, and popular youth visions of the Japanese home and family. In R. Ronald & A. Alexy (Eds.), *Home and family in Japan: Continuity and transformation* (pp. 25–46). New York, NY: Routledge.

White, M. (2002). *Perfectly Japanese: Making families in an era of upheaval.* Berkeley, CA: University of California Press.

Yamada, M. (2005). *Meisou suru kazoku: Sengo kazulu moderu no keisei no kaitai* [Runaway family: Decline in the post-war family model]. Tokyo: Yuhikaku.

Yamada, M. (2008). *Konkatsu jidai* [*The age of partner hunting*]. Tokyo: Deisukabaatouenteiwon.

Michelle Henault Morrone
Department of Human Care
Nagoya University of Arts and Sciences
Japan

VIKKI BOLIVER

AFTERWORD

Around the globe, widening participation policy makers, practitioners and researchers continue to focus almost exclusively on the 'domestic' population. Consequently, the barriers to higher education access faced by those who lack full citizenship rights, or who lack full fluency in the national language, are frequently overlooked. As this book shows, citizenship status in both its legal and cultural senses, and the language fluency of both prospective higher education students and their families, matter a good deal for access to higher education and for access to the labour market benefits that a university degree 'ordinarily' provides. The absence of full citizenship rights and a lack of full language fluency undoubtedly constitute additional barriers to access for those from socioeconomically disadvantaged backgrounds, but they also impede access even for those who are relatively socioeconomically advantaged.

Depending on the specific national context, refugees and asylum seekers may be unable to access higher education at all; may see their higher education options restricted as a result of policies which dictate where they are allowed to live; and may even find that they are permitted to study but not to graduate with a degree at the end of their course. Spouses of highly skilled and highly educated migrant workers, who tend to be classified as a 'dependent' for visa purposes, may find their higher education plans thwarted by uncertainties around the length and location of their spouse's employment, and by the unknowable probability of their own chances of ultimately being granted permission to enter the graduate labour market and recoup the costs of gaining a degree. Even those studying abroad on international student visas are left in doubt as to whether they will be permitted to work and live on a permanent basis in the country in which they gained their degree, all the more so in contemporary climates of volatile immigration policy.

Migrant origins can prove a major obstacle to higher education access even for those with full citizenship entitlements if language proficiency is limited. For some citizens with foreign-born parents (sometimes referred to as 'second generation immigrants'), parents' lack of fluency in the national language may prevent them from realising in time which educational choices need to be made in order to access higher education further down the line, and in some national contexts there are no second chances. Internationally higher educated professionals who have been actively recruited by the nation state to work in key areas such as healthcare may find that limited language proficiency inhibits their professional performance and

M.-A. Détourbe (Ed.), Inclusion through Access to Higher Education, 159–160.

progression, and that educational opportunities for improving language competency are of limited availability or efficacy.

The cross-national focus of this book highlights the relevance of citizenship and language to higher education access in all nations. The barriers to access faced by non-citizens and the non-fluent differ in nature and magnitude from one country to the next, but the challenges presented are remarkably similar cross-nationally and no country is exempt. Moreover, these issues affect growing proportions of the populations living in developed countries. Today more than 244 million people live in countries other than those in which they were born,[1] including more than 2.5 million international students currently studying in the member states of the OECD.[2] In such a context, it is clear that widening participation policies, practices and research must bring considerations of citizenship and language to the fore. At its core, this means expanding the remit of widening access beyond the 'domestic' population to include those from migration backgrounds irrespective of legal or linguistic status, recognising the key role of higher education in social inclusion.

NOTES

[1] UN statistics for 2016. Retrieved from http://www.un.org/sustainabledevelopment/blog/2016/01/244-million-international-migrants-living-abroad-worldwide-new-un-statistics-reveal/
[2] OECD statistics for 2012. Retrieved from https://stats.oecd.org/Index.aspx?DataSetCode=RFOREIGN

Vikki Boliver
School of Applied Social Sciences
Durham University
Durham, United Kingdom

ABOUT THE CONTRIBUTORS

Rashed Al-Haque is a researcher and public policy analyst. He holds a PhD in Educational Studies from the Western University in Canada. His doctoral research explores how federal citizenship and immigration policies intersect with international education policy, vis-à-vis international student recruitment and retention in Canada. As a critical policy scholar, he is also interested in public policy issues, multi-level governance, and comparative and international education. He recently published in the *Comparative and International Higher Education Journal* on how Canada's citizenship and immigration policies marginalize international students.

Cui Bian is a researcher at the Research Institute for International and Comparative Education of Shanghai Normal University in China. She researches issues about student mobility and internationalization of higher education in a global context; she is specialized in the study of French higher education, with a focus on internationalization issues in universities and *grandes écoles*, from a historical, socio-political and cultural perspective. She publishes papers in English, Chinese and French and her recent publications include two books, *International students in French universities and grandes écoles: A comparative study*, Springer & Higher Education Press, 2016 and *Studies on the system of entrance examinations and selections in French higher education institutions* (in Chinese), Central China Normal University Press, 2017.

Vikki Boliver is Professor of Sociology in the School of Applied Social Sciences at Durham University. She is best known for her work on socioeconomic and ethnic inequalities in admission to highly selective universities and for her research on patterns and processes of intergenerational social mobility. Recent articles include 'Exploring ethnic inequalities in admission to Russell Group universities' published in the British Sociological Association's flagship journal *Sociology*. Professor Boliver is Principal Investigator on projects funded by the Economic and Social Research Council and the Nuffield Foundation which explore the fairness of university admissions policies. She is a member of the Centre for Global Higher Education Research where she is leading research into alternative providers of higher education.

Julia Carnine holds a doctorate in Sociology from the University of Toulouse based on fieldwork in France, China and the United States. She is a member of LISST-CERS (CNRS-UMR 5193) with over 17 years' experience in higher education directing international programs in the United States, China and France. She is the Director of the Dickinson College in France Study Abroad program, and a lecturer at the University of Toulouse Jean Jaurès. Her research is published in peer reviewed journals: *Presses Universitaires de France, Editions de Paris Ouest* in France, *Journal of Overseas Chinese* in China.

Marie-Agnès Détourbe is a senior lecturer in English Studies at INSA Toulouse and the Graduate School of Education (ESPE) of Toulouse, France. Her research has focused so far on institutional quality assessment mechanisms in Higher Education (e.g. *Les enjeux de la qualité dans l'enseignement supérieur. Le cas des universités britanniques* [A comprehensive study of institutional assessment mechanisms in British higher education], PUM, 2014); she considers that evaluative mechanisms provide an interesting analytical lens for the study of higher education systems as they encode specific values and priorities. She is also interested in the study of higher education from multiple perspectives, especially English for Specific Purposes/ ESP (e.g. "Mapping specialized domains through a wide-angled interdisciplinary approach: The case of British higher education and research," *IJLS*, Vol. 11(3), 2017) and, more recently, international comparative education. She is the associate editor of the peer-reviewed ESP journal in France, *ASp*.

Gaële Goastellec is a sociologist, professor at the University of Lausanne, Switzerland. Her main research deals with the socio-historical comparison of higher education systems, especially with regard to access and social background characteristics. Her latest books include, with C. Kamanzi and F. Picard (Eds.), 2017, *L'envers du décor, Massification de l'enseignement supérieur et justice sociale*, Presses de l'Université du Québec; with G. Felouzis (Eds.), 2014, *Les inégalités scolaires en Suisse. Ecole, société et politiques éducatives*, Peter Lang; and with F. Picard (Eds.), 2014, *Higher Education and the fabric of societies. Different scales of analysis*, Sense Publishers.

Michelle Henault Morrone is Professor of Comparative Education at the Nagoya University of Arts and Sciences, Nisshin, Japan. She has lived in Japan for over 25 years and is interested in how a culture designs its educational environment, affecting the development of its students, its future citizens. Her main research topics are related to the problematic handling of change in Japanese society and culture. Influenced by anthropological methods, her approach focuses on narrative inquiry and ethnography. Her recent academic contributions include "The Culture of Japanese Medicine," in the *Introduction to Healthcare for Japanese-speaking Interpreters and Translators*, edited by I. Crezee and T. Asano, John Benjamins Company, 2016, and "The Father Image in Japan," *Father's Involvement in Children's Lives; A Global Analysis*, Springer, 2013.

Nadezda Kulikova is currently a sessional faculty in the Department of Educational Psychology and Leadership Studies at the University of Victoria, Canada. She holds a PhD in Educational Leadership and Policy from the University of Utah, USA, and has additional academic background in linguistics and teaching foreign languages.

Her research interests include international and comparative education, higher education policy and leadership in educational organizations, and she has taught extensively both face-to-face and online in Russia, USA and Canada.

Vincent Latour is Professor of British Studies at Université Toulouse – Jean Jaurès, France. His research focuses on Franco-British and wider European comparative studies, with particular emphasis on multiculturalism, immigration and minority communities. His recent publications include "The Securitisation of British Multiculturalism," in *The Politics of Ethnic Diversity in the British Isles*, edited by R. Garbaye and P. Schnapper, Palgrave-Macmillan, 2014, and "The Sarkozy Years: Attempting to Define a New Paradigm for Diversity Governance in France," in *The Sarkozy Presidency: Breaking the Mould?*, edited by G. G. Raymond, Palgrave-Macmillan, 2013.

Norah Leroy is a teacher educator in the Graduate School of Education (ESPE d'Aquitaine) at the University of Bordeaux, France. Her doctoral research focuses on the specific contribution teacher educators of foreign languages make to early language learning and teaching within the education systems of England, France and Scotland. Previously, she was a secondary school teacher of both English and geography during her teaching career in England and France. Her most recent publication is an article in a special issue of the *International Review of Education* in 2017, titled "Modern foreign language teachers – don't leave those kids alone! Linguistic-cultural 'give and take' in an ad-hoc tutoring scheme."

Régis Malet is Professor of Education (University of Bordeaux) with extended expertise in the field of comparative education. His research topics are teacher education and identities, school cultures and diversity. He is the director of the Laboratoire Cultures, Education, Sociétés (LACES EA7437) and the deputy-director of the ESPE d'Aquitaine. Previously, he held a position as director of the Faculty of Education in the University of Lille. He has also been the President of AFEC (*Association Francophone d'Éducation Comparée*) and the Editor of *Éducation Comparée* for one decade. He has been a visiting scholar in various universities all around the world. Professor Malet has been on the editorial board of various international journals in education. He is a member of the Canadian Research Chairs College of Reviewers as well as an expert for European programs and the French High Council for the Evaluation of Research and Higher education (HCERES).

Yuliya Miakisheva is an instructor at the York University English Language Institute in Toronto, Canada. She teaches English as a Second Language to university students and internationally-educated medical and legal professionals. She has participated in assessment and training of the internationally-educated nurses (IENs) as part of the Post-RN for Internationally-Educated Nurses Program at York

University. Her research interests include English for Academic or Special Purposes, Intercultural Communication, and Blended Learning.

Himabindu Timiri has a PhD in Organizational Leadership, Policy, and Development from the University of Minnesota. Her interdisciplinary research interests overlap the fields of gender, migration and education. Her dissertation was a study of gendered subjectivities among 'dependent' immigrant women from India in the US using a critical narrative analysis of their experiences. She has a master's in literary studies from the Université du Québec à Montréal. Her master's thesis raised a critique of gendered Orientalist representations of India in contemporary Quebec novels.